THE
BIG CAT
MAN

An Autobiography

JONATHAN SCOTT

FOREWORD BY

DR RICHARD LEAKEY

BRADT

First published in the UK in August 2016 by

Bradt Travel Guides Ltd
IDC House, The Vale, Chalfont St Peter, Bucks SL9 9RZ, England
www.bradtguides.com

Published in the USA by The Globe Pequot Press Inc,
PO Box 480, Guilford, Connecticut 06437-0480

Text copyright © 2016 Jonathan Scott
Photographs copyright © 2016 Jonathan and Angela Scott
Illustrations copyright © 2016 Jonathan Scott
Edited by Caroline Taggart
Proofread by Janet Mears
Designed and typeset from the author's files by David Scott and Pepi Bluck
Original cover design by David Scott, adapted by Pepi Bluck
Cover photograph: Jonathan with Kike by Angela Scott.
Reproduction: Fiona Cox at Creative Design & Print (Stamford) Ltd
Production managed by Sue Cooper, Bradt & Jellyfish Print Solutions

ISBN: 978 1 78477 033 4   (print)
e-ISBN: 978 1 78477 500 1   (e-pub)
e-ISBN: 978 1 78477 401 1   (mobi)

British Library Cataloguing in Publication Data
A catalogue record for this book is available from the British Library

Printed in Turkey
Digital conversion by www.dataworks.co.in

THE
BIG CAT
MAN

For Angie, the best thing
that ever happened to me.
Your unconditional love, courage
and perseverance have been an
inspiration to all of us.

CONTENTS

FOREWORD

At this moment when the very future of the famous Maasai Mara's wildlife is at a critical crossroads, the publication of this work is of great importance. Jonathan Scott has produced a book that captures the magic of the Mara and his personal story will be of interest to the millions of television viewers who have enjoyed the spectacle of the great cats of the Mara as told through the various episodes of the BBC's *Big Cat Diary*.

In the last months of 2015, there was a tragic incident where the widely known Marsh Lion Pride, made internationally famous by Jonathan and Angie, suffered losses from having eaten poison on the carcass of a cow that the pride had killed inside the Mara National Reserve the night before. Three of the Marsh Lion pride died, and whilst I have no doubt that in time the pride will grow again, the incident was a very public wakeup call to the conservationists and wildlife lovers of the world. Is the Mara wildlife there forever? As human numbers increase, the pressure on wildlife and wild spaces also increases and, inevitably, there are some hard decisions to be made.

In the narrative that follows we learn a great deal about Jonathan and why over the years he has become so deeply passionate about saving the big cats of Africa. The leopard, lion and cheetah that he has photographed and written about have become in many ways an integral part of many families living in England and beyond. His passion and love have been infectious. The enormous audiences that have enjoyed *Big Cat Diary* and much of the associated popular journalism can in large measure explain why the Maasai

Mara remains the most popular destination not only for western tourists visiting Kenya, but also increasingly for growing numbers from Asia. Jonathan and Angie can certainly be applauded for their work to boost the popularity of the Mara.

Having said this, I must however emphasise that the vast majority of Kenyans, young and old, have never had the joy of seeing these great creatures on their television sets at home. *Big Cat Diary* is a product of a British corporation and our Kenyan outlets cannot afford the licence fees to show the series on prime time. This is sadly the norm for most wildlife documentaries made in Kenya: Kenyans do not see them. Is it really difficult to understand, then, why popular demand to protect the Marsh Lions, the leopard and all the big African creatures seems to be largely a foreign concern? Films about Kenya's wildlife must be shown in Kenya, without exception.

I know that Jonathan and Angie, along with many film-makers, share this viewpoint and are doing what they can. The magical tales incorporated in this book and shown on film must be enjoyed by Kenyans too. At the end of the day, the Kenyan wild animals and wild places will only survive for future generations if the Kenyan voters and people push for them. The next episode of *Big Cat Diary* should have Kenyans clamouring for it to be released in their country.

Jonathan has been very candid about his own life, sharing the good, the uncertain and the bad. He has had a complex moulding of his character to become the person he is and many readers will identify and empathise with his ups and downs. He writes of a successful career, but without denying or trying to hide some of his doubts or curious choices that he had to make. This makes the story personal and particularly interesting.

As I write this foreword, Jonathan is again on the front line, drawing attention to the plight of the lions in the Mara once more. Can the Mara survive as a prime wildlife-viewing area, bringing huge benefits to Kenya through tourism and providing amazing support for the Maasai people who are the custodians of the area and who gain substantial revenues to operate their County Government?

The story of wildlife/human conflict is complex, but to me there are some very clear choices that the government, both County and National, must make and uphold. The rules for a successful National Park, Reserve or Sanctuary are broadly similar. Wildlife can be managed sustainably if it can feed itself, have a large enough area to breed and have genetic diversity to sustain viability. The rules are not unlike those for running ranches for cattle.

In Kenya, we are allowing the rules to be broken. Domestic stock is competing with wild species for grass, browse and water. There are too many animals to sustain and numbers must be reduced. It seems obvious to me that if the competition for grazing and browse inside a protected wildlife area is too intense, the wildlife will be lost. Cattle, sheep and goats must be excluded at all times and there really is absolutely no room for compromise. At present, many incursions into the National Parks and wildlife County Reserves occur under cover of night. Animals are herded in at dusk and brought out at dawn. Tourists are perhaps thus not offended, but the damage to the area from overgrazing is no different, be it daylight or darkness.

My information is that the owners of large herds of cattle, sheep and goats have in many instances sold their own land or leased it to conservancy organisations for wildlife conservation. So, if they do not then sell their herds as well, they have to graze them in the Parks and Reserves when they can. Some livestock will even be trucked in from considerable distances so that the animals can graze in the protected areas. This cannot continue if the wildlife is to survive.

At night, cattle and other stock are very vulnerable to predators and quite often cattle and goats in wildlife areas get killed by lion or leopard. The stock owners are outraged and often retaliate by spearing or poisoning the predators. Who can win such a fight? It makes no sense, and if we are serious about preserving our wildlife, part of the action must be the total exclusion of domestic animals from protected areas.

As we move deeper into this century, the impact of climate change can only make the conflicts worse. Massive flooding or extensive drought is predicted for at least the next thirty years. In these new circumstances, clear thinking and political resolve will become increasingly critical and reactive strategies will not work unless planned and executed over long-term periods. The problems are not going to take care of themselves and the moment for resolve is now. Landuse policy must be formulated and practised to the letter.

This book, the great pictures, the films and the words are a wonderful record. I hope it will be a stimulus for action. It would be a tragedy if the world in 2050 could only read about what we have now. The readers would rightly curse us for our lack of resolve. The Scotts are doing their part and I salute them.

Richard Leakey, FRS
January 2016

CHAPTER

01

IN SEARCH OF AFRICA

Man is a brief event on

this continent; no place has ever

felt older to me, less touched or

affected by the human race…

the wild animals belong here.

———————————————————

Martha Gellhorn
Travels with Myself and Another

The cheetah crouched and then in one glorious movement leapt on to the bonnet of my safari vehicle. It was September 2003 and the first season of *Big Cat Week* was underway in Kenya's Maasai Mara. The programme's predecessor *Big Cat Diary* had been running since 1996; now we were back on BBC1 with more great animal characters to share with our audience of over six million people. All three of our big cats were performing like never before: Bella the leopard was accompanied by two adorable cubs of just three months old, while the Marsh Pride of lions were up to all their old antics with a bunch of boisterous cubs of their own. But there was no doubting who the star of this year's show was going to be. Kike the cheetah sat confidently on the roof of my vehicle, her long ringed tail dangling languorously through the roof hatch centimetres from my face as I explained to the audience that there was only one wild cheetah in our area who treated vehicles as if they were termite mounds – Kike.

When I glanced up again I saw to my horror that Kike had turned so that her bottom was poised directly above my open roof hatch. Not only that, but she was straining her hindquarters in a way that could mean only one thing. Cheetahs routinely use termite mounds as an aerial perch from which to survey the surrounding plains for prey or for predators that might be lurking in the grass. They also use them as places to deposit strong-smelling messages for other cheetahs that might pass this way in the form of urine – and, yes, faeces. I grabbed a toilet roll from the dashboard and managed to catch the first of the incredibly smelly droppings as they rained down on my head, but I missed the one that ended up in the canvas seat cover housing my telephoto lenses. Cameraman Toby Strong could barely contain himself as he struggled to keep the video camera steady and of course the audience loved it. From that moment I became 'the bloke the cheetah crapped on'. It was a small price to pay for having carved out a life for myself in Africa, the sort of life that most people can only dream of, as an author, photographer and television presenter, sharing my passions with my wife Angie – a world away from the reality of a child growing up on a farm in England.

I was two years old when my father died of an inoperable brain tumour, prompting my mother to sell our home in London and move to Cuba Farm, a smallholding located near the picturesque village of Cookham in Berkshire. My father had bought the farm a few years before he died and it had always been his dream to retire there. After serving with distinction in the Royal Engineers during the Second World War, he had become the Senior Architect and Surveyor to the Duke of Westminster's Grosvenor Estate in London, but he loved horses and had a natural affinity for the English countryside: his beautiful sketches and woodcuts of country scenes testify to that. The thought of his young family growing up surrounded by green fields and idyllic woodlands rather than in the bleak streets of post-war London would surely have pleased him. That was reason enough for Mum to apply herself to making a living raising a handful of Jersey cows and a dozen saddleback and large white pigs, along with scores of chickens and rabbits, supplementing her income by taking in a lodger and breeding corgis and bull terriers. On occasion we would help her milk the cows or watch in fascination as she prepared to defend herself, pitchfork in hand, against a cantankerous old sow threatening to roll on a dozen newborn piglets. Life on a farm is not for the fainthearted and my sister Caroline and I would stand wide-eyed as our much older brother Clive castrated the young pigs with a

razor-sharp scalpel (nonchalantly discarding the testicles for the poultry to gobble up) or deftly wrung the neck of a chicken before plucking its feathers. One of the hardest things to comprehend was the need to fasten rubber bands around the long tails of the latest litter of corgi puppies to comply with breeding standards and produce the requisite 'docked' tails. Harder still was knowing that, come market day, the silk-eared piglets and doe-eyed calves that we had named and helped to nurture – each with a character of its own – would have to be rounded up and loaded into the farm truck, never to return. Farm life provided me with a close-up view of our relationship with domestic and wild animals and helped prepare me for the harsh realities of life on the African plains.

It was back-breaking work for Mum and margins were slim. Tractors broke down and pigs leapt out of van windows on their way to market; foxes played havoc with the geese and the chickens; cows kicked up a storm in the cowshed; and you could guarantee that just when Mum was concluding a sale of one of the puppies all hell would break loose as the corgis went for each other's throats – or bit the postman. Dogs were always to the fore on the farm and Caroline and I each had our own corgi – mine was named Sugar, hers was Bella. My love of cats was yet to emerge. Our cats were outdoor cats, unnamed felines who earned their bowl of milk by controlling the rats and mice.

Caroline is eighteen months older than me and we were inseparable. Outwardly I was a happy, hyperactive child, bursting with energy and mad about sports, while she was more serious and reserved. But beneath that optimistic exterior was a darker side that I would struggle to conquer over the next thirty years.

I no longer remember the name of the boy I was playing with at home on Cuba Farm that fateful day in the late 1950s. It was certainly a friend from my primary school Challow Court, someone of my own age, no more than eight or nine years old. But the other details are etched in my mind as vividly as if it were yesterday, not fifty-five years ago. We were climbing up and down a mountain of hay bales stacked to the ceiling of the grain store. At some point I slipped and fell with my legs apart on to the metal rim of an empty grain bin. I landed with a sickening crunch and uttered a startled yelp that brought Clive running to see what the matter was.

Despite the excruciating pain my instinct was to act as if nothing of any consequence had happened. I was barely able to stand, let alone tell him the truth. Scared and embarrassed beyond words, I pretended that I had fallen and hurt my shin, even though there was no sign of a cut or bruise. There was no way I was going to suffer the embarrassment of allowing someone to examine my private parts.

Looking back it sounds ridiculous. But that fateful decision – to choose silence over truth – proved a turning point in my life. Despite some impressive swelling and bruising (which would necessitate minor surgery years later), not to mention barely being able to sit astride my beloved new bicycle, I was resolute in my determination not to tell a soul what had happened. I became two people – the confident, outgoing person that others saw and the inward-looking observer who became convinced that the injury had precipitated some disease process that would one day kill me, just as the brain tumour had killed my father. Compounding the situation was the fact that at the age of four I had contracted rheumatic fever, necessitating endless visits to hospital that continued well into my teens, for X-rays, blood tests and antibiotics to ensure that there had been no damage to my heart. Surely it was only a matter of time before someone discovered the secret of my fall. Conquering my fears and the obsessions they nurtured would prove far more challenging than facing up to charging elephants or an angry leopard in Africa.

In contrast to this sense of inner darkness, there were carefree days exploring the fields and woodlands with Caroline, with Clive always there in the background as a steadying influence. The hedgerows and thickets became our playground, somewhere to collect flowers and grasses to press and keep in our scrapbooks, along with birds' feathers, acorns and fir cones – natural treasures that held us in their thrall. We

would return home with our jam jars filled with sticklebacks and, best of all, frogspawn, delighting in the anticipation of watching it hatch into dozens of tadpoles in our garden pond, then marvelling at the miracle of their metamorphosis into tiny frogs. I particularly loved to wander through Redlands, the patch of woodland bordering one of our fields, hoping for woodpeckers and jays, squirrels and foxes, riveted to the spot as a stoat streaked into the open, then bounded and leapt over the tall grass to pounce on an unwary rabbit. All of this was fertile material for my sketches and drawings, a talent that I had inherited from my father.

Dad had attended Christ's Hospital (or CH, as it is known), the 'bluecoat' school founded in 1546 by King Edward VI to support and educate orphan children. Its original home had been in the old Greyfriars buildings in the City of London; by my time it had relocated to Horsham in Sussex, where it is to this day. The CH legacy was in my family's blood. In addition to my father, my Aunt Sybil, godfather Jack Palmer (a private banker who assumed a fatherly role to our family) and sister Caroline all went there. Dad had later been a school governor and his staff of office, emblazoned with the CH crest, rested in the corner of our living room, along with his ceremonial army sword and scabbard. Everything he turned his hand to seemed to have borne fruit and to my young eyes CH was the foundation of all of that.

With Caroline already at the girls' Christ's Hospital School in Hertford, the pressure was on me to win a place at the boys' school two years later. I will never forget the day that the brown envelope arrived with my exam results and my mother called me into her bedroom to tell me that I had failed. The enormity of that word was almost too much for me to comprehend. I was beyond disappointment. Not going to CH was unthinkable. Wearing the Tudor-era uniform of long yellow stockings, grey breeches with three silver buttons at the knee, a long blue cassock with high collar cut away at the front to show the white clerical band and large silver buttons from neck to waist, along with a leather belt and silver buckle, might sound out of step today – it did to some people back in the 1960s – but to me it was the ultimate badge of honour.

The day my results arrived, my mother walked me down the lane past the lush green fields of our farm to the place where I would catch a lift to the primary school I was soon to leave. How could this be happening when all I had ever wanted was to follow in my father's footsteps? You only got one chance at the exam, or so we had been told. But my mother was incapable of accepting defeat, and was determined that I would go to CH. Apparently I had been unwell around the time of the exam. By lobbying the School Treasurer she saw to it that I was offered another opportunity. Nothing was left to chance. A change of school and intense tutoring in the three Rs by my godmother made certain that I was accepted this time.

I adored my mother. She was an optimist by nature, believing that you could overcome adversity by facing up to it, that perseverance and sheer hard work would see you through. That attitude has inspired me throughout my life. I never saw her cry, though she must have at times. She was like a rock to our family. As I grew older, though, I came to recognize the toll that my father's death had taken on her. She had wanted a large family and had suffered a number of miscarriages between Clive's birth and Caroline's: the thought that something terrible might happen to one of us preyed on her mind and was almost more than she could bear.

As a healthy balance to life at home with Mum and Caroline (Clive had married and left the farm by this time), CH was a world of men. It offered the gift of multiple friendships – a stimulating contrast to the rather isolated world I had enjoyed on the farm. I loved boarding school, though the angst of Father's Day always reminded me of just how much I missed having my father there to witness my successes and drove me even harder to make him proud of me. Luckily being good at sport counted far more than being clever. If you were on the rugby team or boxed you were 'someone'. That meant you were unlikely to be bullied, and the fact that the school was a melting pot that cut across race and class promoted the positive attributes of the finest public schools without the sense of elitism that pervades many of them.

It was during this time that a visitor from South Africa brought me a copy of Sir Percy Fitzpatrick's classic tale of farm life, *Jock of the Bushveld*. The farm in question bordered the great Kruger National Park, a wild stretch of bush country replete with lions and leopards, elephants and buffaloes, and bore little resemblance to my own existence. The edition I pored over was something to behold, a weighty tome bound in leather, the text brought to life by beautifully graphic pen and ink sketches of the day-to-day happenings on the farm, with each colour plate separated by a piece of rice paper. Not a day passed without the author regaling me with some triumph or disaster of spirit or flesh as the craggy old Boer farmer went about his business, pushing back the wilderness as he scratched a living from the parched earth. Always by his side was Jock, his faithful bull terrier, flop-eared but tough as teak. My favourite parts of the story were the battles with the lions, hyenas and leopards. The leopard was portrayed as a creature of almost supernatural powers of stealth and cunning, the ultimate challenge for both man and dog in their attempts to keep their precious livestock safe.

From the moment I read *Jock of the Bushveld*, books took on a totally different meaning in my life. They became objects of wonder rather than just a tedious part of school lessons, while the leopard would continue to fire my imagination like no other wild creature: to my young mind it was as much a part of the spirit world as it was a denizen of the veld.

It was a big day when a black and white television appeared in the sitting room at Cuba Farm. Until then we had snuggled up around

a log fire in the evenings to listen to *The Archers* on a crackly old radio, with the gravel-voiced Walter Gabriel our favourite, or sat enthralled by Charles Dickens' dark tales of *Nicholas Nickleby* and *Oliver Twist*. All this paled by comparison to the stunning visual depiction of our world that television now revealed, particularly series like *On Safari*, with wildlife filmmakers Armand and Michaela Denis bouncing around wild places in Africa in their open-top jeep, or dive masters Hans and Lotte Hass exploring the underwater world. What young boy could fail to be mesmerised by stingrays and sharks, with the mermaid-like Lotte in her fishnet swimsuit to please the eye as she and her husband explored the magic of the coral reefs? But what really stands out from those teenage years is the memory of sitting in a cinema watching *Born Free*, the true story of George and Joy Adamson's triumph in returning the wild-born lioness Elsa to the wilderness of Meru National Park in Kenya. Its stirring effect was reinforced by a talk that a fresh-faced teacher gave to the sixth form one evening, illustrated with colour slides of his travels around the world on a gap year. I sat there aching to do something like that – to be free of studying and to *live*. Grey old England looked drab and pale by comparison to the splendour of the African savanna.

By the time I completed my schooling at CH, I had been accepted by Queen's University in Belfast to read zoology. Biology and art had always been my favourite subjects; now I had the chance to learn more about animal evolution, in particular the evolution of animal behaviour, or ethnology, a science that was in its infancy when I first went to Queen's. I was more interested in *how* animals lived than in the way their kidneys functioned, and while the university specialised in parasitology I knew I eventually wanted to focus on something more tangible.

I graduated four years later with a decent Upper Second, determined to achieve my ambition of 'doing something with wildlife'. I wasn't quite sure what that might mean, but preferably not studying for a doctorate in something observed under a microscope. When I expressed those sentiments to my Professor of Zoology he looked me straight in the eye and asked, 'And do you have a private income to fund your dream?' I didn't – and he was right. Natural history had always been the great British pastime, pursued by gentlemen on the family estate with retriever at heel and double-barrelled shotgun under one arm – or by the less financially well endowed with their butterfly nets and binoculars, out on a ramble in search of birding rarities. While I might have listened to my professor's sensible advice to 'either take a doctorate or get a job', I was far too smitten with my idea to be deterred by words alone. Another member of staff suggested a stint teaching at a school in Zambia, which was perhaps closer to my ideal of exploring Africa, but still wasn't quite what I wanted. I decided to take a year off in the land of opportunity: America.

After nine months humping sheets of gypsum wallboard up and down stairs in New York, I had saved enough money to see more of the continent. During university holidays I had spent time hitching around much of Western Europe, camping or sleeping rough on park benches, so I felt ready for whatever lay ahead. I packed my rucksack and headed up to Boston, onwards to Nova Scotia and Prince Edward Island in Canada, then to Quebec, quickly awakening the nomad in my veins. On my return to Long Island I bought my first car, a $300 blue Comet Mercury that subsequently leaked oil all over the USA and Mexico. That car spelt a different kind of freedom. Now I didn't need to rely on anyone for a ride. I set off on my own with nothing but a sleeping bag and a map, determined to zigzag my way across North America, focusing on the parks and wilderness areas wherever possible. It didn't matter that I was travelling alone – in fact I preferred it. With no fixed itinerary I was free to let destiny take its course and make friends along the way.

In those few short weeks hitching and then driving across North America I experienced life in the early 1970s in all its technicolor rawness and glitter. I tested myself by travelling on my own, sleeping in my car and confronting the unexpected head on, from a bad case of mistaken identity involving gun-wielding cops in California to a car full of Mexican conmen intent on stripping the moving parts from my stricken vehicle late one lonely night near Acapulco. Nevertheless, I was charmed by the warmth and friendliness of a people who, with unbridled generosity and a genuine pride in being American, would invite a stranger into their homes: 'Have a beer, stay for lunch, sleep over.'

There was no doubt that America offered many of the things I loved about life, especially people who believed in shaping their own destiny through hard work and a positive outlook.

The grandeur of the landscape and the beauty of the parks engendered the sense of freedom and adventure I was looking for, with the thrill of seeing herds of bison and caribou and the thought of the Arctic wolves and great brown bears that preyed on them to stir the imagination. But it wasn't enough to make me want to settle down – not yet, not now. I was more certain than ever that I didn't want to go back to university to study for a doctorate. The continent that had beguiled me since childhood now beckoned. That place was Africa and to travel there I needed to head home to England to earn some money.

A few months later, having lodged at my Mum's house in London and replenished my savings, it was time to move on. While harbouring ambitions of hitchhiking the length of Africa on my own, I had spotted a newspaper advertisement looking for people to participate in an overland journey from London to Johannesburg by Bedford truck – a giveaway at £475. There are vague memories of an initial get-together in a smoke-filled pub somewhere in London, a mix of Aussies and New Zealanders along with the Brits and a smattering of folks from other European countries. By the end of the evening I had signed up along with thirty-six fellow adventurers for a three-month journey with Encounter Overland in two rickety old blue and orange Bedford trucks. The trip had all the elements I was looking for: the chance to explore the great outdoors and take some photographs without any of the worries that normally attend life. We would have a roof over our heads – canvas tents and camp beds, to be precise – and a staple diet of packet food to supplement the fresh meat and vegetables we would buy along the road.

I had always enjoyed drawing and taking photographs – as witnessed in a letter I wrote to my mother aged twelve: '*Please could you bring my camera and a film and some flashbulbs. I will pay you the money in the holidays.*' Having snapped away with a simple point-and-shoot camera during my year in America I was determined to buy a 'real' camera for my journey through Africa. I finally settled on a Canon EF camera body that was built like a tank and looked indestructible – just what was needed given the rough ride it was about to endure. Better still, it offered shutter priority, a semi-automatic function that meant all I needed to do was to set the shutter speed and press the button. At £175 that single purchase consumed most of my savings, leaving me with just £35 to buy a multipurpose 80-250mm Tamron zoom lens. I wish I had known then that buying the best piece of glass to put in *front* of the camera – preferably a Canon – is far more important than paying good money for a camera body with lots of fancy functions and settings that you will never use. Despite dabbling in the dark room at school and inconveniencing the rest of the family with black and white prints floating in the bath, I didn't really

have a clue about the most important elements of photography. But armed with my Canon and a rudimentary feel for composition I felt as if I knew what I was doing.

From the first day in the back of the truck I was determined to live and breathe every moment of the experience. With the canvas tarp rolled up each morning, weather permitting, I was going to stand and let the sights and smells envelop me, suck in the fresh air and feel the sun and the wind on my face, marvel at the changing scenery. First, though, before our African adventure could begin, we had to get out of Europe.

That should have been the easy part, but someone identified a problem with the rear differential on one of the trucks, necessitating a four-day wait in Rouen while a new part was shipped and fitted. Meanwhile, as one of my companions recently reminded me, we 'cleaned out the French pastry shops'! Most of us didn't know a differential from a gearbox, but we would soon enough. Without a 'diff' to deliver four-wheel drive when the going gets tough, life in Africa would be untenable. Roads in the Central Africa Republic (CAR) and Zaire in particular could become impassable in a matter of hours during the rainy season, with potholes the size of a small car. It was November and, as if to remind us that winter was closing in this far north, it snowed as we adjusted to life under canvas. The days of comfortable beds and mattresses were over. Most of us were greenhorns when it came to travelling rough; some like myself had backpacked around Europe and got used to sleeping on a park bench or in the back of a car. But this would be different.

Keith Miller, our team leader, was an affable and laconic Englishman with a friendly northern accent, an unruly mop of ginger-blonde hair and permanent five o'clock shadow. Cigarette in hand,

Keith was a 'no bullshit' kind of guy who had undertaken countless overland journeys through Africa and Asia. That, together with the fact that he was older than most of us, gave him a genuine presence and maturity. Nothing fazed Keith, from crawling under a vehicle to dealing with a stroppy immigration officer; none of us doubted his ability to get us safely to our final destination in Jo'burg. What made the trip special for me was the mix of Aussies and New Zealanders, some of whom were on their way home after the mandatory antipodean two-year working vacation in Europe. I loved their refreshingly forthright 'say it as it is', 'get stuck in' approach to life, providing just the right counterbalance to the British reserve. We would soon find out who the team players were, whether helping others to put up their tents or packing and unpacking the trailers. During my time in London I had worked as a lifeguard at Harrods Club in Barnes and played for their rugby team; I was determined to stay fit during the trip. Armed with a book of Canadian Air Force Keep Fit Exercises I managed to get most of the group to join me during our lunchtime breaks under the pretext that many hoped to climb Mount Kilimanjaro as we passed through Tanzania and would need to be in good shape to reach its snow-capped summit. Most people's enthusiasm had withered by the time we emerged on the far side of the Sahara Desert, but one or two stuck with it.

Crossing by ferry from southern Spain, we made our first footfall in Africa at Algeciras. Morocco's stark and ruggedly beautiful Atlas Mountains, where the North African lion once roamed, loomed into view, soon merging with the epic sandy wastelands of the Algerian Sahara and the promise of cloudless nights and a blanket of stars. The pock-marked sand tracks strapped to the sides of the trucks soon proved their worth and made us realise just how much we took for granted Keith and our drivers' expertise at nursing our vehicles through every eventuality. As we headed for Niger we passed through the oasis city of Tamanrasset, stopping to buy tins of condensed milk and bars of chocolate as treats on our way south – all overlanders dream of the food they are going to eat next time they hit town, regardless of expiry dates or weevils. Tamanrasset is the chief city of the Algerian Touareg, fiercely impressive tribal people dressed in flowing white tunics and blue-black turbans, as starkly beautiful with their fierce demeanour and aquiline features as their haughty camels.

The sparkling purity of Niger's desert country gave way to the ugly cityscapes of Nigeria, hot and humid as hell, with mosquitoes aplenty. We stopped for a couple of nights at a dive of a campsite in the city of Kanu. There were plenty of people with something to sell, from easy sex to fistfuls of marijuana. Almost everyone was taking dope in those days, but I didn't smoke and initially felt no great urge to get high. I was having far too good a time to need even greater stimulation, or so I thought.

Caught up in my African adventure, I suddenly felt that I could have a puff of marijuana on my own terms, find out what people found so alluring about it, but without the risk of getting hooked. I'm not sure what mix was in the packet of weed that one of the ever-smiling and friendly Aussies bought from one of the wide boys doing the rounds at the campsite. In no time at all I was as high as a kite and hallucinating – people morphed into bears or whatever other outlandish creatures we wished to imagine. I oscillated wildly between euphoria and paranoia as we mingled with the members at Kanu Country Club, rubbing shoulders with expats in blazers and ties and exotic ladies of the night with figure-hugging mini-skirts and bedroom eyes. By the time I regained my equilibrium the following morning my eyes felt so light-sensitive and my guts so wretched that I knew I never wanted to risk experiencing anything similar again.

There were the inevitable mishaps as we made our way south, such as when we inadvertently blocked a saloon car trailing in our dust near the Nigerian border. Those of us standing in the back of the truck tried to get the attention of our driver, but by the time we did the damage was done. When we arrived at the border it transpired that the vehicle that had been eating our dust belonged to the Chief Immigration Officer, who was none too pleased at being delayed by a bunch of scruffy overlanders. I don't know how many packets of cigarettes, bottles of whisky or dollars it took to sort out the situation, but I do know that we waited for many hours until the forms we needed to complete materialised. Just another day on the road for Keith.

Our crossing of Cameroon came and went so quickly that it barely registered. Not so the CAR, one of the poorest and most remote countries we visited, all luxuriant green banana trees, isolated villages and narrow pathways, with women carrying huge plastic containers filled with water on their heads. So it came as a thing of wonder when we reached the capital, Bangui, with its mouth-watering French patisserie, polished glass shelves laden with fresh croissants and cream pastries, not to mention some stunningly beautiful hookers who proved too much of a temptation for a couple of the lads on the trip. But the air of modern city living evaporated as we set off into the rainforest again. From CAR to Zaire it felt as if we were travelling through a dark green hothouse, the crowns of the trees so closely stacked together in places that they shut out the daylight, one enormous dark canopy spreading in every direction.

Not long after we entered Zaire one of the group took some photographs near a military establishment, even though we had been warned not to do so. Soldiers in camouflage kit and black shiny sunglasses, with cigarettes hanging from their mouths,

ABOVE There is a gap of fourteen years between my brother Clive and Caroline and myself. My mother was desperate to have a large family, but the war and health issues conspired against her.

LEFT My love of animals was nurtured growing up on Cuba Farm.
RIGHT House Captain of Coleridge A, Christ's Hospital, 1968.

ABOVE These photographs of Dad and Mum went everywhere with me.

ABOVE Overland through Africa, 1974–5 (photo: KIM GOTTLIEB).

ABOVE Fishermen in dugout canoes, Luangwa River, Zambia.

ABOVE Richard Leakey at the burning of 12 tonnes of ivory in Nairobi National Park,
18 July 1989, an event that led to a worldwide ban on the ivory trade.

Above With the Marsh Pride in Musiara Marsh,
not far from our stone cottage at Governor's Camp.

Above I am notorious for getting stuck in the Mara – if there is a big hole I will be sure to find it.
Opposite The Marsh Pride are so used to safari wagons that they will
sometimes rest in the shade of a vehicle.

ABOVE LEFT Game catcher Jan Oelofse in Namibia during the filming of *Wild Kingdom*, 1984.
ABOVE RIGHT A female leopard pauses to drink along the Olare Orok seasonal river.

ABOVE A Kenya Select rugby squad, 1981. I am third from the left and
Kenyan rugby icon Jimmy Owino fifth from the left in the back row.

ABOVE Lilac-breasted rollers: one of the highlights of birdwatching in the Mara.
FOLLOWING PAGE The Mara Buffalo Female, 1984. I had waited all day – twelve hours – for her
to emerge. It was the briefest of encounters, but provided the cover shot for *The Leopard's Tale*.

insisted that we unpack all our gear from our trucks and trailers while they spooled through our friend's precious film, exposing it to light. Keith's earthy diplomacy and sweeteners eventually had us safely back on the road.

We had been travelling for a month. It was December; the beginning of the rainy season brought a humidity that was almost overwhelming. Whenever we stopped to brew up tea we played Oliver Twist, stretching our hands out for more as we gulped down each tin cupful. We took it in turns to do the cooking and the shopping and on one occasion I mistook the engine oil for the cooking oil as we prepared what should have been a feast of fresh steak and onions. A feast it wasn't.

Sleeping was like resting your head in a sauna, kicking out the mosquito net in the fug of half sleep and then suffering death by a hundred mosquito bites. Despite rigorously taking Nivaquine from the start of the trip to guard against malaria, I began to feel feverish a couple of weeks later, just as we reached the place where we would stop for a day or so to allow those who had signed up for gorilla trekking in the fabled Virunga Mountains to head off into the forest. Somewhere along the way I had picked up a toxic combination of amoebic dysentery and giardia as bedfellows to my malaria, ensuring that I alternated between teeth-chattering chills and a raging fever with a headache from hell. Feeling rough wasn't the word for it. I remember parking my camp bed in a clearing in the forest, wracked by fever and dehydrated by the endless calls of nature. An Aussie friend who had nursing experience administered water and whatever pills were required so that when the truck was ready to set off again I was on the mend. By that time one of our drivers had been forced to return to the UK after the mosquito bites he had scratched raw turned into ugly tropical ulcers and he became too ill to continue.

Potentially far more serious to our wellbeing was the afternoon we stopped for a drink at a local bar in a remote village in Zaire. Overlanders measure time by the breaks for meals or a coffee; better still a cold beer. Waitresses collected our money after each round of drinks, so when we were finally ready to leave we were surprised to find there was money still owing. Everyone insisted they had paid in full and that one of the bar staff was taking liberties on the assumption that we would pay up just to keep the peace. Word soon spread that something was amiss and the mood soured as a noisy crowd gathered around the trucks. The threat of mob violence is always lurking in the wings in a situation like this – a robbery, road accident, someone knocked from their bike, a sense of injustice all potential triggers for mayhem.

Just when things looked as if they were going to turn really ugly a vehicle drove up. A smartly dressed man in a dark suit stepped out of his car and the crowd fell silent. Wealthy and influential businessmen in this part of Africa are known as *wabenzi* due to their fondness for Mercedes Benz vehicles that act, along with the size of their stomachs, as visible signs of their status. Keith spoke with the man, who then talked to the crowd. He pulled a wad of money from his pocket and handed some notes to the waitress who had insisted she had not been paid. He told us that while he was sure it was just a misunderstanding, he did not want visitors to go away with bad memories of his country. We were soon on our way again, relieved that sense had prevailed and grateful for the diplomacy of our mystery friend.

I am not exactly sure where I bought the small ivory carving that would haunt me in years to come. I think it was Kisangani (formerly Stanleyville), 2,000 kilometres upstream from the mouth of the mighty Congo River, home during the 1880s to Tippu Tip, the infamous Zanzibari who traded ivory and slaves. I remember a man with a basket unwrapping packets of green banana leaves, each containing ivory, and choosing one particularly beautifully piece with a woman's head carved on it. The sheen and texture of ivory make it exquisite to the human eye and to the touch. Seduced by the beauty of the piece, I never gave a thought to where the ivory had come from. What I can be sure of now is that an elephant died to make that carving possible – a young elephant of perhaps six to ten years of age, judging by the size of the tusk it was fashioned from.

There was no stigma to buying ivory in those days and I did not even consider that the killing was almost certainly the work of poachers. Back then there were more than a million elephants in Africa. But during the 1980s, 60,000 were killed each year for their ivory, reducing the population within a decade from around 1.2 million to 600,000 by 19 July 1989, when the Kenyan President Daniel arap Moi (on the advice of Dr Richard Leakey, then head

of the Kenya Wildlife Service) burned a stockpile of 12 tonnes of ivory in Nairobi National Park. With a street value of three million dollars, it represented the loss of 2,000 elephants. That momentous gesture helped secure a ban on the sale of ivory later the same year. I was there to photograph it and as I watched I was reminded of the carving I had left in South Africa at the end of my journey, along with a carved wooden head of a Maasai warrior I had purchased in a street market in Dar es Salaam. They had been my most treasured keepsakes from the overland trip and I fully intended to return to collect them. But by the time I went back to South Africa many years later I knew all about the carnage wreaked by the ivory trade and had no desire to set eyes on the carving ever again.

As we ascended the steep road winding its way out of the rainforests of Zaire into Rwanda, I looked back down the pathway, thinking that I had never seen anything so vast and pristine in all my life: even today the Democratic Republic of the Congo (DRC), as it is now called, has the greatest extent of tropical rainforests in Africa, covering over 100 million hectares, a dense swathe of dark green foliage reaching to the sky. But that vast expanse is an illusion. In West Africa alone ninety per cent of the rainforests have already disappeared.

Though they cover less than two per cent of the earth's surface, the world's rainforests are home to fifty per cent of its plants and animals and are crucial to our supply of fresh water. They are also the lungs of the earth, storing carbon and helping to keep the global climate stable. And they yield a wealth of medicinal plants, leading them to be called 'the world's largest pharmacy'. Despite all this, 145,000 square kilometres of rainforest are lost each year to logging, unsustainable agriculture, cattle ranching, mining and exploration for oil, in the process destroying more than 50,000 species of those same animals and plants. At that rate – according to Professor E O Wilson, the doyen of biologists who was pioneering the study of the evolution of behaviour when I was a student at Queen's – a quarter of all species on earth could be exterminated within fifty years due to loss of habitat.

The opening up of the forests by the logging industry precipitated a devastating influx of meat hunters to feed their workers. A study commissioned in 1999 found that the bushmeat trade in Central African rainforests involved the equivalent of 10 million head of cattle. Today there is a silence sweeping over these green and fertile landscapes, some of which are devoid of all life – aptly described as 'Empty Forest Syndrome'. Hardly surprising when 155 million people live on less than a dollar a day each in West and Central Africa, but at this rate by 2030 eighty per cent of the world's remaining rainforest will have vanished.

One thing I could be certain of was that I was not a rainforest person, the kind who found the stifling hothouse of the tropics cosy, who willingly embraced the constant dampness and fungus, the leeches and tropical ulcers. I need the lightness of the open places, the savannas; I only have to think humidity and I begin to pour with sweat. The primatologist Dian Fossey certainly earned my respect by surviving eighteen years in an environment like this. Wracked with emphysema and in poor health much of the time, Fossey dedicated her life to trying to save the few hundred mountain gorillas (currently estimated at 380) that live in the Virunga National Park in Rwanda before she was murdered in her cabin with a blow to the head from a *panga* on Boxing Day 1985.

Pangas are ubiquitous implements in Africa. As you travel through the continent you soon get used to the sight of people carrying these lethal-looking 'garden' tools. Large, flat Crocodile Dundee-sized knives the length of your forearm, they are used as farm implements to cut back sugar cane, branches and vegetation. Depending on mood and circumstances, those same pangas can be wielded as weapons that can slice off a hand or an ear or bury themselves into someone's head with fatal consequences, as had happened with Dian Fossey. So when we passed through a quiet and isolated village early in our journey across the rainforest and men came running towards us, shouting and brandishing their pangas, it was with considerable relief that we saw their stern appearance transformed into laughter at the surprise and alarm so evident on our faces. But in 1994, twenty years after I completed my overland journey and almost ten years after Fossey's death, an estimated 500,000–1,000,000 people were killed during the Rwandan genocide, hacked to death with those same pangas, as members of the Hutu majority went on a deadly hundred-day rampage: twenty per cent of the country's total population and seventy per cent of the minority Tutsi then living in Rwanda were slaughtered as the world looked on. What does that say about the human condition?

Malaria and dysentery may have sapped my energy reserves, but not for long. I was galvanised by the thought of the next leg of our journey, a safari through the Serengeti in Tanzania and the Maasai Mara in Kenya, the savanna Africa that had been the catalyst for my journey. The former domain of Dr Bernhard and Michael Grzimek, the German father and son with the unpronounceable surname, the Serengeti had been immortalised in 1959 with their epic book and Oscar-winning documentary *Serengeti Shall Not Die*, which recorded how they took to the air in a small plane in order to observe the seasonal movements of zebras and wildebeest.

I had seen the film and read the book. With my farm upbringing, love of wild creatures and thirst for adventure, how could I not be motivated to try to follow a similar path to those pioneering scientists and filmmakers?

I could barely contain my excitement as we crossed from Rwanda into Tanzania, skirting the shores of Lake Victoria before rumbling up to the entrance gate marked Serengeti National Park. It wasn't long before we saw our first lions as we navigated our way through the treacherous black cotton soils in the Western Corridor with its dense acacia woodlands and hard-biting tsetse flies, heading east towards the ancient granite outcrops of the Maasai Kopjes. I was in heaven, my heart bursting with the realisation that there was still a place like this where animals of every description roamed free.

Somewhere along the languorous course of the Seronera River, in the centre of the park with its three-billion-year-old rocks, we came across a leopard. We had been told to keep a sharp eye out for 'the spotted one' as we drove past towering yellow-barked acacia trees that lined the banks. These elegant 'fever trees', as they are known, grow near water, the sort of place where mosquitoes love to breed. Although the trees' seductive shade makes them look like the perfect campsite, if you are not careful to sleep under a net you might come away with the malarial parasite coursing through your veins and the mother of all fevers.

We had hired a game ranger to show us round and with the leopard resting at the base of one of the trees and partially veiled in long grass we were desperate for a better view. Eager as our guide was for a good tip, he was adamant that we must not go off road, warning us that David Babu, the Senior Warden, sometimes lay in hiding for wayward drivers and guides, staking out the area just as a hungry leopard might wait in ambush for its prey. If we were caught off road the ranger risked losing his job and we would feel the wrath of the warden, along with a heavy fine for our drivers and even the possibility of being banned from the park. I had dreamed of my first meeting with a wild leopard. As a child I had waited patiently for the leopard to emerge from its cave at Regent's Park Zoo in London; even then, I thought that this had to be the most sublimely beautiful and graceful of all the big cats. The fact that this particular leopard was in no hurry to move, just his bluish-green eyes and spotted head visible in the swaying grass, only increased my desire to get to know this member of the cat family a lot better at some point in my life.

After the highlights of the Serengeti, the Maasai Mara was little more than a break on our way to Nairobi. Just time for a morning game drive around Lake Nakuru which, beautiful as it was, proved disappointing. The tens of thousands of greater and lesser flamingos that normally transform the edges of the lake into a pink paradise had vanished for richer feeding grounds further north at Lake Bogoria. The splendour of the world's finest bird spectacle would have to wait. As we began to climb out of the Great Rift Valley and away from Nakuru I could see in the distance a smaller lake where the pink of the elusive flamingos dotted the shoreline. I was determined to head back for another look. But for the moment my first priority was to have my precious photographs developed in Nairobi and then to head for the post office to pick up the bundle of letters that I felt sure would be awaiting my arrival. The streets of the city were lined with jacaranda trees – surely one of the most captivating sights when in full bloom, their ripe blossoms creating a carpet of lilac along the highway into town.

The following day I returned to the camera shop to collect my contact sheets with thirty-six thumbnail images printed on each page. All my films were black and white – I couldn't afford colour.

With a shake of his head and an apologetic look on his face the technician handed me a large brown envelope. As I tore open the package with trembling hands I imagined his manner indicated commiseration for the amateurish quality of my photography. Nothing could have prepared me for the shock and disappointment of finding virtually all my images ruined. Sheet after sheet was as black as night, except for a handful of pictures taken in the Sahara where the light had been so intense that it had given a correct exposure. The rest were beyond saving. All those stunning landscapes and busy village scenes, the atmospheric sunsets and sunrises, that amazing woman with tattoos on her face in the market in Niger, the Serengeti with its lions and elephants – that leopard. Nothing!

What an idiot. If I had read the instruction manual I would have known that it was impossible to synch my camera with a non-Canon lens to give me automatic exposure. Instead, with the Tamron lens set to the electronic exposure setting, I had been shooting everything with the lens stopped down to f/22 – the smallest aperture. I could not have wished for a more painful wake-up call as a fledgling photographer. The lesson was clear: take nothing for granted, read the manual, familiarise yourself with your camera and lenses, and take some test shots before heading off on an important assignment or the holiday of a lifetime.

We had a few days R&R at a campsite in Nairobi, during which I kept my promise to myself to head back to the Rift Valley in search of the elusive flamingos. While everyone else was busy catching up on some creature comforts – hot showers and a change of clothing, lazy days by the swimming pool, pastries and coffee in downtown Nairobi – I hitched a lift past Limuru tea country and down into the Rift Valley towards the lakes. When I reached a wide bend on the rutted tarmac overlooking the dry bush near Lake Elmenteita

I jumped out, camera in hand, and strode down through the long grass towards the water. I hadn't a clue as to what I would find along the way – might there be lions or buffaloes lying up among the patches of thick bush, perhaps a leopard watching from the acacia forests? I kept to the open wherever possible, taking note of trees I might climb if something large and dangerous suddenly emerged. I got the fright of my life as a family of warthogs erupted from under my feet, exploding from their burrows with blood-curdling grunts and squeals, showering me with soil. There were herds of waterbuck, too – large, shaggy-coated antelopes, the males bearing impressive sets of knurled horns that could easily skewer a lion if they were cornered; goodness knows what they might do to me.

I was rapidly discovering that I was a novice when it came to walking through game country, but I was determined to immerse myself in the sight of those flamingos, even if only for a moment or two. Nothing in my upbringing in England could have prepared me for the excitement of this. I had never felt so alive. I snapped a few photographs and then hurried up to the road, hitching a ride back to the campsite, feeling a sense of utter elation as I picked the ticks off my legs. I had kept my promise that I wouldn't waste one precious moment of my time in Africa, soaking up every spine-tingling element of the safari experience I hungered after.

Kilimanjaro, the highest free-standing mountain in the world at 5,895 metres, would be the next challenge, but to climb it would mean leaving the overland trip while the trucks carried on to Mombasa for a week on the coast. My New Zealand chum Bob Paine was the only other member of the group who still fancied the climb. Bob was a great guy, quiet and gentle, but a sportsman with a nose for adventure and bags of determination. Off we went by bus to Moshi in Tanzania, the starting point for the ascent, where we could hire some warm clothing. Climbing Kilimanjaro is pretty much one long hike requiring no mountaineering skills: 55 kilometres to the top, then 55 kilometres back to base, normally over the course of five days – three up and two down, though to acclimatise properly seven or eight days at altitude are recommended. However, because there was a fuel shortage in Tanzania at the time, vehicle movements were restricted on Sundays. That meant we would have only four days to climb the mountain and descend again: only by getting back down on Saturday would we arrive in Kenya in time to meet up with the rest of the group before they departed for Dar es Salaam. Keith had told us that they wouldn't wait if we failed to return on time.

There were huts situated at 3,000, 3,500 and 4,500 metres where we could sleep – bare timber shacks with holes in the planks and rats to keep us company. But they would shield us to a degree from the wind and the cold.

The key to climbing the mountain is simple: don't turn it into a race. Our porters jogged alongside us most of the time with our kit balanced on their heads, reminding us in Swahili to go *pole pole* – slowly slowly – to take it easy. Bob and I were both pretty fit, but we knew that fitness wouldn't protect us from altitude sickness; it can literally strike out of the blue. Two of our climbing companions were Dutchmen who had pedalled their way from South Africa to

Tanzania and sported the muscular legs of professional athletes, but when they decided to push ahead one of them had to be sent back down.

By 3,500 metres our hearts were thumping in our chests, then in our throats; our heads were pounding. We scrutinised the faces of people on their way back down, from teenagers to pensioners; some looked terrible and could barely speak, while others waved and smiled as if they were returning from a walk in the park. We were told to go easy on the food as we climbed higher: it was best to stick to porridge, nuts and chocolates. I was ravenous and ate all my food before tucking into some of Bob's and soon felt as sick as a dog. Our guides then woke us in the dead of night and we stumbled off into the darkness, trudging along in the footsteps of the person in front as we snaked our way up the final thousand metres or so. By now it was mainly loose scree that slipped from under our feet, so that at times we barely made any headway.

We weren't sure if the guides get you up early so that you reach the summit at sunrise, or because the scree is more manageable when icy cold, or just so that you cannot see how much further you still have to climb: apparently rock slides are more likely once the sun comes up and your footing becomes more unstable. I felt grim by the time we got to Gilman's Point (5,685 metres) at the rim of the crater and stayed just long enough to take in the thought that this particular volcano last erupted 150,000 to 200,000 years ago. I couldn't wait to get off the mountain. My hands and face were puffy and I knew that the only way for me was down. I waited while Bob hiked the final two hundred metres to Uhuru Point and then we went slip-sliding down over the scree on our bottoms.

We now faced a new challenge, yomping all the way back down to the YMCA in Moshi before nightfall. When we woke the next morning and struggled out of bed Bob and I just looked at each other. I had had surgery for a torn cartilage at university and our knees had taken such a pounding on the way down that we could barely walk. A few hours later we gratefully jumped on a bus with a chassis so warped that we drove crab-like along the road, narrowly missing cows and people as we hurtled back towards Kenya.

The final leg of the trip was one long gallop down the 921-kilometre TanZam highway, the main trade route between the Tanzanian port of Dar es Salaam and landlocked Zambia. There was a sense that the best of our safari was coming to an end as we roared past dusty towns and villages with their warrens of non-descript shops and offices. Convoys of trucks spewing noxious black diesel smoke hauled copper, cattle, textiles and farm produce from city to city. In years to come truckers on routes like this would be the catalyst for HIV/AIDS to rage like wildfire through Africa. Guesthouses and bars sprung up along the highways as the sex trade moved in to service the demand, with the plague of HIV spreading silently into the surrounding villages: what could be better for the working man after a long day on the road than a beer and some roast meat shared with a girlfriend before retiring to bed? Those chums of ours in Bangui had been lucky – the days of free love with no consequences were coming to an end, as I was soon to find out for myself.

I was elated by what I had seen of the African continent. Three months on the road had opened my eyes to how starkly different each of the fifty-two countries were. North Africa was defined by its Arab culture and harshly beautiful landscape, the contrast between its rugged mountains and the grandeur of the Sahara Desert a thing of wonder. West Africa was more humid, more malarial and less Arabic in its ways, while the east – particularly Kenya and Tanzania – was my kind of Africa: a land of high steppes and dry heat with chill nights to temper the equatorial sun. More importantly to me, it was a land filled with wild animals. Travelling south along the TanZam highway I began to feel the 'end of holiday blues', as the things I loved most about Africa slipped away, particularly the friendliness of a people freed from their colonial legacy. Here in Southern Africa the Europeans were still in charge; the mood felt different, the people more guarded and reticent. Zambia was still dominated by white settlers, many of them Brits or Afrikaners from South Africa; the capital Lusaka a somewhat drab and surly city with characterless shops full of green malachite carvings and garish copper artwork. We barely had time to stop.

On arrival in Johannesburg, I bade farewell to my fellow travellers and headed for Bishop Timothy Bavin's residence, where my mother and sister-in-law, Clive's wife Judith, awaited my arrival. Our plan was to visit Judith's brother Philip, who had settled in South Africa many years earlier and married into a local family. We then set off on a two-week trip around South Africa, visiting Kruger National Park, in those days a bastion of white Afrikaner society run with military precision. Clive and Judith's great friend the Reverend Simeon Nkoane, a member of a religious order called the Community of the Resurrection, drove us there and I had my first taste of apartheid: under the Segregation Act Simeon was directed to separate accommodation and had to endure some silly remarks from one of the officials about men in women's clothing – he was wearing a long white cassock befitting his status as a priest. The look of contempt on the faces of the white officials in Kruger observing how friendly we were with Simeon was quite a shock.

After Mum and Judith returned to England I moved into St Peter's Priory in Rosettenville, a suburb of Johannesburg, where the Community of the Resurrection was based, with Simeon as my mentor. This might imply that I held strong religious views.

I didn't. I had attended Sunday School at Cookham Church as a child, sung in the choir and for a while thought the best part of getting confirmed was the sip of Communion sherry. I certainly enjoyed the ritual celebrations of Easter and Christmas – the feeling of family and community; the carol service with all those lusty ancient songs echoing around the church – but could never accept the literal interpretations of the gospels. In fact I was far more fascinated by the life and work of the avant garde painter Sir Stanley Spencer, who had been born in Cookham and could often be seen pottering around the village. Spencer's unique brand of art opened my eyes to a different world to the one I inhabited. His painterly stories were far more exciting to lose myself in than the word of God, helping the time to pass until the vicar's sermon was over. Spencer's powerful imagery gave expression to his innermost thoughts, allowed him to lay them bare and explore them, something that until now I had had little idea how to do.

Despite my reservations about a conventional God, staying at St Peter's was an enlightening and liberating time in my life. The resonance with CH, a life marked by ritual and order with people in clerical gowns, made me feel at home. Here were men from different backgrounds moulded together by a common faith in God and humanity. Love and compassion were their guiding principles, allied to a rock-solid belief in something greater than themselves and their own selfish needs, a conviction that a meaningful life demanded more than material success. They led a simple existence of solitude and contemplation, of quiet and prayer, offering pastoral care and conferences to the wider community. Never far from their thoughts was the struggle against apartheid. Each evening the brothers assembled for service in the small chapel – hour-long sessions of contemplation and quiet as I succumbed to the sense of calm that came with singing the psalms and hymns so familiar to me from childhood.

CHAPTER

02

AFRICA
MY
HOME

The darkest thing about Africa has

always been our ignorance of it.

———————————————

George H T Kimble

AFRICA TODAY: THE LIFTING DARKNESS

Having exorcised the urge to continue on my travels around the world, and with St Peter's Priory as only a temporary base, I needed to address the challenge posed to me by Professor Owen at Queen's University. Were my dreams of working with wildlife destined to become nothing more than a pastime or could I really make a career out of my passion?

By now I had discovered that there were three pathways for someone who wanted to 'do something with wildlife'. I could follow the traditional academic route with the hope that I might be able to spend time studying predators here in Africa for a MSc or PhD. That would gain me a few years in the field but then what – teaching? That didn't sound very exciting. The second option was to find work in the wildlife tourism industry as a guide or camp manager in a park or game reserve. With no experience that seemed unlikely. Finally I could become a wildlife artist or photographer, which would allow me to spend time in the bush collecting material. That seemed the most promising possibility, but was my artwork good enough for me to make a living from it? A fourth option that quickly proved to be a non-starter was to try to join the National Parks Service in Africa as a game ranger. Jobs like that were in great demand, with a long waiting list in places like Rhodesia, as I soon discovered when I wrote to enquire. For a young white man – an outsider at that – in a fast-changing independent Africa, the Parks Service offered an uncertain future. It looked as if art and photography were my best bet, despite my lack of experience.

The disaster with my photographs from the overland journey reminded me that I had to master the technical aspects along with the creativity. Even more important, I needed to learn as much as possible about the behaviour of my subjects. With that in mind I spent time browsing the bookshops for insights into animal behaviour, as well as visiting galleries specialising in wildlife art and photography. The Everard Read Gallery in Johannesburg was of particular note, displaying impressive paintings by international artists such as David Shepherd and Donald Grant, as well as showcasing talented locals such as Keith Joubert, whose work was defined by its graphic originality and abstract approach to his subjects. But the artist who made the greatest impression on me was Leigh Voigt, whose pen and ink drawings I had first seen illustrating a weekly column in the *Rand Daily Mail* written by the wildlife veterinarian Sue Hart. There was something about Leigh's work – its realism particularly appealed to me, as did its incredible vitality, creating a dynamic connection between subject and viewer. Allied to Sue Hart's eloquent words, it resonated with my growing passion for Africa.

It was while leafing through a copy of that same newspaper in the library at St Peter's Priory that I first came across the name Dr Theodore Bailey. Bailey was an American biologist and student of Dr Maurice Hornocker, who had made the study of the mountain lion in North America the focus of his life's work. Bailey had been one of the pioneers of radio-telemetry; his research on the bobcat would have been impossible without the ability to track his subjects with radio collars. When I spotted an article featuring his work on leopards in Kruger National Park it reignited my interest in fieldwork – and my longing to learn more about leopards. I wrote to Bailey asking if he needed a research assistant. I was thrilled when he responded, even though he explained that his wife acted as his field assistant and advised me to go back to university to study for a Masters degree if I was serious about continuing my career in zoology. Fired with enthusiasm, I then made an appointment with Professor John Skinner, the head of the prestigious Pretoria Mammal Research Institute that had featured in Sue Hart's newspaper column. My overriding memory of that meeting is an uncomfortable conversation with the professor's secretary while I was waiting to see him. I sat and listened as she pondered what it might be like if apartheid were to disappear, and contemplated the 'unimaginable' distress she would feel having to sit in a cinema full of black people.

Professor Skinner was warm, friendly and clearly passionate about his work. Antelopes were his area of particular interest and he wondered how I would feel about studying the feeding biology of impala or elands rather than focusing on big cats. When he realised I was not to be dissuaded, he wrote to Queen's University to find out more about my academic credentials and suitability for a scholarship: I would need funding for a 4x4 vehicle and a bursary to support the writing up of the project at Pretoria University. He proposed a broad-based ecological study on large predators in one of Rhodesia's parks or reserves – possibly Wankie, now Hwange National Park. Hwange was to achieve worldwide notoriety many years later as the home of Cecil the lion who, in 2015, was shot illegally by an American dentist, first with bow and arrow and then forty hours later finished off with a high-powered rifle. The event brought shame on the already embattled trophy-hunting industry and made lion conservation headline news around the world, while forcing the dentist into hiding.

I was elated on hearing that my application had been successful. My long-suffering mother and family back in the UK were equally overjoyed to know that I was going to settle down and follow a more conventional career path, rather than continuing to 'bum around Africa', as my uncles and godfathers feared I was intent on doing for the foreseeable future. But I was almost immediately overcome with doubts about my decision. On the academic level, was I bright enough to deal with the maths and statistics that my thesis would involve? More importantly, how would I adjust to life back at Pretoria University while writing up my thesis, given its place at the very heart of Afrikaner society?

I spoke to Simeon Nkoane about my concerns. He had already acted as my confidant and mentor when an American girlfriend from a casual liaison during my overland trip told me she thought she was pregnant. She had been a passenger on another overland truck and we hooked up one night on our way south, agreeing to meet up again at the end of our journey. We bought a pregnancy test kit in a chemist's in Johannesburg and sure enough it proved positive, prompting us to make an appointment at a clinic. Based on the examination the doctor thought my friend was indeed pregnant and ordered another test, while giving us both a stern lecture about morality and commitment. In that moment all our dreams came crashing to earth. We agonised over what we might do – we barely knew each other. Simeon, who had seen hundreds of young women in similar situations in the townships, proved a rock of good sense and compassion, rather than simply scolding us. Fortunately the second test proved negative and we went our separate ways, chastened by the experience of the downside of casual sex.

Simeon wanted me to make my own decision about the opportunity Professor Skinner was offering me. To me it seemed disingenuous and hypocritical to profess my abhorrence of apartheid, yet accept a scholarship to study at a South African university. As a visitor and outsider I would be receiving an education beyond the reach of the vast majority of the country's citizens. When I wrote to Professor Skinner expressing my doubts and regrets he responded with a withering rebuttal of my decision, ending with the memorable words: 'If you are to take your argument to its logical conclusion, then I suggest you become a missionary in a black African country.' I could well understand his frustration. He had been incredibly welcoming and generous in trying to make my dream come true, but in the end I am grateful that I turned my back on an academic life and chose the freedom of my next destination, Botswana.

Inspired by Leigh Voigt's artwork, I decided to experiment with the painstaking technique that she had mastered. I had seen other examples of stippling or pointillism – in fact I had dabbled with it when illustrating my thesis at Queen's – but nothing that compared with hers. She rendered flesh and fur with a mix of dots and pen strokes, building up a wonderful range of tones and textures. Her drawings were masterly in the way she 'modelled' her subjects by leaving parts of them as pure white, forcing the eye of the beholder to complete the shape. She was just as adept at adding colour to her artwork. By the time I left St Peter's I had made a start on creating a collection of pen and ink drawings of my own.

At this time, many artists were maximising the revenue from their original artwork by selling limited edition prints. Wildlife art had always been popular in the UK and even more so in North America, where trophy hunters paid handsomely for paintings and bronze sculptures featuring big game such as lions and elephants. The fashion at that time was for highly detailed artwork showing every feather of a bird's plumage and every nuance of a big cat's fur – a form of super-realism that was very eye-catching and technically superb, but sometimes lacking in mood or emotion.

Much as I admired attention to detail, I was captivated by artists who could reveal the essence of their subject in a few lyrical brushstrokes, or suggest feelings of movement through a blur of wings or horns. I was greatly impressed by the Canadian Robert Bateman, who often chose to make his animal subject a detail in the larger landscape – a tiny wren lost in a maze of ivy or a leopard writ small in the sculptural tapestry of the gnarled limbs of a fig tree. Bateman is as much a master of backlight and sidelight as the great wildlife photographers and while there is an element of photographic realism and attention to detail in his work you always know that you are admiring both a painting and a work of art. He would be a source of constant inspiration to me over the next few years, both as an artist and as a photographer.

As for myself, I had no pretensions to being creative with my art. I have never progressed to exploring colour and painting with a brush, at least not since school art classes under the tutelage of the inimitable and bohemian Miss Todd, who was as original in her approach as Stanley Spencer. She was a true eccentric with extravagantly decorated signature hats and voluminous white skirts, a free spirit who livened up our week with her unconventional ways in what was otherwise a very conventional school. Her apartment above the art school was adorned with huge sweeping works of her own, romantic landscapes and quasi-religious tableaux. She encouraged us to break free, embracing art as a way of expressing our innermost feelings, whether casting a pot of clay on a stone wheel or giving rein to our emotions with vivid splashes of colour on canvas. Some frowned on her methods, but most of the teachers adored Miss Todd as much as we did – though when she encouraged one of her classes to take off their clothes on a hot summer's day some people thought that, rather than liberating her young charges, this was taking art a step too far.

Despite this early influence I knew to play to my strengths. My skill lay in rendering exactly what I saw down to the minutest detail while retaining a sense of the subject's character. Adding the intangible element that brings a drawing to life and fires the imagination fascinated me. As Einstein reflected, 'If what is seen and experienced is portrayed in the language of logic, we are engaged in science. If it is communicated through forms whose connections are not accessible to the conscious mind but are recognised intuitively as meaningful, then we are engaged in art.' Drawing had allowed me to excel in biology classes that often involved illustrating a plant or animal, a dissected specimen or item of taxidermy. My reward was not just in the pleasure I got from drawing but in gaining marks that helped to move me towards the top of the biology class at CH. It also fostered a sense of closeness and connection to my father.

Having turned down Professor Skinner's offer, I decided that I no longer wished to remain in South Africa: I wanted to be free of the oppressive atmosphere that apartheid cast over that wonderful land. It was Simeon Nkoane who recommended that I head north to Botswana. At considerable risk to his own safety, he had helped a number of young black activists to flee their homes, finding them safe havens in places like Botswana once it became apparent that they were likely to be targeted by the security forces in South Africa. He bade me farewell with a letter of introduction to the head teachers at a school in Botswana's capital city, Gaborone. After that, a chance meeting with Bodo Muche, the taxidermist at Botswana Game Industries, led to an introduction to the naturalist

Tim Liversedge. Tim and his wife June lived on a double-storey houseboat called the *Sitatunga* after the rare marsh antelope that lives in the Okavango Delta, the magnificent seasonal wetland that draws visitors to Botswana from all over the world. June was a cordon bleu cook and together they made a charismatic couple, hosting small groups of wealthy clients on the houseboat that provided the ideal platform for viewing wildlife in terrain often shrouded by a four to five metre blanket of papyrus.

Tim was just the inspiration a young aspiring naturalist like myself was looking for – proof of what might be possible. The fact that he could paint and sculpt made him all the more impressive. Some evenings after yet another delicious dinner on the boat, he entertained visitors with slide shows of his colourful and emotive wildlife photographs. I was mesmerised by the beauty of the Delta and by Tim's skills in capturing it. He was something of a loner, quiet but strong and resolute; he did not suffer fools gladly and allowed nothing to stand in his way. Only with that kind of attitude, I decided, could you achieve the seemingly impossible. In time I would discover similar characteristics in just about all the top wildlife filmmakers and photographers I met, some of who stamped their claim on a particular area with the ruthlessness of a territorial lion. The Liversedges in the Okavango and Alan and Joan Root in the Serengeti are just two examples of couples who took their vision and inspired others to help them make it a reality.

The Okavango is best seen down low at water level or from on high in a helicopter. More remote and inaccessible than the Mara-Serengeti, vast tracts of the Delta are off limits to vehicles due to the flood that arrives each year at the end of the rains, transforming the land into a patchwork of palm-fringed islands set amid blue and green tongues of clear fresh water flowing over the yellow sands of the Kalahari Desert. It feels totally different from the

Mara-Serengeti's broad sweeping plains and scattered acacia trees – yet its unique character makes it one of my favourite places in Africa, a watery wonderland. During my time there, there were encounters with stroppy bull hippos defending their patch of water with fierce snorts of alarm, creating menacing bow waves as they duck-dived or surfaced ahead of the boat. From low down you suddenly realised just how huge these two to three tonne behemoths really were – and the sheer speed with which a four-metre crocodile could launch itself out of the water in an explosive lunge after prey.

Little wonder they call the Delta the Jewel of the Kalahari. At first light the crystal-clear waters sparkle like a carpet of diamonds as herds of lechwe antelope bound through the shallows; or become a turbulent lake of silver and white spume as the heavy black shapes of an army of five hundred buffaloes plough a path through the water as they head towards fresh grazing.

More than anything this is a birder's paradise. At night we would load our guests into the boats and chug slowly along the fringes of the papyrus, marvelling at the sight of half a dozen bee-eaters huddled together for warmth on a single drooping reed stem as radiant as a string of emerald-green pearls. Sometimes we would pinpoint the red eye-shine of one of the Okavango's most sought-after birds, the Pel's fishing owl, a tall buff-orange avian predator that Tim and June wanted to study in more detail. There was even talk that, given my zoological background, I might be able to help them collect the data they were looking for. The Liversedges had raised young fishing owls at Shakawe, high up on the Panhandle, a long narrow gully on the edge of the Delta: their camp there was the starting point for safaris aboard the *Sitatunga*. They had discovered that the owls often perched close to the water's edge, watching for the tell-tale ripples of their prey before plunging into the water feet first with talons outstretched to snag a fish or freshwater crab. They would eat only the nutritious brain of a tiger fish, leaving the rest to the scavengers.

We would use a spotlight to catch these handsome owls at night so that Tim and June could ring, weigh and measure them. While I kept a tight grip on the feet of a newly caught adult, I asked Tim if they ever used their beaks to defend themselves. At that moment the owl bent forward and attempted to take a chunk out of my hand. We should have known better than to release the owl the following morning, as it was immediately mobbed by an aggressive fish eagle intent on knocking it out of the sky, illustrating perfectly how these two impressive birds of prey normally avoid competing with one another by operating at different times of the day or night.

Spending time on the *Sitatunga* was a glorious introduction to what living in the African bush might be like. To find myself in one of the planet's greatest wildlife paradises seemed almost too good to be true. Waking each morning to the hauntingly beautiful cry of fish eagles and the sonorous honking of hippos was beyond my wildest dreams. Better still, I was in the company of a couple making a living from their talents on the back of plain hard work. However, despite the opportunity to entertain the likes of author Wilbur Smith and his charming wife Danielle, I could tell that Tim was frustrated by having to attend to his fledgling tourism business: in his heart he wanted to devote more time to artistic endeavours. He had dreams of becoming a wildlife filmmaker, while June had determined to develop her love and talent for stills photography. In time they would both excel in their respective fields and with June's business savvy they carved out their own niche in this particular Garden of Eden.

I had brought my oversized cardboard portfolio of pen and ink drawings to show the Liversedges and during my time on the *Sitatunga*

I added a number of sketches to the collection. I was particularly pleased with a detailed drawing of a martial – Africa's largest eagle – perched on a branch in heraldic pose with a monitor lizard clasped in its powerful talons. It was the perfect subject for my style of drawing, given its dark crown and spotted white chest and legs. One evening when all the guests had departed for home we headed for a night out at Shakawe Fishing Camp, owned by the Liversedges' friends Barry and Elaine Price. I took my drawings along to show them. After a dinner of fresh tilapia washed down with plenty of beer and wine we headed for the wooden walkway where the boat was moored ready to take us back to the *Sitatunga*. With my portfolio under his arm Tim tripped as he got into the boat and toppled into the water, still clutching my precious drawings. As he surfaced, spluttering with embarrassment and laughter, I noticed my portfolio floating beside him. June shouted at Tim and he quickly retrieved it; then we headed for the *Sitatunga* as fast as we could. We dried the portfolio with towels and with more than a little trepidation unfastened the ribbons. To my delight and Tim's immense relief the drawings were in surprisingly good shape, with only one or two a little soggy at the edges – the waterproof ink had held fast.

I later entered the drawing of the martial eagle in an art competition organised by the Botswana National Museum. While it did not win,

the eminent rock-art expert Alec Campbell, curator of the museum and newly created art gallery, was sufficiently impressed to ask if he could buy it for their permanent collection. I had made my first sale as a wildlife artist.

After a few unforgettable weeks in the Okavango it became apparent that, whether working on the fishing owl project or helping with guests on the *Sitatunga*, I was surplus to requirements and likely to distract Tim from his obligations to the tourist enterprise. He and June decided to 'let me go'. There were no hard feelings; they flew me back to Francistown, where I met up again with the taxidermist Boda Mucha and his boss Peter Becker. It was Peter who put me in touch with Jack Bousfield, the proprietor of Botswana Birds and Game, a game-capture operation on the outskirts of town. I had my doubts about the animal-capture business and soon discovered that Jack's quarantine facility resembled a rather shambolic mini zoo. The cages were small and unimaginatively conceived, so it was fortunate that most of the inhabitants did not stay for long. Quite what future lay in store for them in zoos and safari parks in Europe and America I could only imagine. But I knew that working there would provide me with the perfect opportunity to collect more material for my artwork.

In the evenings I would work on drawings of the various animals that I was able to observe up close. There were bat-eared foxes with large black eyes and enormous ears, a beautifully marked long-legged serval cat and a number of caracals or desert lynx with piercing pale blue eyes and tufted ears. I was particularly fascinated by a couple of exceedingly friendly and vocal spotted hyenas, and by a small pack of wild dogs that had been dug from their den as pups. Wild dogs would become an important part of my life in years to come.

The mainstay of Jack's business was birds – everything from small seed-eaters such as the cordon bleus, fire finches, melba finches and common waxbills to the larger ground hornbills, secretary birds and saddle-billed storks. Most lucrative of all were the rare and beautiful wattled cranes and dazzling pygmy geese that were Jack's speciality. There were plenty of stories to remind us to be careful how we handled the animals and birds, from the fish eagle that sank a talon clean through the meat of one man's thumb to the goliath heron that, with one rapier-like thrust of its beak, impaled the nose of the man who tried to catch it by dazzling it with a flashlight while his accomplice closed in with a net. My encounters with Jack's animals were tame by comparison: a slash through the finger from a caracal's razor-sharp dew claw as we treated the cat with antibiotics for mange, reminding me how lightning quick and tough they are; and a stamp on my outstretched hand as I fed a dead rat to a feisty secretary bird. The luckiest escape of all was when a saddle-billed stork spied my approach as I went to peer through the coin-sized peephole in the door of its pen: it slammed its bill as far as it could through the hole, ending just centimetres from my eye.

As a sideline, Jack collected the occasional snake to be used for extracting venom to make serum to treat snakebite: the South Africans were the continent's leading exponents in treating snakebites. I had always been fascinated by snakes and lizards: the pet shop along the High Street in Camden Town had been a highlight of childhood visits to my Auntie Florence and her husband Stan in London. I started with green lizards and graduated through slow worms to grass snakes. I can still smell the pungent excrement that the grass snakes expelled from their cloacas when first captured, though fortunately once they settled down they stopped doing this. However pleased my aunts, uncles and godparents may have been to see me, they always viewed my visits with a degree of trepidation: would I depart with the same number of 'pets' as I had arrived with? Sometimes the inevitable happened and the house would be turned upside down until the truant was discovered – or not.

One morning a member of staff at Jack's called me to come and capture a large Egyptian cobra that had been discovered sheltering beneath an empty water drum. Armed with my Heath Robinson catching stick – a willowy branch to which I had tied a length of cord and fashioned a noose – we lifted up the drum. As we did so the two-metre-long cobra spread its impressive hood, allowing me the chance to drop the noose over its head. I quickly tightened the noose around its neck and picked it up by the tail. But when I raised the snake off the ground its weight snapped the catching pole, causing the broken end to swing back towards me in an alarming fashion. With the cord slackening, the cobra sensed freedom, slithered forward and reared up defensively in my face. I remember in the sharpest detail its large shiny black eyes, its mouth agape to reveal the fleshy white sheaths of its glistening fangs and flickering forked tongue, the dark opening of its trachea resting in the floor of its mouth. I dropped the stick before the cobra could strike and watched as it made a hasty retreat into the undergrowth.

Jack rarely came to town, preferring the freedom of life at his Lazy J ostrich camp at the edge of the Delta. There he could smoke his pipe, enjoy a beer and plot how he might make his fortune, whether ostrich farming or masterminding a tourism venture out on the Makgadikgadi Salt Pans, which were his great love. He always had a twinkle in his eye and a pipe in his mouth and could charm anyone with his white beard and moustache and gypsy ways. He

ABOVE Corporal Abnel Mwampondele on patrol for poachers, removing the wire snares
they have set along game trails in thornbush country, Serengeti National Park, 1988.

ABOVE Maasai elders dancing and singing traditional songs out on the Mara plains.
FOLLOWING PAGE The Mara River is the lifeblood of the Reserve, vital to the migratory herds.

ABOVE Zawadi's cubs along Fig Tree Ridge, 2000. Safi is the little female on the right.
Like her mother, she went on be a star of *Big Cat Diary*.

ABOVE Half-Tail drags an impala kill into a croton thicket along Fig Tree Ridge
to conceal it from hyenas and vultures, 1996.

ABOVE Julian Pettifer opening an exhibition of the photographs from *The Leopard's Tale* in London, 1985. Julian was my co-host on *Africa Watch* in 1989, my first taste of live TV.

ABOVE Still following leopards quarter of a century later: Bahati, daughter of *Big Cat Diary* favourite Olive, was born in 2010 and now has cubs of her own.

ABOVE Zawadi with her daughter Safi, then aged three months, along Fig Tree Ridge, New Year's Day, 2000.

ABOVE Zebra stallions fighting. Note the worn teeth of the old stallion on right.
FOLLOWING PAGE Scarface (one of the group of males known as the Four Musketeers)
mating with a Paradise female, 2015.

reminded me that there is something about Africa that encourages each individual to give full rein to their dreams and aspirations in a way that is intoxicating to observe. Around the campfire Jack would regale his visitors with lively tales about escorting aristocrats and film stars into obscure corners of Bechuanaland (as Botswana used to be called), or how he turned a tidy profit as a crocodile hunter on Lake Rukwa in Tanzania, where by his own estimate he shot 53,000 crocs for their much sought-after skins.

Jack had a miraculous knack of walking away from crashes in light aircraft, but the seventh proved fatal. After Jack's death, his son Ralph (who was with Jack when the plane crashed and caught fire) and partner Catherine Raphaely established Jack's Camp out on the Pans in his memory.

But Jack was still very much alive when, in mid 1976, his nephew Colin Swynnerton and I decided that it was time to leave Francistown and travel overland back to East Africa, where Colin had been born and raised. Planning to take in as many of the wildlife areas as possible, we bought an old VW Combi double-cab van, not unlike the minivans that swarmed over the game parks of East Africa in those days – the dreaded zebra-striped buses that epitomised mass tourism there. Despite their poor reputation, minivans are tough, comfortable and much more economical to run than the 4x4 vehicles favoured by the more traditional upmarket safaris, which mimicked the old hunting safaris romanticised in the books of Ernest Hemingway. We welded a couple of forty-gallon drums together to ensure we had plenty of fuel and stashed them in the back of the pick-up. Colin's warm and eccentric character and years of living close to nature made him an ideal companion for the trip.

Just prior to our departure I was thrilled to negotiate the production of a set of prints of my drawings through Howard Swann Publishers in South Africa. With Christmas imminent, Howard suggested I come down to his offices in Johannesburg and sign the prints to make them a limited edition. But I had run out of time and could ill afford the cost of the journey. Swann paid me a modest advance against a royalty of ten per cent of the recommended retail price of a hundred rand per set of four images – the princely sum of ten rand, the cost of a meal. We agreed that he would send a set of prints to me in Nairobi. As it turned out, my inability to travel to Johannesburg and sign the prints proved fortunate.

Colin and I set off in late October, known in this part of the world as 'suicide month' because the brain-numbing heat in the build-up to the rains makes tempers liable to spark at the slightest provocation. On arrival in Lusaka we headed for the tourism information office to enquire about conditions in South Luangwa

and Kafue National Park, wilderness areas teeming with wildlife. The lady in the office explained that the rainy season had set in and the parks were closing. The roads would soon be impassable, particularly given that we were in a minivan: there were areas of black cotton soil that Martha Gellhorn (writer, journalist and Ernest Hemingway's third wife) wisely noted had the consistency of chewing gum and should be avoided at all costs – go round it, not through it.

I was all for accepting this disappointing news at face value, but Colin was having none of it. His motto after a lifetime spent in Africa was never to say no until you find out for yourself that you cannot do something. Like Keith Miller, Colin knew there was room for negotiation in just about any scenario. While we did get stuck and had to dig ourselves out on more than one occasion, we reaped the reward of making ours a real safari, with spectacular game viewing and all manner of exciting times in the bush along the way. I never forgot that lesson in life: we all have our own idea of what is possible and too often let our fears hold us back.

Colin also proved his mental toughness and grit on another occasion. We were on our way to Kafue National Park when we were stopped by a group of soldiers manning an army roadblock on a bridge. We had been warned to be careful; we were two young white guys from Botswana travelling through Zambia at a time when the war against apartheid was gaining momentum. Freedom fighters were being trained in the art of bush warfare in Zambia and Botswana and every so often South African security forces would mount an attack or act of reprisal with bombs and grenades in cities like Lusaka and Gaborone.

We produced our passports and explained the nature of our journey. The soldiers were bored, waving us through with sour looks to speed us on our way. But no sooner had we started the engine and begun to move off than they came running after us, shouting and yelling for us to stop. I am not sure if the soldiers had been drinking already, but when they searched our vehicle and found Colin's precious supply of beer they were all set to help themselves. Colin loved nothing better than a cold beer each evening at the end of a long hot dusty drive and wasn't about to abandon his precious ritual for anyone. He knew that the best way to handle this situation was to be assertive and above all to stay calm. To be intimidated by figures of authority without good reason is to lose the psychological war – 'Don't say more than you have to and don't back down' was Colin's motto. He made it quite clear that we had a long journey ahead of us with little chance of resupply and that he was not giving up his beers. One of the soldiers pulled out a copy of Mao Zedung's *Little Red Book* and waved it aggressively in our faces, telling us that this was the new way: the Chinese brand of socialism had found a receptive audience in this part of Africa. But Colin stood his ground. Eventually the soldiers allowed us to leave and Colin popped the cap off a beer in celebration.

The tsetse flies in Zambia's game country proved even more testing and irritating than the authorities. Further north, in Tanzania and Kenya, they are referred to as 'Dorobo', after the legendary local hunters and bowmen, because of the sharp jab of pain the flies inflict when they bite. Tsetses sometimes carry the parasite that causes sleeping sickness, so it is better to avoid being bitten in sleeping-sickness country if you can. Our vehicle was often full of the noisy insects and it became a lively contest as to who could zap the most flies without rolling the car.

Colin's Uncle Jack had always been adamant that you could sleep anywhere in the bush, protected from the wild animals by nothing more than a mosquito net. Colin lived by the same rule, despite the fact that Jack also told the story of how his young nephew had had his nose and upper lip bitten off by a spotted hyena when camping in one of South Africa's game parks on a family safari. With that in mind, I always made doubly sure that my mosquito net was securely tucked in around my sleeping bag. Even sleeping in a tent is no insurance against the unexpected. A young female lion researcher who was camping out in the bush in a little pup tent once woke to find that a male lion had lain down against the tent, pinning her arm beneath his 180-kilogram body. Barely daring to breathe, let alone move, she eventually fell asleep, quite expecting never to wake up again. When she did it was with a huge sense of relief to find that the lion had moved off, leaving his palm-sized pug marks as proof of her close encounter.

Once you have slept out under the stars in wild country, the thought of cocooning yourself inside a tent seems sacrilege; though if you do it is foolish to leave the zip open, as one man learnt to his cost in the Serengeti when a lion grabbed him by the head. How much more exciting it is to awake to the ghostly shapes of a family of elephants passing through your campsite or even to have a lion or leopard pad quietly past. Each morning we would scout around our latest campsite, interpreting the footprints and scats left by nocturnal visitors. We had plenty of adventures as we headed north, reacquainting ourselves with the wonders of the Mara-Serengeti. Looking at the album of photographs of our trip that Colin put together I can see we took some risks too: there am I on foot, taking photographs of bull elephants in Lake Manyara. That was before I learnt just how fast they can cover the ground. At least this time when I arrived in Nairobi I knew my photographs would be correctly exposed, if a little blurred from all the excitement.

CHAPTER

03

THE
MARSH
LIONS

The word *enthusiasm* first appeared

in English in 1603 meaning

'possession by a god'. It is derived

from the Greek adjective *entheos*,

'having the god within'.

Internet definition

When Colin and I arrived back in Kenya in late 1976 we sold the VW combi to help finance our stay and I went in search of my old university chum Paul Pavlides. Paul, who lived in Nairobi, cautioned me that it was exceedingly tough for expats to get work permits, but a fortuitous introduction to Jack Block, the proprietor of Block Hotels, proved a turning point. Jack had a philanthropic streak and was known for his generous support of artists and photographers, so I showed him my drawings. Liking what he saw, he walked me across the corridor to the office of his brother Tubby, who immediately bought a number of the originals. So too did the friendly American manager at the Commercial Bank of Africa where I had just opened an account with the proceeds of my sales; each original earned me around £150 – a lot of money in those days. Jack meanwhile offered to help me obtain a residence permit so that I could stay in Kenya and gain more experience as a wildlife illustrator.

Paul and I had played rugby together at university, so I eagerly joined him and his friend Boris Tismimiezky for one of their training sessions at Impala Rugby Club. Despite all my efforts to keep myself fit, touch rugby played at over 1,700 metres soon had me gasping for breath. Afterwards Boris introduced me to Jock Anderson, the managing director of a tour company called Root & Leakey Safaris. This was owned by legendary wildlife filmmakers Alan and Joan Root and anthropologist Richard Leakey, all of them icons of Kenya's European community. Jock was looking for someone to help run a tented camp that Root & Leakey had just opened in a quiet, shady spot along the Mara River, a few kilometres north of the boundary of the Game Reserve – an ideal opportunity for me.

Getting Jock's undivided attention would be the hard part: he was known to his friends as the 'oldest teenager in town' due to his love of pretty girls and an ability to woo them that was the envy of many a younger man. After hours of vying for Jock's ear with the bevy of women at the bar I managed to tell him my story. He had seen and heard it all before, of course: everyone who visits Kenya falls in love with its heady mix of white coral beaches and big game safaris, its warm and friendly people and sunny climate. He was inundated with requests to give some young buck a chance to spend time on safari in the bush. He made no promises, telling me to come and see him after Christmas. By then I had successfully applied for my Kenya residence permit. My persistence paid dividends and I got the job.

My role at Mara River Camp was to act as the in-house naturalist and to keep an eye on how things were running behind the scenes. No salary, just board and lodging. That suited me fine; my only stipulation was that I was allowed to take visitors out on game drives. Mara River Camp soon became legendary among safari guides, young and old. It wasn't so much its idyllic location or its proximity to some of the best big-cat game viewing in the Mara. From the hot-blooded safari guide's point of view it was more the fact that it had the highest density of airline stewardesses in Kenya – girls working for SAS, Lufthansa and KLM all relished the opportunity to spend their days off on safari in the Mara and twinkle-eyed Jock was only too happy to vie for their business. Guides from the other camps and lodges kept a keen lookout for our distinctive blue and grey Land Rovers and spent as much time ogling the female talent through their binoculars as they did looking for lions. Things got even better when Jock and his business partner, an Irishman by the name of Joe Oxley, opened up a nightclub in downtown Nairobi called the Pasha Club. The Pasha provided the ideal night-time romancing venue at the end of the flight crews' two-day safari. We were the envy of the town with pretty girls on our arms, though this way of life was hardly likely to foster long-term relationships. Perhaps it was just as well I wasn't looking for one.

One of the safari operators who used to bring his guests to Mara River Camp on a regular basis and who had good contacts with the airline crews was a man known as 'Bwana Drum'. He had survived a horrendous crash as co-pilot in the Police Air Wing during the Emergency (also known as the Mau Mau Uprising, the conflict that raged across Kenya in the 1950s and led eventually to independence), when a radio aerial sliced through a wing of his plane on a low-level reconnaissance flight. He had served with distinction as a member of one of the 'pseudo gangs' that helped to infiltrate Mau Mau living in the Aberdare Forests, an action for which he was awarded the George Medal. He used to carry a copy of his autobiography *Bwana Drum* in a brown paper bag to share with his guests on safari in the days when you kept quiet about having served in the colonial forces in pre-independence Kenya.

Bwana Drum was a crack rifle shot who had represented the national shooting team for many years (witnessed by the number of decorations on his official team blazer) as well as winning the World Sniper Championship. He was as tall and wily as he was charming, someone who knew how to impress his safari guests from the minute they stepped into his safari wagon for their first game drive in Africa. Before long he would stop his vehicle and raise a finger to his lips to stifle the chatter of his guests, then lean out of the window and listen intently.

'Did you hear that?' he would enquire. To which everyone shook their heads. 'I'm sure I heard lions – that soft *aagh* that lionesses use when calling their cubs', imitating the sound perfectly before continuing. Up would go his hand again as he slowed to a halt. The guests fell silent as he scanned the countryside with his binoculars, sniffing the air, 'Lions – I can smell the musty odour of their scent on the bushes.'

By now the clients were almost beside themselves with excitement and anticipation. Bwana Drum continued once more, heading for a croton thicket where half a dozen tawny shapes including a litter of small cubs sprawled in the shade – just as his game spotter had assured him they would be, having located them earlier that morning in that very spot. Bwana Drum had the pretty stewardesses swooning in disbelief at their Great White Hunter's powers of perception, vying for his attention around the campfire after dinner with one of them not uncommonly sharing his tent the same evening.

By contrast to Bwana Drum's harmless duplicity, I was fortunate to have Joseph Rotich, a Kalenjin safari guide, as my mentor. Joseph had worked for years with Alan and Joan Root on their various filming adventures around East Africa and was known to all as *Bwana Chui* – Mr Leopard. If there was a leopard hiding in a rocky outcrop or skulking among the long grass, Joseph would surely find it. He was the same age my father would have been, a warm and honourable man who exuded a quiet dignity. He had served in the

King's African Rifles in North Africa during the Second World War and proudly gave me an old black and white photograph of himself as a young man in his army uniform, asking for help in retouching the frayed borders and removing the spots of brown pigment. I could see that his ears had been pierced to create the long folds of skin that were part of the rite of passage among members of his tribe. In more recent times it has become quite usual for people to have these long loops of skin surgically removed and Joseph had done that.

The only time I ever heard Joseph raise his voice was when I chastised him over some innocuous mishap at camp with the damning words 'How could you be so stupid?' I never for a moment thought Joseph was stupid – just that he had been careless, but to Joseph it was like a son being disrespectful to his father; worse still, calling someone stupid was viewed as a legacy of the colonial era when whites looked down on blacks. Nothing could have been further from my mind and I never forgot how hurt Joseph was by my thoughtless choice of words.

I was in awe of the old man's intuitive understanding of the Mara's landscape and its wild creatures, his uncanny knack of finding the right track leading back to camp in the dead of night. It wasn't just Joseph's ability to see with razor-sharp clarity. He knew *how* to look, interpreting all the nuances of the environment like a detective collecting evidence at a crime scene. Joseph would spend long periods sitting quietly at a vantage point, scanning the open plains or acacia thickets through his binoculars, taking particular note of the prey animals: did they look nervous or alert, were they literally 'pointing' to the big cat, hyena or wild dog that had caught their attention? These are all things you can learn, but some people seem to have a sixth sense when it comes to wildlife and Joseph was one of them. He was born to his trade.

Having Joseph as a mentor reminded me how much I missed the father I had never known. In today's world of mobile phones, videos and Facebook there would have been a visible record of his life. I could have watched him move, listened to him speak, absorbed his essence. Instead I made do with a black and white photograph of him in his army uniform, taken when he was in his twenties, revealing a strong face with cropped hair and neatly trimmed moustache. That photograph, placed carefully in a leather frame, went everywhere with me, alongside a picture of my beloved mother.

Having someone to pass on wisdom accumulated over a long and eventful life is a blessing: aside from Joseph, I had been fortunate to know people like Bob Hailey, my basketball coach at CH, and the inimitable Professor David Halton at university, men of strong beliefs and compassion. But mentoring is not unique to us humans; I would witness it in lions and elephants as they nurtured their young or less experienced relatives through difficult times, such as when, during a terrible drought, an elephant matriarch led her family to a precious source of water that she remembered from years before, or when the youngsters in a pride learned from the older and more experienced lionesses how to bring down large, dangerous animals such as buffaloes. At what level of consciousness this transfer of information occurs I can only ponder; what I am certain of is the powerful influence for good that certain people have had on my life, simply by being true to themselves and available in my hour of need; and of the ability of the written word to inform and inspire, distilling the brilliance of ancient minds and passing their essence down through the ages.

It is hard to describe the euphoria that I felt living in the Mara in those early days. There is nothing quite like the joy of becoming one with a piece of wild country, breathing its very essence until you are no longer an outsider looking in, but a part of the whole. I would be up before dawn each morning, savouring a mug of tea or coffee around the dying embers of the campfire in the company of our Maasai watchmen, their red *shukas* (robes) pulled tight around their shoulders, long-bladed spears glinting in the firelight. Then we would climb into the battered old Land Rovers and head out on safari, the sense of anticipation almost unbearably exciting. Would today be a big day, when we might come across lions battling to pull down an old bull buffalo – the ultimate heavyweight contest between predator and prey – or would Joseph find us that elusive leopard skulking around the magnificent rocky outcrop known as Leopard Gorge? That was what made each day different: you simply never knew what you might find.

I was working in Africa's finest wildlife area, home to all the most charismatic 'big game' that I had read about as a child in England. I had to pinch myself for fear that I might wake up and find that it was all a dream.

But despite all my excitement, there were many times when I slipped back into an inner world filled with doubt. The fears and anxieties surrounding my childhood fall were capable of ambushing me when I least expected them, prompting a bemusing sense of unreality known as dissociation that would descend like an invisible cloud, especially during times of stress. All through university and my early days in Kenya these feelings of unreality would return without warning and might last for weeks or even months.

Dissociation is the very opposite of living in the moment and experiencing the vitality that I so loved in my other life. Confusion and uncertainty eat away at your confidence. Going out could be daunting while I was feeling so strange. I would see someone that I recognised coming towards me, only to find as they drew closer that it wasn't them. Something as simple as crossing the road could become a major endeavour, taken to absurd extremes by anxiety. I am not sure how old I was when I finally felt able to tell my family about my fall and consequent descent into turmoil, but it was long after I left school.

My mother was always incredibly supportive, staying calm when my anxieties reached fever pitch – anxieties that no amount of tests or specialists could cure, given that I was still light years away from being able to admit that it was my mind that needed healing, not my body. When I visited England, Foyle's bookshop on Charing Cross Road in London became my most productive haunt – and not just for its wildlife books. Sooner or later I would head for the medical section, working my way along shelves lined with thick volumes from *Gray's Anatomy* to *Medical Symptoms and Signs of Disease*.

I would stand for hours engrossed in whatever I found, waves of panic sweeping over me in the certainty that I had discovered something significant to match my symptoms – symptoms that emerged wherever I looked, demanding that I head back to the doctor or hospital for yet more tests to reassure me. I insisted on having a swollen lymph gland removed from my neck – just to be sure – and at one point began to obsess over the idea that the muscle in the left side of my jaw was getting larger. The speculative extraction of a wisdom tooth provided only temporary relief. Surely it must be a tumour? This in turn prompted me to follow a ritual that continued for years, waiting until I was on my own, then taking two mirrors off the wall in my mother's living room or wherever else I might be staying, to compare one side of my face with the other, checking for signs of change, quickly putting the mirrors back on the wall at the first sign that someone might discover my improbable behaviour.

At some point in the 1980s the mirrors stopped coming off the wall and I could look myself in the eye again without needing to check. The problem was that sooner rather than later I would find something else to worry myself sick about, trapped by my inability to live with uncertainty. It was like a roller coaster; there were lulls between the storms when I felt normal, but while I never completely broke down I was often filled with despair and frustration.

Initially I was so taken with the new and exciting world I had discovered in the Mara that I allowed nothing to stand in the way of my exploring it. If someone told me of a particularly interesting sighting − a lioness with small cubs, perhaps, or a mother cheetah at a den − I would do my best to drive to the spot, even when it meant grinding up the rockiest hillside or fording a marsh. In those days road maintenance was non-existent and everyone drove off road. New tracks emerged according to the season and your ability to find a way from one game-viewing area to another. Knowing the right places to cross the network of *luggas* or intermittent watercourses that divided up the plains could save you time and lessen the likelihood of being stuck for hours. But inevitably I would sometimes find myself wedged tight on an enormous rock or sink the vehicle up to its axles in the black cotton soil. We didn't have radios or mobile phones back then and I would race against time to try to get myself out of trouble before Joseph or some other driver-guide spotted my predicament and berated me for my stupidity.

Joseph would wag his finger and remind me of all he had taught me – where to cross a particularly tricky lugga, or when to attempt to ford marshy ground during the long rains. He would shake his head and chuckle, 'Jonathan, Jonathan, Jonathan – when will you ever learn?' Jock was understandably far less amused whenever the mechanics jacked up my vehicle to assess the damage done to the gearbox, differentials, shock absorbers or spring hangers.

There was plenty of excitement for my guests, too, from the rhino who side-swiped the vehicle to trying to avoid a charging buffalo with a slipping clutch. And I have never forgotten the over-zealous Japanese visitor who opened the door of the Land Rover as we watched the Marsh Pride playing with their cubs one evening nearly forty years ago. When I chided him for even thinking of getting out of the vehicle he told me that the lions looked so friendly and cuddly, he just wanted to play with them. He had no concept that these were truly wild creatures.

Having recently witnessed Notch, the cantankerous old female of the pride, send a young Maasai warrior scrambling into the nearest thornbush when he came over the crest of a rise and surprised her and her sister with young cubs, I knew just how dangerous lions could be when provoked. Notch charged towards the youth, skidding to a halt with an angry grunt as he disappeared into the bush. She had tried exactly the same a few weeks earlier. On that occasion the Maasai had been armed with a spear and simply stood his ground, shouting at the lioness and prompting her to turn and hurry back

to her cubs. This time she was not for turning, stalking forward again as I hurried to cut her off with my vehicle, gesticulating to the young warrior to get into the car. After hesitating for a moment he clambered in, albeit on legs that had turned to jelly, his arms and shins torn and bloody from his brief encounter with the acacia bush. It was some hours before he felt confident enough to continue on foot. Next time I met my new best friend he was riding a bicycle.

One of my duties helping oversee the camp was the weekly supply run to Lolgorien or Kilgoris, small threadbare towns nestled in the high country an hour or two from camp. Here we could stock up on fresh drinking water at the Catholic Mission and purchase supplies of beef or a whole goat for the staff, along with maize meal, cooking oil, margarine, sugar and salt. If anyone was sick from malaria or suffering from some other ailment, there was a clinic and dispensary to minister to their needs. The murram road (an unpredictable mix of gravel and sand) threading its way through the bush en route to Lolgorien was a nightmare to navigate at the best of times, but during the rainy season it became almost impassable, with numerous muddy and waterlogged tracks leading off into the treacherous black cotton grasslands. Even with the magic four-wheel-drive lever engaged it was always touch and go as to whether we would escape having to dig ourselves out.

There were occasional sightings of packs of wild dogs or a cheetah to transform our quest into a game drive and the staff always viewed these outings with unbridled enthusiasm, pleading for the chance to accompany me days before I was due to set off. After weeks away from home I put this down to 'camp fever', with escape for a few hours a highly prized treat. I would drop the men off at the butcher's around ten o'clock in the morning and arrange to meet them again a couple of hours later, by which time I would have filled the plastic drums with water and chatted to the missionaries to catch up on the local gossip.

When I returned I was often perplexed to be met by one of the staff to say that they still hadn't finished at the butcher's. There would be some convoluted story about how the butcher was waiting for a fresh side of beef to be delivered or that they needed to go in search of the goat herder or that the shop had closed and it would take another hour to finish off business. It was only many months later that someone tipped me off to the fact that it took 'fifteen minutes max' to buy meat from the butcher's, unless you arrived late, which we never did. Meanwhile the men were whiling away the hours with the good-time girls who ran a lucrative business of their own in a one-room 'hotel' next door and were only too happy to offer their nubile services for a fee. The price we were paying for beef and goat meat was evidently subsidising the men's fun. But over the years I watched as many of my friends among the driver-guides and camp staff succumbed to the ravages of AIDS; the dramatic loss of weight and sunken eyes, whispered references to their being 'slim' or a 'sufferer' telling their own story, the consequences inevitably feeding back into the villages and leaving the elderly to nurture the young.

In time Joseph taught me how to read the signs of the wild and in particular what alarm calls might lead me to a leopard, the creature I most wanted to study and photograph. The incessant high-pitched yelp of a silver-backed jackal was always worth investigating, as was the guttural chatter of vervet monkeys among the treetops or the ear-splitting screech of a bush hyrax alarm-calling from a rocky outcrop. Though Joseph could sometimes conjure up a glimpse of a shy leopard for his visitors, the trade in spotted cat skins had taken a terrible toll, with upwards of 50,000 leopards killed each year in Africa during the 1960s and '70s. Consequently when I first arrived in the Mara the leopard population was at an all-time low. Leopards that had become habituated to vehicles soon disappeared, with rangers and unscrupulous professional hunters implicated in their demise to the point where Jock warned me not to tell rangers if we saw a leopard. Those that had survived were incredibly wary and primarily nocturnal in their habits. Given how masterly a leopard is at concealing itself through cunning and the camouflage of its spotted skin, your only chance of seeing one, let alone photographing one, was if you were lucky enough to be driven by Joseph.

In my first year in the Mara I saw a leopard on only two occasions – both by chance. The first was a large male who had stashed a Thomson's gazelle carcass in the top of a boscia tree and who soon bolted with an angry grunt as vehicles gathered. The second was a fleeting glimpse of a beautiful young female who ghosted across the track as we headed back to camp one night. Joseph knew this leopard – and so did the *askaris* who occasionally spotted her in camp. We would sometimes hear her calling as she patrolled the riverine forests, uttering that wonderfully guttural 'wood-sawing' grunt that leopards use to mark their territory, call large cubs and find a mate.

I soon realised that working with leopards was going to have to wait. I had a lot to learn first. Meanwhile, finding lions was relatively easy, given the open nature of the terrain and Joseph's knowledge of the best places to search. Joseph introduced me to a pride of lions that occupied a territory just inside the Reserve, some twenty minutes' drive from Mara River Camp. I named them the Marsh Lions because their 50-square-kilometre territory included an area called Musiara Marsh that was a Mecca for all manner of wild animals: not only the lions, but elephants, buffaloes, waterbuck and a myriad of water birds. During the dry season the Marsh was also the focal point for tens of thousands of wildebeest and zebras attracted by the perennial supply of fresh water and lush grazing: it was the perfect ambush site for the pride.

I kept meticulous notes in my diaries of what I saw each day, gradually getting to know the big cats as individuals – first the lions and cheetahs and later the leopards. It allowed me to indulge my scientific interests without having to write up my data and submit it to a university. I had the best of both worlds. I was living in the bush, watching wild animals, studying their behaviour, and writing, photographing and drawing what I saw.

There were plenty of characters to liven up life in camp, from actors to politicians. The Hollywood movie star Burt Lancaster was as rugged and self-assured in real life as he was on the big screen, while the politician Bruce Mackenzie, former Minister of Agriculture in President Jomo Kenyatta's government and at one time the only white MP in post-independence Kenya, certainly knew how to hold his audience's attention. Mackenzie's daughter Margie managed the Firmin Gallery in Nairobi, which would become the main outlet for limited edition prints of my drawings. With his substantial bulk, bristling handlebar moustache and booming voice, he reminded me of the British comedian and musician Jimmy Edwards, whose acquaintance I once made in a Nairobi nightclub in the days when my moustache was a bit on the thin side. By contrast Edwards was founder and lifelong member of the Handlebar Club, an apt description of a moustache that spread from one ear to the other. Reaching for the hand of the lady I was with, Jimmy asked if she had ever been kissed by a 'real' moustache? Having nearly asphyxiated her he turned to me with evident relish and offered to send some 'cuttings' from his own moustache to spruce mine up a bit.

I first met Bruce Mackenzie through the safari guide Ian Ross, who was a good friend and regular visitor to Mara River Camp in the 1970s. Ian was a carefree spirit with an easy manner that went down well with the KLM stewardesses who were the staple fare of

his safari business. He always had a twinkle in his blue eyes, along with a story to share as to how he might make his fortune, narrated between nervous puffs on his cigarette. The latest of these ventures involved starting a safari business based in Kampala. He explained that Mackenzie wanted to help Uganda tourism to get back on its feet and was willing to finance the whole project, including new safari vehicles and a mobile tented operation for upmarket clients. Ian reckoned the time was right; would I join him?

I knew that beneath his portly and jovial demeanour, Mackenzie was a shrewd businessman with contacts stretching across the continent; he understood East Africa from the inside out, and had the ear of Idi Amin, the notorious President of Uganda, who was keen to promote new business ventures. I listened one evening as Mackenzie regaled us with the wonders of Uganda and how we might make a handsome living by setting up shop ahead of the wave of investment he felt sure was soon to follow. Exploring a new country renowned for its big game certainly promised opportunity and adventure but, before Ian and I could meet up with Mackenzie again to finalise the deal, the light aircraft he was travelling in from Kampala was blown out of the sky. An incendiary device concealed in a wooden carving of a lion's head (some say it was a *real* lion-head trophy) – a parting gift from Idi Amin before they set off – exploded as they neared the Ngong Hills on the outskirts of Nairobi, killing the pilot and all three passengers, one of whom was an arms dealer.

The bomb was said to be Amin's revenge for Mackenzie's role in what became known as the Raid on Entebbe when, on 4th July 1976, Israeli Mossad agents rescued hostages from a plane that had been hijacked in Tel Aviv by a Palestinian terror group and diverted to Uganda. Amin was sympathetic to the Palestinian cause and had personally welcomed the hijackers to his country and deployed Ugandan soldiers to help guard the hostages. Mackenzie, who doubled as a British and Israeli intelligence agent, flew one or more Mossad operatives over Entebbe Airport in his private plane so that they could photograph the situation on the ground. This proved crucial in allowing the Israelis to neutralise the Ugandan air force when the raid took place a week after the hijacking. Three hostages were killed, along with all six terrorists and forty-five Ugandan soldiers, in a rescue mission that lasted barely ninety minutes. Mackenzie had also apparently helped to persuade President Jomo Kenyatta to allow the Israeli planes to refuel in Kenya on their way home, so he had done a great deal to alienate Amin.

The death of Bruce Mackenzie spelt the end of our Uganda safari dream, but I kept in touch with Ian and always enjoyed his visits to camp – until the day dawned that reminded me yet again just how important it is to savour every moment. It was Christmas 1980 and, as I had often done before, I headed down to the coast for a few days' break. On my return to Nairobi I found a scrap of paper on my bed with a scrawled message from Ian and his long-time companion Annette Kampinga. Ian and Annette had just arrived back in town with clients who wanted to purchase sets of my wildlife prints. Could I join them that night for New Year's Eve dinner at the Norfolk Hotel? That way I could meet their guests and sign their prints.

The Norfolk was Kenya's most iconic hotel, its Delamere Bar a favourite watering hole for safari guides and hunters of old, somewhere they could entertain in style and catch up on the gossip as they passed through town. It was a tempting offer, but I had just completed a nine-hour trek over pot-holed corrugated roads from Mombasa and I was due to set off again early next morning for the Mara. There were no mobile phones in those days and no landline at the house, so I couldn't answer; I settled instead for a nice relaxing bath and went to bed.

That night Ian and Annette were killed in a horrendous explosion that ripped through the hotel. As I prepared to leave Nairobi for the Mara a friend waved me down with a startled look on his face: he told me that he had just seen a green Toyota Land Cruiser in the Norfolk parking bay and feared it was mine. He said it was like seeing a ghost. But it was Ian's safari wagon, not mine.

The Norfolk bomb blast killed twenty people and injured eighty-nine. Once again it was said to be retaliation for Kenya's support of the Raid on Entebbe. Al-Hamid, the Moroccan passport holder who had occupied the room directly above the dining room prior to the explosion, had already boarded a plane for Saudi Arabia by the time guests assembled for dinner. Jack and Tubby Block, who owned and managed the Norfolk and had been so pivotal in helping me to live and work in Kenya, belonged to a high-profile Jewish family, making the hotel an even more attractive target.

I had come close to terrorism before as a student in Belfast, when the 'Troubles' were taking hold. Those years were marked by student protests and Civil Rights marches with Bernadette Devlin ,our Joan of Arc, alongside the giant student leader Tom McGurk, all fiery red beard and rousing oratory. There were rowdy debates at the Students' Union, pitting Catholics against Protestants, Liberals against staunch Conservatives, occasionally ending with chairs and tables flying through the air. We soon became familiar with the strident voice of the firebrand Protestant leader , the Reverend Ian Paisley, with his rallying cry of 'No Surrender' in response to calls for a united Ireland.

Full of idealism and indignation at the bigotry that polluted the social and political landscape, the students went on the march. Paisley vilified Queen's as a hotbed of opposition to Ulster's remaining part of Britain and led his supporters to the Elms Halls of Residence, where I was living. Once, when students attempted to march into town to protest at the steps of City Hall, we found our paths blocked by the massed ranks of blue-coated Royal Ulster Constabulary. With icy contempt they looked us square in the eye while booting us in the shins and kneeing us in the groin in retribution for our Catholic sympathies. Playing rugby against the RUC or the Paratroop Regiment also always gave the opposition the opportunity for some student bashing and a punch-up.

People used to ask me why on earth I would choose to go to university in Northern Ireland, when bombs were going off in pubs and cinemas, and sectarian gangs and British soldiers were shooting it out on the street. But travelling across the Irish Sea had been my first big adventure after years at an all-boys' boarding school. Aside from Queen's being an outstanding seat of learning, people in Ireland were so friendly and life so rich in the living that I never thought of leaving.

Even this sort of experience doesn't prepare you for friends being killed by terrorists. My generation may not have had to fight in a world war as my father did, but this tragedy put a very different perspective on the carefree existence I had been enjoying in Africa. A few months later, Ian and Annette's families joined us on safari to celebrate the lives of their loved ones and scatter their ashes in the Mara, the place that had meant so much to all of us. We stopped for a moment in a beautiful stretch of country known as Paradise Plain, home of the Paradise Pride of lions and the place where more than twenty years later a lion called Solo and a cheetah cub known as Toto would become stars of *Big Cat Diary*. Ian and Annette would have chuckled as the wind picked up just as we tossed their ashes into the air, blowing their remains back in our faces as if mocking our sadness at their passing. Ian was never one for regrets. He lived in the moment with great gusto.

During one of my visits to Jock's offices in Nairobi, his secretary handed me a slip of paper notifying me that there was a package to collect from the main post office. The sender was Howard Swann in South Africa. I ripped the package open, my hands shaking with excitement, overwhelmed to see the beautifully designed artwork featuring my drawings on the front of the portfolio with my biography on the inside flap; the four pen and ink drawings were printed on an off-white tone. I could hardly contain myself as I ran back along Kenyatta Avenue to show them to my friends. Now I had something tangible to support my dream of making a living from my passion.

One day a driver whom Jock employed to bring guests down to Mara River Camp from Nairobi approached me with a proposition. He told me that he had acquired some books of counterfeit Reserve entrance tickets and that between us we could make some money by selling them to the guests staying at the camp. The normal procedure was to pay our entrance fees to the rangers stationed at Governors' Camp inside the Reserve, but this way, the driver suggested, we could circumvent that system and make a tidy profit. According to him, the rangers were also selling forged tickets to camps such as ours. When I asked him if he wasn't worried that I might say no to his idea, he seemed genuinely perplexed – even more so when I told him that I wasn't interested in his scheme.

I let Jock know about the scam and he in turn told the former Chief Game Warden of Kenya, Jack Barrah. Jack had spent many years helping in negotiations with the Maasai that led to the setting up of the Mara Reserve in 1964 and had successfully opposed a massive wheat-farming project by the UN's Food and Agriculture Organisation, which would have involved ploughing up two-thirds of the entire area. After Jack's post was Africanised he was retained by the Kenya government as a special adviser to his successor, a two-year appointment that lasted twenty years. Jack had made a name for himself during the Emergency when one Saturday afternoon he tracked down a notorious Mau Mau gang holed up in the rough at the Karen Country Club and preparing to attack. He collected a couple of Bren gunners from the police station and flushed the gang out of the rough, killing eight of them, including General Mwangi Toto, their Nairobi commander. When the Club Secretary complained that there had been golfers on the course at the time, Barrah famously replied, 'Don't worry – next time I'll shout "Fore!" before firing the first shot.'

In those days your entrance ticket entitled you to drive wherever you pleased – in and outside the Reserve – with each person paying their daily fee to the Narok County Council, who administered the area. Jack advised me that next time the ranger and the sergeant in charge came to the camp to sell us some tickets, I should forward the signed and dated receipts to him. I did and, as expected, they proved to be forgeries. Thanks to this evidence the ranger and sergeant were arrested and in due course appeared in court in Nairobi. On the given day I drove up to Nairobi as a witness for the prosecution. Much to my surprise the sergeant was defended by one of Nairobi's top criminal lawyers, and the Senior Warden, whose brother was the MP for Narok, sat with the sergeant in court in a very obvious show of support. It looked to me as if the ranger was going to be hung out to dry. However, the Governors' Camp driver who had accompanied them to Mara River Camp had since gone on leave, never to return, while the police handwriting expert failed to appear in court. Not surprisingly, when I spoke to Jack a while later he said that the case had been dismissed for lack of evidence. Nonetheless it pointed to massive fraud involving the looting of Reserve revenues, with everyone from the lowliest rangers right up to the most senior officials taking a cut. How to ensure all the revenue is accounted for continues to challenge management to this day.

Corruption not only robbed the Maasai at grass-roots level of any real financial return from tourism, but it took its toll on the Mara's big cat population too. It was apparent that the authorities had not only chosen to turn a blind eye to the poaching of leopards, but were actively involved. The same was true of the illegal killing of large black-maned lions by trophy hunters who had 'strayed' into the Reserve from hunting concessions on the periphery. This was only possible with the blessing of corrupt officials. At one point the East African Wildlife Society sent a team to the Mara to investigate complaints from the tourist industry that it was becoming almost impossible to find a large male lion in northern parts of the Reserve. Questions were raised in Parliament and not long afterwards, in February 1977, all hunting was banned in Kenya, along with the

lucrative trade in wildlife curios sold to tourists. In years to come
some people blamed the failure to develop a coherent and well-
regulated wildlife policy allowing consumptive use of wildlife –
trophy hunting, game ranching and the sale of wildlife products
– for the massive decline in Kenya's wildlife populations outside
protected areas (in some instances *within* protected areas too); up
to seventy per cent of the large animals have been lost in recent
decades. The assumption was that if people see no financial reason
to value wildlife, they have little incentive to protect it. One thing
was certain, though: the ban put an end to the killing of lions and
leopards within the Reserve.

What it didn't stop was the slaughter of Kenya's black rhinos.
According to reports from the 1960s, there were once 150 to 200
of them in and around the Mara Reserve. In my first year there I
once saw nine rhinos in a single game drive between Mara River
Camp and Paradise Plain, an area of approximately 100 square
kilometres. By 1983 only eleven survived, while Africa's overall
black rhino population plummeted from 60,000 in 1970 to 3,000 by
the late 1980s. On one occasion in the Mara Triangle I came across
a freshly killed rhino lying on its side like a giant granite sculpture.
My guests, who had been so excited at the prospect of seeing a
rhino, sat in silence, the stench of death overpowering as thousands
of flies buzzed around the carcass and blood oozed from the place
where the rhino's horns had been hacked from its prehistoric head.
I drove to Serena Lodge to report the incident to the official who
would later become Senior Warden of the Reserve. He thanked
me and said that his men would investigate. I later heard that a
vehicle with rangers had been seen in the area much earlier that
morning. There was little doubt that members of the field force
were involved in the demise of the Mara's rhino population, with
poaching said to be helping to boost the re-election campaigns of
top officials in Narok.

CHAPTER

04

WILD KINGDOM

Nowadays we don't think much

of a man's love for an animal…

But if we stop loving animals,

aren't we bound to stop

loving humans too?

Alexander Solzhenitsyn
CANCER WARD

While I soon made lots of friends, I was always aware that not having been born in Kenya made me a bit of an outsider on a deeper level. Everyone knew everyone because they either went to school together, served together in the Kenya Regiment during the Emergency, were related by birth or marriage or were going out with someone's brother or sister who lived here. 'Are you married or do you live in Kenya?' is a well-known refrain with more than a dash of truth to it, given the easy-going way of life and insularity of the European community. When it came to doctors and dentists everyone had an opinion on who you must see to fix your back, deliver your baby or treat the latest bout of malaria.

Living for five years at Mara River Camp, whose directors Richard Leakey and Alan and Joan Root were known to everyone, allied to my artistic abilities, provided an entrée to the local community to whom safari was a way of life and wildlife art a passion. Everyone had bronze sculptures or paintings celebrating Kenya's dramatic landscape and spectacular wildlife prominently displayed on the walls of their homes or on their mantelpieces, along with black and white photographs and drawings of the handsome nomadic tribes and their favourite wild animals. The fact that between 1977 and 1981 I came to Nairobi during the rainy season to play flanker for Impala Rugby Club also gave me some 'street cred'.

While I might not have been educated at the Duke of York, Prince of Wales or Saint Mary's School in Nairobi, having been brought up overseas proved an asset rather than a liability when it came to competing with my generation in Kenya. There was no shortage of young white Kenyans who wanted to do what I was doing. The difference was that by the time I arrived in Kenya I had seen something of the world, and my university degree gave me a boost when it came to asking for help, whether from Jack Block or Jock

Anderson. The discipline of life at Christ's Hospital followed by four years at Queen's had taught me to value every opportunity offered to me as a precious gift. If there was a party down at the coast or a safari headed for northern Kenya I wasn't about to abandon my job at Mara River Camp to take off on a 'jolly'. While my friends did not always approve of my doggedness and tried to put me under pressure to conform to local custom, I stuck to my plan regardless. I knew what I wanted and at that stage that was far more important than the approval of my friends.

My first proper girlfriend in Kenya was Jock Anderson's secretary Hilary Mitchell, a sweet-natured girl who came from a close-knit Kenya family. Her father, Louis Mitchell, had been Assistant Commissioner of Police during Jomo Kenyatta's presidency and her mother Evelyn described herself as the 'oldest son' of four daughters. There was never any question as to who ran the Mitchell household at Kiambethu Farm in Limuru – about an hour's drive north of Nairobi – where all three children, Fiona, Arnie (with whom I played rugby) and Hilary, eventually built houses on the family property. The rambling farmhouse with walls fashioned from tea-packing cases overlooked the stunning high green country with neat lines of tea bushes that characterises the Limuru Highlands on the outskirts of the city. Evelyn's father, Arnold McDonell, was a pioneer who, quite apart from being the first person to grow tea commercially in Kenya in 1918, went on to build All Saint's Church and found Limuru Girls' School for his daughters and granddaughters to attend.

The strong sense of family and community resonated with me. But while I loved my visits to the Mitchells' farm, it made me appreciate just what a gift my mother had given me in encouraging me to follow my dream – even if it meant living on the other side of the world from her. That ability to set her children free was something that Evelyn found hard. The old European settler families tended to keep their children close – a legacy of their pioneering spirit and loyalty to the clan.

During a visit to London a couple of years after we met, Hilary and I decided to get engaged. We headed down to Hatton Garden, famous for its diamond merchants and jewellers, and picked out a handsome diamond ring – or so we thought. Just to be sure that I hadn't been taken for a ride, I took the ring to Harrods and then to Mappin & Webb in Knightsbridge, where my mother had always shopped. When the jeweller scrutinised the ring with his eyeglass it quickly became apparent that the diamond had a number of dirty-looking inclusions and that we had been sold a dud. I immediately cancelled my cheque and took the ring back to a very unhappy jeweller. That evening Hilary told me with evident relief that perhaps it was for the best, as she felt uncomfortable getting engaged without speaking to her family first. I think we both knew that this was as close as we would ever get to the altar together and decided to go our separate ways. When Hilary headed to America for an extended holiday, I started a series of liaisons with airline stewardesses whom I met on safari in the Mara. There was no turning back after that.

I now established a Nairobi base for myself at Colonel Terence Conner's home in Westlands. I had met 'the Colonel', as he was known to everyone, through his love of rugby and friendship with the Mitchells: he rarely missed a big match and used to drive up to Kiambethu Farm every Sunday for lunch, or for one of Evelyn's famous cream teas. He was a larger than life character who had been born in India, schooled in England and then spent time back in India as a tea planter before signing up for a career in the Indian Army. He served with distinction during the war in Burma and when he retired after thirty years in the Indian Army he settled in Tanzania, as active and resilient as ever, running his coffee farm at Oldeani, not far from the spectacular Ngorongoro Crater, with his trademark discipline and attention to detail.

The Colonel loved safari: in his home there were tiger skins from India and leopard pelts taken from stock-raiding predators shot on his farm, stools made from elephants' feet and living-room sofas covered with zebra skins. There were elaborately carved wooden doors from the Far East and prints of oil paintings of wildlife and beautiful oriental women scattered around the house. The colonial lifestyle was all the Colonel had ever known, but he had a genuine respect and fondness for his loyal house servants, Asthmani and Amina, who on his death inherited enough money to ensure they had a comfortable retirement. He was always kind and generous, firm but fair, though his generosity was not to be taken as a sign of weakness. Once, when well into his eighties and regardless of his own safety, he walked into the middle of an irate throng of people intent on beating a thief to death and demanded justice – not mob justice, but a fair trial for the miscreant. If a thief had tried to break into his house he would have reached for his glasses and his walking stick to challenge them rather than hiding under his bed. The Colonel married late and never had children. I knew that given the life I had chosen and my love of sport I helped fill that void. He was a great friend to me – and to many people.

On one occasion when my sister Caroline was visiting from England the Colonel joined us on safari for a few days. We drove to a bend on the Mara River where a particularly cantankerous old bull hippo known for its cavernous yawns and huge canine tusks rested up. I parked, telling the Colonel to stay in the car while I walked cautiously down the nearest hippo trail to check on the bull's whereabouts: it had been raining and the pathway was steep and muddy underfoot. Just as I reached the bottom of the trail the bull, who had been dozing beneath the surface of the river, erupted into life and came thundering towards me from midstream, ploughing a deep furrow through the water as he picked up speed. To my horror, as I attempted to escape I found the Colonel blocking my path, woolly pompom hat pulled down over his ears, scarred knobbly knees protruding from his baggy white shorts, point-and-shoot camera at the ready. He turned and immediately fell flat on his face in the mud, rubber flip-flops pedalling madly in the muck as I scooped him up by his shorts and hauled him bodily up the hippo trail, expecting the bull to chomp me in the backside at any moment. Fortunately the hippo veered off and plunged back into the water.

The same bull almost killed me on another occasion when I walked down to the river and surprised him resting up behind a patch of bush close to a sandbank. It is always a shock to realise just how quickly big animals such as hippos, rhinos and buffaloes accelerate from a standing start. I took a photograph over my shoulder as I ran back to the vehicle, imagining that it might prove to be my last. The hippo fills the frame like a giant bloated potato with three legs off the ground. I can still hear the rasping hissing noise of him inhaling and chomping his massive jaws like a butcher sharpening a knife. This time the bull spun off in front of my vehicle, throwing up a cloud of dust over the startled passenger standing and looking out of the roof hatch as I legged it round the back. Though it is permitted to get out at hippo points along the river, I have learned that it is much safer to stay near your vehicle, given that hippos can outrun any man and are liable to charge if you get between them and the water.

My life in the bush would be punctuated with emotional highs – peak experiences – that I not only lived for but actively sought out, balancing the periods of anxiety and introspection. I was by now supplementing my board and lodging by selling my prints and original drawings to visitors to Mara River Camp as well as through the wildlife art galleries in Nairobi. Having bought two hundred sets of my prints at cost from Howard Swann, I turned them into a signed limited edition and the market in Nairobi was sufficiently buoyant for them to retail at around £20 a set – many times more than I would otherwise have earned. This encouraged me to start printing my own editions.

The art paper I used to print my drawings was imported by a company called Kenya Stationers and when the CEO Pravin Shah (known to everyone as PV) saw my artwork and discovered that I was also a keen photographer he invited me out for lunch to talk about his own love of safari and photography. PV had already published a number of colourful souvenirs and postcards promoting Kenya's wild places and we agreed to produce a simple photographic guide to East Africa's most visible and beautiful birds. I wrote to Canon Cameras asking if they would be interested in sponsoring my work and was overjoyed when they agreed to pay me the generous sum of $1,000 for publicising the equipment I was using. As a result,1981 saw the publication of my first book: *A Souvenir Guide Book to African Birds*. PV and his son Noopy became great friends of myself and Angie and years later published two popular safari guidebooks that we created. Noopy was brutally shot dead by thugs in 2011 – a tragic sign of just how violent Nairobi had become.

It did not take me long to realise that while taking photographs was an efficient way of collecting material for my drawings there was money to be earned from the photographs themselves, but only if you were shooting the right kind of film. Initially I wasn't: I was using black and white film – it was all I could afford. But as my drawings began to generate an income, I was able to upgrade my Canon cameras and lenses and to invest in Kodachrome 64 – the holy grail of transparency films among professional wildlife photographers, revered for its sharpness and true-to-life colours.

Just as I had been an enthusiastic follower of the British magazine *Animals* dating back to the first issue in 1963, I was now also an avid collector of *Swara*, the monthly periodical of the East African

Wildlife Society. My drawings and photographs had already been published in *Swara*'s predecessor *Africana* during my first year in the Mara. *Swara* was edited by Peter Davey, a keen wildlife photographer with a particular interest in birds: he ran an upmarket safari operation called Bateleur Safaris. Peter encouraged me to submit some of my images to the Frank Lane Picture Agency (FLPA) in the UK and before long I made my first sale – a series of photographs of four young lionesses of the Marsh Pride catching and playing with a wildebeest calf. It was a quick lesson in the business end of things, too, when Peter told me he would be receiving a percentage of the income from my sales for introducing me to FLPA.

When David Keith Jones took over as editor of *Swara* he encouraged me to start publishing illustrated articles, the first being a story on a pack of wild dogs known as the Aitong Pack that I had

been following just outside the Mara Reserve. David gave me the confidence to believe that I could write *and* take photographs. Some of my safari guests left me rolls of film in lieu of a tip. Others agreed to buy cameras and lenses for me in the USA, where prices were half those in the UK. I was on my way to becoming a photographer and, with the purchase of my first Toyota Land Cruiser, enjoying a degree of independence. Word was also getting round that there was a young Englishman with a love of big cats living in the Mara who could draw a bit and had a story to tell about the cats that he was following – and the wild dogs too.

It was at this point that the award-winning English journalist Brian Jackman visited Mara River Camp to write an article for the magazine *Wildlife*. I was able to introduce Brian to both the Marsh Lions and the Aitong Pack, which proved to be the highlights of his visit. Brian lived and breathed Africa from his home in rural Dorset, where songbirds and butterflies, wildflowers and oak trees competed for his attention along with foxes and badgers – the same fauna and flora that I had been happy to leave behind in search of adventure on a grander scale.

When Brian's article appeared in print he was approached by the book publishers George Allen & Unwin asking if he knew anyone who might be interested in writing a personal narrative about the Mara. Brian kindly suggested me, adding, 'I might be able to help out with the narrative if Jonathan doesn't fancy the idea of being a professional wordsmith.' It wasn't a matter of not fancying the idea – at that point I simply did not have the experience to write 60,000 words, and I knew that time was of the essence: the French photographer and balloon pilot Yann Arthus-Bertrand and his wife Anne had arrived in the Mara in 1979 and were also working on a book on the lions I was following. So I accepted Brian's offer, which is how *The Marsh Lions* came about.

Brian already had a literary agent, the wonderfully enthusiastic Mike Shaw at Curtis Brown. He kindly agreed to take me on too, but I had to battle hard to ensure that I was billed as co-author of the book. Despite his enthusiasm, Mike had the unnerving habit of appearing to be on the verge of falling asleep whenever we met. On this occasion I made sure his eyes stayed wide open. While I had huge respect for Brian's journalism, the book was based on my diaries, collected over the five years that I had been watching the Marsh Pride (along with visits from Brian), and could not have been written without my detailed notes for him to craft his story around. I was determined not to become simply 'the photographer'. An Author's Note was added, clearly explaining my involvement.

In the end Allen & Unwin lost out to Elm Tree Books, a division of Hamish Hamilton, in the bidding for the book. Elm Tree offered a more generous budget, allowing for colour throughout instead of lots of pen and ink drawings and only a smattering of photographs to keep costs down. I was delighted to see my wildlife photographs in print, particularly given that Allen & Unwin had been far more impressed with my drawings. They were right, of course. There were lots of great photographs of African wildlife, but my drawings offered something unique. In *The Marsh Lions* they featured prominently as chapter openers, mirroring the personal approach that we had chosen for the narrative.

With a UK book club taking 10,000 copies, along with American and paperback editions, *The Marsh Lions* was a bestseller and front-cover copy in the prestigious *Sunday Times* colour supplement. We were thrilled when Virginia McKenna, who had played Joy Adamson in the film of *Born Free*, read *The Marsh Lions* on Radio 4. With her wonderfully sculpted features and quiet compassionate ways she always reminded me of Angie – both are gentle souls with a steely inner strength; people who listen.

Working on *The Marsh Lions* was a huge learning experience for me and with Brian's generous encouragement I was able to graduate to becoming an author in my own right in the years to follow. The book's success prompted Seaphot Picture Library in the UK to approach me to represent my photographic images. Seaphot had started out primarily as an underwater picture agency, before quickly expanding their range to become Planet Earth Pictures (PEP). The 1980s and 1990s were the heyday for specialist image libraries such as PEP, with many of them showcasing their best photographs through stock directories – catalogues of high-quality photographs aimed both at generating editorial sales (for use in books and magazines) and at attracting the far more lucrative world of advertising. All I needed to do was to send in my latest submissions and the rest was done for me: editing, labelling, cataloguing and filing. For years PEP provided first me and then Angie and myself with an steady income.

Everything changed when the mega picture libraries such as Getty and Corbis, which hold tens of millions of images, gobbled up the smaller brands, stripping out all but the most lucrative images and returning the rest. The advent of the World Wide Web allied to digital technology saw a massive proliferation of images, leading to a crash in value for most photographers' work. Photographs could now be transmitted instantly, with the whole world a shop window for sales. A lot of photographers suffered, but Angie and I survived these transitions by being careful to nurture a number of sources of income aside from our photography: hosting safaris and lecturing along with television and radio work, artwork and books.

My connection with Alan and Joan Root opened my eyes to the possibilities of wildlife filmmaking, and of the dedication it involved. A new release of theirs would be a major event, with standing room only at the Nairobi Museum or whichever venue was showing it, and I always tried to be there. *The Year of the Wildebeest* and *Mysterious Castles of Clay* are just two in a long sequence of their award-winning films. The latter focused on the intricacies of life in a termite mound, while at the other end of the spectrum *The Year of the Wildebeest* told the story of the epic migration of wildebeest and zebra through the Mara-Serengeti ecosystem, an area of some 25,000 square kilometres. Alan and Joan always saw the big picture as well as the detail. They were unrivalled as naturalists, seeking out the scientists in their area of interest to gain the very latest information and blending it with their own observations and masterly storytelling. Inspired by their example and by what I was seeing in the Mara, I knew that one day I wanted to travel to the Serengeti to tell the story of the migration through my own eyes in book form and to go in search of the elusive wild dogs that had piqued my interest in the Mara.

By this time television crews and series producers were regularly seeking my advice as to the best places to film their quarry. One such enquiry came from the popular ATV series *Nature Watch*. Produced by Robin Brown and with the highly regarded Julian Pettifer as presenter, it focused on people such as myself who were living and working in the wild and passionate about animals. It was a simple idea that worked brilliantly due to Julian's sharp intellect and ability to ask the right questions while putting his guest at ease. Shortly before *The Marsh Lions* was due to be published, I was thrilled to be approached to see if I would be interested in being featured. I knew this would be great publicity for the book, especially as the BBC Natural History Unit had already agreed to camp with Brian and myself for two weeks to film the Marsh Pride for a programme called *Ambush at Maasai Mara*. It was to be narrated by David Attenborough and form part of the BBC's popular *Wildlife* on One series. This gave me the chance to take David on a game drive around Musiara Marsh to show him the lions I had come to know so intimately. He remarked on how 'busy' the Mara was and how competitive it must be working among all the other photographers attracted to the area.

He was right, of course, but I have always been determined not to let anything cloud my view of the Mara's unique abundance and beauty. Everyone has the right to be there, whether first-time visitors or cinematographers working for major television channels. Without the 300,000 tourists who visit every year, there would be no Mara. While we should never forget the emotional bond we share with wild creatures and how vital that is in enriching our lives, like it or not wildlife must pay its way in Africa. The fascination I derive from being in the field makes me focus all my attention on whatever I happen to be watching to the exclusion of everything else. I simply refuse to let other people spoil my day, however noisy and disruptive they may sometimes be!

Although Mara River Camp remained my base until 1981, I sometimes took time off to act as a safari guide for companies specialising in private tented safaris. One such operator was Peter Davey's Bateleur Safaris, among whose clients were the television presenter Marlin Perkins and his formidable wife Carole. Marlin was the anchor of the long-running American television show *Wild Kingdom* and each year he and Carole hosted a 'by invitation only' safari to East Africa for their friends and supporters. I was invited to drive one of the vehicles for this safari and as a result became close friends with Warren and Ginny Garst, a delightful couple who produced and filmed *Wild Kingdom* and spent long periods at

Mara River Camp. They were passionate conservationists who particularly loved the chance to collaborate with scientists working in the field.

In 1979 the Garsts had asked me if I would be interested in doing a screen test for them. Marlin Perkins was by now in his seventies and Don Meier Productions were looking for new faces to freshen up the show, young people who understood wildlife, were knowledgeable and articulate, and could perform on camera. My heart sank when Warren wrote to say, 'I think you might fit our requirements, but I have difficulty convincing Don Meier with the short test film we made…You weren't very sexy in that.' Fortunately, when Don saw some clips from the *Nature Watch* show he agreed to hire me.

My first assignment was in Ethiopia, focusing on rare species such as the gelada baboon, walia ibex and birds of prey called lammergeyers, wild inhabitants of the ruggedly beautiful Simien Mountains that are famed for dropping bones on rocks to crack them open to feed on the marrow. Accommodation was primitive and the cold soon caught up with Ginny in the form of a nasty attack of double pneumonia that would later hospitalise her. My role was to record pieces to camera against a suitably dramatic backdrop to open and close the show. In those days it was not uncommon to use a crude version of today's teleprompter – a white board held alongside the camera with my lines writ large in bold type. I shudder now at how wooden my performance was: it was certainly a world away from the informality and intimacy we eventually developed for *Big Cat Diary*.

Getting good sync-sound on location is always a challenge for the technicians and can prove a nightmare in open country, with the wind howling into the microphone (at times it is nigh impossible in the Mara with all the vehicles coming and going, as we found to our

cost when recording *Big Cat Diary*). Much to my delight the solution was to fly me to Chicago, where the sound could be re-recorded at Don Meier's headquarters. This meant having to watch myself on a big screen with the original commentary replayed through my headphones while I tried to 'lip sync' my new commentary to the old. Fortunately there were computers to help nudge the words into place. This was heady stuff. From sleeping in a tent in the wilds of Africa with no salary to staying in fine hotels in an upmarket part of Chicago and becoming a member of the Screen Actors Guild was seductive, to say the least. That first programme was followed by a series of exciting shows: some featured animal capture on location in Zimbabwe and Namibia, while another had me starring alongside Marlin Perkins and an Eagle Scout at a river crossing in the Mara in an episode covering the great migration.

While I relished my new role, those early experiences with *Wild Kingdom* soon revealed an element of filmmaking that I wasn't at all comfortable with. It was not uncommon – particularly in the USA – for producers to set up sequences to make them appear as if they had been shot in the wild. Game farms and private wildlife sanctuaries in Southern Africa sometimes doubled as locations offering 'animals for hire'. At its worst, captive animals might be sacrificed to achieve the required result. Was it right to stage events that mirrored real wildlife behaviour, with possible lethal consequences for the animals and without the audience being any the wiser? The answer had to be no.

This deception wasn't confined to moving images; stills photographers were sometimes culpable too. I remember shortly after I arrived in Africa looking with a mix of incredulity and admiration at a portfolio of big cat images published by the award-winning *Time Life* photographer John Dominis. A copy of his book *Africa's Big Cats* is tucked away in my study in Nairobi, a slim volume with some unforgettable photographs of big cats in action. The most memorable of them shows a big male leopard about to pounce on a young baboon that has turned in a last desperate effort to confront its adversary. You could not conjure up a more dramatic photograph. The leopard is coiled, about to pounce; the baboon has its mouth wide open with a look of utter desperation.

I later read that the scene had been set up among the desert sands of Botswana, using a captive male leopard that could be hired for filming. Knowing what I now know about leopards, I should have guessed something was amiss when I first saw the image. It shows a patch of sandy terrain – the sort of open country where it would be highly unusual for a baboon to allow itself to become isolated and where leopards would normally avoid exposing themselves to view. Leopards generally steer well clear of baboons during daylight for fear of being mobbed and possibly injured or even killed (I would later witness both Chui and Half-Tail high-tailing it from a troop of aggressive baboons when surprised in far less open country).

Under normal circumstances a baboon would run for its life rather than turn to defend itself – unless it already knew that there was no escape. Many years later Dominis admitted that the shot had been set up and that they had gone out into the bush with the captive leopard in a pick-up and released it among troops of baboons to get the shot they were looking for.

But it still doesn't add up. Trying to photograph a leopard hunting a baboon in these circumstances would have been pure chaos. The closeness of the photographer to the action, the angle, the open sandy terrain, plus the back-to-the-wall posture of the baboon all make one wonder if the shot wasn't taken within a confined space. One thing is for certain: Dominis' photograph helped to perpetuate the myth that baboons are the leopard's favourite prey. This just isn't true. Though leopards do sometimes kill baboons, they mainly do it at night or when they are able to launch a lightning strike from cover and escape with their victim into a cave or impenetrable thicket.

Two of the most exciting stories I worked on for *Wild Kingdom* were with the legendary game catcher and professional hunter Jan Oelofse. Jan lived in Namibia, one of the most starkly beautiful countries on the continent. Far removed from the savanna Africa that I had fallen in love with on television as a youngster, Namibia is a blistering-hot desert land, famous the world over for the golden sand dunes at Sossusvlei that tower 300 metres into the sky, as well as for its desert elephants and rhinos. Formerly known as South West Africa and under the jurisdiction of apartheid South Africa, Namibia was settled by Germans and Afrikaners, tough farming people who established themselves on this rugged terrain, in the process eradicating large segments of the predator community. Lions and hyenas soon disappeared from farmland and even the wily and adaptable leopards felt the wrath of the ranchers, who trapped, shot and poisoned them. As numbers of these larger and more powerful predators were exterminated or diminished on private land, cheetahs flourished, sometimes taking calves and small stock when wild prey was in short supply. Jan had made catching and translocating cheetahs his speciality, though in his forthright manner he admitted that in the early days, when he was struggling to make a living on his ranch and cheetahs were eating into his threadbare profits, he had hunted one down in his safari vehicle, chasing it until it was exhausted and then driving right over it.

There was something very attractive about the old stereotype of the African 'White Hunter'. Big-game hunters had an aura about them. Hardened by growing up in Africa, they were sons of the earth whose fathers and grandfathers had farmed the same stretch of wild country passed down through the generations, learning as children to shoot lions and buffaloes, then serving in the military before going on to become professional hunters or entering the Parks Service. Such men lived exciting lives, building roads and

opening up the bush, chasing poachers and controlling the large predators and other big game that menaced humans and their livestock. In this respect Jan was the real deal, a character straight out of a Hemingway novel, with steel-blue eyes and a black cowboy hat covering his bald head, a man whom other men admired for his toughness and whom women often found irresistible.

I had first come across Jan Oelofse in a dramatic series of pictures published in *National Geographic* magazine. They showed him manhandling a cheetah into the back of a truck by the root of its long spotted tail and the scruff of its neck after the cat had been treed with the help of a pack of Jan's dogs; I am not sure now if this was one of his domestic cheetahs or a wild one, but it looked mighty impressive. During our stay in Namibia we based ourselves at Mount Etjo, Jan's 25,000-hectare game ranch. One of the shows we filmed included some thrilling scenes on a neighbouring ranch, where helicopters were used to drive herds of hartebeests, oryx and zebras into capture pens known as *bomas*. Sheets of plastic were concealed in bush country to form a wide-mouthed funnel that gradually narrowed until it reached a holding pen; from here a ramp led up to a truck in which the animals were transported by road to their final destination. As the animals ran towards the pen, men hidden in the bushes would pull the sheeting across the neck of the funnel to prevent the herd from escaping.

In his early days with the Natal Parks Board in South Africa, Jan and his fellow rangers had driven the wild herds to the capture point on horseback. Helicopters, with their speed and manoeuvrability, have made the whole process much quicker and easier. By pioneering the boma-capture technique Jan helped to transform the way national parks and game reserves managed their animal populations. Now, if it was necessary to control numbers, animals could be captured and translocated rather than shot.

The oryx – large, muscular antelopes with rapier-like horns – were particularly dangerous and sometimes men clutched a metal door in front of them as a shield when attempting to corner one. Once they were safely in the holding pen our job was to lean over the walls, place plastic tubing over their metre-long horns and then hammer the tubes tightly in place to prevent the oryx injuring one another in the truck. I once managed to give myself a black eye when a particularly feisty beast reared up as it felt the plastic tube touch its horn, and rammed it straight back into my face.

Next up was a trip to Zimbabwe to film at Viv Bristow's Lion and Cheetah Park in Harare: this meant yet more 'capture' shows featuring captive lions, ostriches, crocodiles and helicopters. By now I had a far clearer idea of what it involved to work on *Wild Kingdom* and elements of it made me very uneasy.

The programme-makers and their sponsors at Mutual of Omaha knew what kept television audiences glued to their sets – action-packed shows with presenters featured in a hands-on 'cowboy in Africa' role. Game capture with the thrill of the chase – all dust and running animals – provided the ideal scenario and the sponsors were constantly pushing for adrenalin-packed programme like these. Shows featuring scientists and their work were considered dull by comparison. The problem was that many animal-capture techniques had evolved over the years to reduce the stress on the animals and lessen the danger to the human participants. This meant that the need to run the animals to a standstill and then noose them or manhandle them in nets was replaced with more sophisticated techniques such as Jan's boma-capture method or tranquillising drugs and helicopters. It was much more humane for the animals, but the powers that be felt it made for less exciting viewing.

I spoke to Warren and Ginny about my reservations. Television shows like the BBC's *Life on Earth* and *The Living Planet*, fronted by David Attenborough, were the benchmark as far as I was concerned – they demystified the world of animals without losing any of the magic, rather than relying on tales of nature 'red in tooth and claw' for their appeal. I wrote to Don Meier about my feelings and to tell him that I felt unable to continue working with *Wild Kingdom* if it meant putting the lives of animals at risk in order to please the sponsors. While agreeing that things had to change, he reminded me of the huge influence for good that *Wild Kingdom* had had in America, helping to sensitise and educate millions of children about the natural wonders of our world, the issue of poaching and the work of scientists in places like the Serengeti. He ended by saying, 'You are a communicator, and a good one… Good communicators, with integrity, are needed… My feeling is that you will do more for wildlife and conservation by being part of *Wild Kingdom* than you will accomplish in few other endeavours.'

While this may well have been true, I was beginning to establish myself as a photographer and author who spent years studying wild animals in their natural habitat, revelling in the fact that as much as possible they remained undisturbed by my presence, even becoming habituated to it. I wanted to be able to look people in the eye when they enthused about the programmes we were making. I certainly had no desire to play a game of make-believe and lie about how we got our footage. *Wild Kingdom* was not alone in filming animals in captivity or controlled environments to ensure that they got the shots they wanted. Thirty years on I fear that the desire to create dramatic wildlife shows, whether filmed entirely in the wild or not, risks diminishing and demonising nature all over again, with titles such as *The World's Deadliest Predators* and *Shark Attack* all too prevalent.

CHAPTER

05

THE
LEOPARD'S
TALE

Happy the man,

and happy he alone,

He who can call today his own:

He who, secure within, can say,

Tomorrow do thy worst,

for I have liv'd today.

John Dryden

TRANSLATION OF HORACE

I was flat on my back in England recovering from an operation on a herniated disc when Roy Wallace wrote telling me something I had waited years to hear. A leopard had given birth to two cubs in a beautiful stretch of country called Fig Tree Ridge, just beyond the northern boundary of the Mara Reserve. Roy was the manager at Kichwa Tembo Camp, where I had made my base for the last two years, and if anything could speed my recovery it was this news.

It was the dry season of 1983 and this wasn't any old leopard – not that seeing any old leopard with cubs wouldn't have been something to marvel at. No, this was a six-year-old female I had called Chui, the Swahili name for Africa's most beautiful spotted cat. Roy also told me that Chui's mother, a shy and wary creature I had struggled to see, let alone photograph, had had cubs six months earlier and that she was currently keeping them at a magnificent rocky outcrop called Mara Buffalo Rocks, a few kilometres to the east of where Chui had given birth. For this reason I named her the Mara Buffalo Female.

Roy's news was beyond my wildest dreams. I had followed Chui for the past six years with only a handful of usable photographs to show for my persistence, though these did include a few precious images of her first litter, born in the area known as Leopard Gorge towards the end of November 1980. Like all leopards, Chui hunted mainly at night, resting up during the daytime in an ancient fig tree or in the cool shady caves along Fig Tree Ridge and Leopard Gorge, at the very heart of her territory. All too often all I could see was a tantalising glimpse of a spotted tail dangling from a horizontal branch. The habit of resting in trees caused the drivers to refer to a leopard as *madoadoa ya juu*, 'the spotted one above' – as opposed to the cheetah, which they called *madoadoa ya chini* – 'the spotted one below' – when they didn't want their guests to overhear them discussing *chui* or *duma*. If the visitors recognised these Swahili names from their guidebooks, it would increase expectations the drivers might not be able to fulfil.

Joseph Rotich had been the first person to mention Leopard Gorge to me, not long after I arrived in the Mara. The name alone prompted my imagination to run wild with thoughts of what the place might look like. In fact, no words can do justice to the magical atmosphere of this ancient rocky fortress. It is a deep cleft in the earth that runs for just a few hundred metres, with massive chunks of rock rising from the ground on either side of its grassy bottom. In places the rocky walls are shrouded by thick patches of croton and leleshwa bush and shaded by euphorbias and fig trees, ideal places for a leopard to rest or to hide her cubs. The Gorge peters out to the west at the point where an intermittent watercourse known as Leopard Lugga cuts across its path, eventually erupting again to become Fig Tree Ridge, a south-facing escarpment of rock.

As I sat in my vehicle, desperately hoping to spy a leopard, I would sometimes encounter Maasai honey-hunters making their way through the rocks. They knew that swarms of bees were attracted to cavities in the fig trees and would smoke them out to collect the honey for their potent home-brewed beer; sometimes they would hack into one of the limbs with a razor-sharp *simi* (tribal knife) to encourage the bees to swarm. Whenever Joseph was in camp he would send word to the Maasai that he wanted to buy some honey to take home to his children. Breaking off a piece of fresh honeycomb to share with me, he told me that it was the food of the gods; certainly I have never tasted honey as good as this.

There is a track that winds its way along Fig Tree Ridge and up through Leopard Gorge, forcing you to crane your neck as you drive carefully along the rutted pathway, checking each nook and cranny, each bush and tree for signs of the leopard you so long to see. Other pathways follow the rim of the Gorge to north and east, the one to the north known as 'the rocky road from hell', a landmine of boulders waiting to hammer your gearbox or suspend you thirty centimetres off the ground by the leaves of your springs. But in those early days there was nothing I would not have given to see a leopard, no matter how steep or rocky the hill.

Once I could find my way to and from Leopard Gorge – a thirty-minute drive from camp – it became part of my daily routine. Whether at first light or at dusk I would make sure at least one of my game drives included a visit there. Yet during my first year in the Mara and despite my best efforts I rarely saw a pugmark or the remains of a kill, let alone gun-barrel nostrils and long white whiskers peering at me over a rocky ledge, or a glimpse of a spotted coat to brighten my day. Joseph fared better, of course. As he so rightly reflected, visiting Leopard Gorge was always an experience in itself: even if you did not see a leopard, you felt its presence and could soak up a little bit of its aura; it was like

visiting the dressing room of a movie star or the rustic den of an author steeped in all the evocative trappings of their life even when they were not in residence.

I had to guard against becoming too blinkered by my fixation, particularly when I was with visitors. In searching for a leopard I might forget to pause long enough to watch the bush hyraxes crammed together in dense huddles to shut out the cold, their warm coats mirroring the smoky grey of the lichen-covered rocks. Or I might fail to notice the male agama lizards frantically bobbing their brightly coloured heads as they displayed to the drab females whose volcanic-grey skin matched their resting place to perfection. Vervet monkeys often gathered to feed on the ripening fruits of the eleodendron and euclea trees and when figs were in season flocks of green pigeons added their bubbling voices as the local baboon troop swaggered among the leafy crowns, squabbling over the best feasting sites. If the vervets were quietly feeding or the baboons were in residence, you could be pretty sure that any leopard in the vicinity would be keeping well hidden for fear of being mobbed.

As well as introducing me to Leopard Gorge, Joseph had also told me about the Mara Buffalo Female, noting how big she was – fifty kilograms or more, the size of some males – and how dark her coat. In 1978 he had taken me aside quietly one evening and whispered that the old female had given birth to two cubs, telling me exactly where to look if I wanted to see them, smiling at the expression of pure joy his news brought to me. My first sight of those cubs – a male and a female – is something I will never forget: two tiny spotted cats, little larger than a good-sized house cat, peering up at me with their pale blue eyes, a mixture of inquisitiveness and suspicion on their bloody faces as they nibbled on a wildebeest calf that their mother had killed earlier that day and dragged to the base of the tree where the cubs now fed. The kill was too heavy for her to hoist into the tree; first she would have to remove the stomach and intestines – if the hyenas didn't scent the pungent odour of fresh meat first and steal it. The mother leopard had already fled from the tree as I approached; but the cubs held their ground – until I reached for my camera. That hint of movement was sufficient to send them bolting for the Gorge thirty metres away.

It would be months before I caught sight of the cubs again, and when I did it was once more at Leopard Gorge. The male was larger and shyer than his sister, keeping to the shadows, but the female – the one I later called Chui and came to know so well – allowed me to watch as she sat on a ledge along the rocks, quietly licking the snow-white fur on her belly and warming herself in the soft rays of the early morning sun.

I was certainly not alone in my devotion to leopards – most visitors on safari long to see one and the fact that they are so elusive, so enigmatic, so charismatic, makes them all the more attractive. This is the cat most likely to enhance both a guide's gratuity and his reputation. When it comes to measuring the success of a safari, a leopard adds a touch of gold.

On one occasion when leopards were still relatively difficult to find and Chui was just becoming independent, I hosted an American family on a ten-day safari. I had guided the Hensons before, but this time they had told me very clearly that their holiday should revolve around finding a leopard. So I was feeling somewhat crestfallen when the safari was drawing to a close with no sign of one. Then on the final chilly morning, as my guests pulled their Maasai blankets a little tighter around their shoulders, standing out of the roof hatches, praying for the leopard we had spent so many hours and days searching for to appear, we found Chui resting high in one of the trees that adorn Fig Tree Ridge.

How she performed that memorable morning, yawning and stretching before climbing languorously from her aerial perch to sit on the sun-washed rocks along the top of the Ridge! My hands were shaking, the Hensons were ecstatic, all of us hushed into silence by the beauty of the moment. The quest to find a leopard suddenly took on an entirely different dimension. Now all those early morning starts were remembered for the joys of the first cup of coffee with a fresh rusk to dunk in it and the incomparable sunrises over game-filled plains; the evenings were celebrated for the exquisite beauty of Leopard Gorge as the sun disappeared beneath the Siria Escarpment and eagle owls shuffled their barred and spotted feathers, the last of the light golden in their huge round eyes. Now the lions and cheetahs we had seen earlier were exalted along with the leopard – before, they had been somewhat disappointing, because they weren't the elusive spotted cat we so desperately wanted to see. Chui's appearance that morning snatched victory from what had seemed like inevitable defeat.

By the time Roy wrote to me about Chui's cubs I was no longer living at Mara River Camp. In 1981, in order to find out what had happened to two males who had been exiled from the Marsh Pride, I had moved to Kichwa Tembo, a tented camp owned by Geoff and Jorie Kent, founders of luxury travel operators Abercrombie & Kent. Kichwa Tembo was located in an area known as the Mara Triangle, to the west of the Mara River. Covering some 520 square kilometres, the Triangle was the genesis of what we now know as the Maasai Mara National Reserve: in 1961 it had become the first area to be given official protection. This was then extended to the game country on the east of the Mara River, including Musiara Marsh and the territory of the Marsh Pride, and converted to a game reserve of 1,821 square kilometres. The Mara attained National Reserve status in 1974 and after various changes in area and administration now covers 1,510 square kilometres; since 2012 it has been controlled by a body known as Narok County.

I had been ruminating on the idea of writing a book on leopards ever since I first went to live in the Mara in 1977. The key was always going to be finding a leopard with cubs to ensure that I could observe plenty of socialising between them: unless they have young, leopards often do very little during daylight hours. I needed a story with strong characters and knew that with Chui's mother being so shy I had little more than an intriguing idea: without powerful images to illustrate it, a book would probably never come to fruition. Now, six years later, with both Chui and her mother visible with cubs, I could only hope that the situation lasted long enough for me to achieve my objective.

By good fortune that year the drought dragged on for month after month, with dust devils whipping across the tattered plains, forcing Chui to cling to Fig Tree Ridge and Leopard Gorge, while the Mara Buffalo Female remained at the Rocks. Normally both leopards would have moved their cubs every few days or weeks as a safeguard against their being found by lions and hyenas. However, with the grass gone and the bushes and thickets stripped bare, they had no alternative but to stay in the most secure part of their range.

There was another factor keeping Chui and her mother anchored to their current locations. They shared part of the same home range, as a mother leopard and her adult daughters normally do. The only way this works without endless and possibly injurious spats is for each of these solitary predators to avoid contact with the other by leaving signs indicating where they are. Scent and the leopard's characteristic rasping roar help them to co-exist mostly without meeting unless they choose to. I found it intriguing to know that Chui and her mother would both have been aware of what the other was doing – aware that each had cubs – as they patrolled their territory.

Favoured birthplaces are essential components of any territory and are jealously guarded. I knew that, if pressed, the mother leopards would fiercely defend the place where they had hidden their cubs. Mother and daughter were locked in a game of hide and seek, with scent-marking, calling and their visual presence all deployed in this battle of wits. Chui was considerably smaller than her mother, who was still in prime condition but had scars to show from encounters with other leopards whose paths she had crossed – her right ear had a deep notch in it. My money would have been on the Mara Buffalo Female if it came to a scrap with *any* other female.

To date, nobody had published a full account of a wild mother leopard raising cubs. Joy Adamson had written about her experiences with the captive leopard Penny, whom she had released into Shaba Game Reserve in northern Kenya, but in nothing like the detail I intended. I knew that other people had similar ideas. I had begun to hear about a private game sanctuary in South Africa called Londolozi, from where the photographer Peter Johnson had returned with some stunning images of leopards, including mating. Londolozi and a neighbouring sanctuary called Mala Mala – both parts of the larger Sabi Sands Reserve – were making a name for themselves as the easiest places to watch and photograph wild leopards. One individual known as the Mother Leopard was attracting considerable attention and would eventually be the star of her own book. But so far nothing substantial had been written on leopard behaviour, which for me meant the thrill of perhaps making discoveries that nobody had written up before.

By the time I returned to the Mara after almost six months in England nursing that back injury, Chui's cubs were about two months old and just beginning to be seen on a regular basis. The Mara Buffalo Female's cubs – a male and a female – were eight months old and highly visible. Each morning I would rise at five o'clock, snatch a quick cup of tea or coffee from the thermos next to my bed, and be in my vehicle no more than fifteen minutes later. I didn't need an alarm clock – I was driven from the deepest sleep by the fear that I might miss one moment in the company of the leopards. The liquid sound of the white-browed robin chat is one of my favourite bird songs – just not this morning, not right now, for I knew that if I heard the robin chat call before I hit the narrow bridge fording the Mara River, still half an hour short of my destination, it would be too late to reach Fig Tree Ridge by first light. I might just as well go back to bed. Given my obsession with these glorious cats, I never lost that particular race against time.

It was imperative that I was in position before the sun came up, arriving with my headlights off so as not to disturb Chui or alert any other vehicle to my location. I would pause a moment to look through my binoculars, enjoying the thrill of picking out the movement of one of the cubs in the half light or spying Chui sitting motionless, listening to the sounds of the dawn. Sometimes she would be suckling the cubs or feeding on a kill hanging in one of the trees further along the Ridge. I would almost certainly be on my own at this time in the morning, praying for enough light to snatch a few pictures before everyone else arrived. I knew that, however conditioned the cubs were becoming, their cautious mother would move them into cover if the press of vehicles became too much. There were days when the light wasn't right for photography or when the leopards played out of sight, obscured in a tangle of bushes, in which case I would take my chances and continue up through Leopard Gorge to Mara Buffalo Rocks in the hope of seeing the other family.

When Chui's offspring were small and less mobile there was a greater chance of being able to catch mother and cubs in the same frame – every photographer's dream. Cubs are at their most persistent in craving their mother's attention when they are little, repeatedly trying to greet or suckle her. But with each new day the cubs were getting stronger and more confident, particularly in honing their precocious climbing abilities, and I knew that it would not be long before they spent more time resting on their own, reflecting the leopard's independent spirit.

To tell the leopards' story I needed to be able to identify the cubs as individuals so that I could explore the differences in their personalities. Fortunately one was much darker than the other – hence my naming them Dark and Light. I soon discovered that leopard cubs always suckle from the same pair of teats, unlike lion cubs, where it is first come first served, with no specific teat order. Indeed, lion cubs are raised in a sort of crèche system and sometimes even suckle from other mothers in the pride. Both lions and leopards have four teats and Light always took the pair closer to his mother's head, ensuring he was easy for her to reach when she licked the cubs as they fed.

Leopards are reluctant to share food – a fact that is consistent with their solitary lifestyle, with each adult generally killing for itself and feeding alone. (I say 'generally' because adult males sometimes scavenge from kills made by females in their territories.) When Light and Dark first started eating meat, at around the age of eight weeks, I saw them feasting together relatively amicably on the remains of a warthog piglet, but it wasn't long before they started to object to each other's presence on a kill. They soon sorted this out, though, and took it in turns to feed rather than squabbling. Leopards are volatile characters and have an explosive way of dealing with adversaries: they brawl with an intensity that would put cage fighters to shame, hissing and spitting, scratching and biting, all four feet flailing.

Once I could identify Chui's cubs I realised just how different in character they were. Dark was bolder and more adventurous than his brother, while Light was shy and craved his mother's attention. I found this fascinating. As a young zoology student I had accepted the scientific doctrine that required human observers to distance themselves emotionally from their study animal and describe things in black and white – a two-dimensional approach that tended to picture animals as 'lions' or 'elephants' rather than recognising the uniqueness of the individual and acknowledging that each animal was a living, breathing entity, not just a 'subject'. Names such as A or B or No 1 or No 2 rob the subject of their individual character. While I preferred names that were not overly anthropomorphic, I never thought of Light and Dark as anything other than unique individuals perfectly adapted to their place in nature. This was never more apparent than when Dark fell from a tree and hurt his back leg: not only did he struggle to survive over the next few weeks but his relationship with his brother was transformed. Now Light was able to dominate Dark, who had become less confident than before, and this seemed to make Light bolder. I was reminded of my own childhood fall and how it had changed my life, how trauma can affect the mind and the body.

Dark gradually recovered from his fall, seemingly with no long-term ill effect, while Light profited from Dark's mishap in becoming less timid around his brother, less willing to back down. How much animals are consciously aware of what happens to them in life is still one of the great mysteries, but when it comes to coping with stress Robert Sapolski's acclaimed book *Why Zebras Don't Get Ulcers* certainly offers some interesting thoughts. He explains how in humans 'prolonged stress causes or intensifies a range of physical and mental afflictions, including depression, ulcers, colitis, heart disease and more. When we worry or experience stress, our body turns on the same physiological responses that an animal's body does, but we usually do not turn off the stress-response in the same way – through fighting, fleeing, or other quick actions. Over time, this chronic activation of the stress-response can make us literally sick – physically and mentally.' As it had me. Humans finding themselves alone on foot on the African plains would be at the mercy of their imagination, the 'what if's?' igniting a sense of impending doom. A zebra, on the other hand, responds appropriately to any signs of danger and then gets back to feeding without any of the angst; life quickly returns to normal. Unless of course the zebra fails to sense the danger lurking in the long grass!

It is an irony that the things we find most alluring about the leopard are precisely those that make it so hard to observe. The beauty we see when a leopard emerges from its rocky hideaway and steps into the daylight, the very quality that takes our breath away, is what helps it to remain hidden. The magnificent pattern of sooty-black spots and rosettes set against the golden brown coat is perfectly designed to blend with the sunlight and shadows of the acacia thickets and forest edges. The leopard's careful watchfulness, the subtleness of its movements, the liquid, almost snake-like way it weaves through the undergrowth, the care with which it places each of its soft pads on the ground, adjusting the weight of its body to balance itself as it glides towards its quarry – all of these help it to remain undetected.

The leopard is a perfect killing machine, a spotted nightmare for a wide range of prey species from grasshoppers to antelopes. There is virtually nothing that it is not capable of killing or scavenging: baby giraffes, a buffalo calf even, have fallen prey to this most adaptable of cats. One thing that I discovered early on while watching Chui and the Mara Buffalo Female was just how active they were when they had cubs and their food requirements increased. They often hunted during the daytime, sometimes coming to water to slake their thirst, avoiding the lions and hyenas that were more likely to be resting up in some shady spot during the heat of the day.

It was fascinating to see Chui waiting until her cubs were quietly resting or asleep after suckling before she slipped away to hunt. I would sometimes see her carrying small prey items back to them: dik dik, African hare, warthog piglets and bush hyraxes, as well as the half-eaten carcass of a young impala, creatures that a lion would not be nimble enough to catch but which were easy for a mother leopard to transport to her hideaway and would provide a substantial meal for small cubs being weaned on to meat. There were times when Chui and the Mara Buffalo Female left their cubs alone for hours – days even – but as Light and Dark became more mobile, Chui would sometimes lead them to the place where she had stashed a kill in a tree, as long as she was sure that there was adequate cover. Mother leopards only do this once their cubs are at least three months old and able to scramble to safety in a nearby acacia bush or up a tree if suddenly confronted by a hyena or lion. Cubs smaller than this are occasionally seen following their mother or being carried in her mouth, but with so many lions and hyenas in and around the Mara it is little surprise to find that many leopard cubs do not survive their first few months.

Once word got round that there were leopards with cubs to be seen on a daily basis, I received messages from as far afield as America and Australia asking the best time to visit. The answer, of course, was 'Pack your bags and jump on the first available plane.' Opportunities like this occur once in a lifetime and you never know how long they are going to last. I loved sharing the chance to watch the leopards and their cubs with visitors – it was a unique time in the Mara and I wanted people to make the most of it. I would always tell guests if I knew where they could find the leopards and share my observations with drivers and visitors.

Yet as a photographer I was sometimes faced with a dilemma, torn between quietly collecting information on the leopards' behaviour and disturbing them as little as possible, and edging forward for the best photographic opportunities. I knew that if I were to do that every other vehicle would immediately follow suit, if they had not moved closer already. So I stayed back, watching through binoculars and making notes, or shooting with my trusty Canon 500mm telephoto and x 1.4 extender – the equivalent of looking through a fourteen-power binocular.

I hated to see these beautiful creatures put under the kind of pressure that now descended upon them, especially as I was one of those who had helped to habituate Chui to vehicles. Visitors and drivers would often chatter at the top of their voices in excitement at seeing leopards like this; thank goodness it was before the advent of mobile phones. Sometimes visitors sat or even stood out on the roof of a vehicle, making their silhouette even more visibly human; or they hung out of the doors or windows, trying to get a better view when the leopards were hidden in a thicket or deep in a lugga. To watch Chui or her mother hissing and snarling as people waved their arms or made noises to attract their attention was almost unbearable. There were days when I just wanted to drive away. But after six years of waiting I could never do that. And, to be fair, I have never forgotten my own eagerness to break the rules on seeing my first leopard in the Serengeti ten years earlier, when all of us tried to persuade the ranger to let us move a little closer for a clearer view of that old male.

Drivers and guides were placed in an almost impossible position. In those days some of the drivers at the tented camps had very little education and could barely speak English, let alone German or French; they simply did not have the confidence or the diplomatic skills to manage their guests. It is no easy task to tell your clients to sit down and keep quiet without making them feel aggrieved. The answer to that problem was for the camp guest-relations manager or guide to brief clients before they left camp – a system that is even more important today, given the proliferation of camps and lodges. Reminding people what is expected of them when watching predators is far easier if they have already been told how to behave.

Inevitably, in a situation like this, someone was going to get hurt. A mother leopard can be very aggressive in defence of her cubs, reacting to a real or perceived threat with a terrifying charge. Male leopards can be fierce, too, and are larger and more powerful

than females. On one occasion a shy male who was persistently harassed by a vehicle not far from Mara Buffalo Rocks ended up charging the car, leaping through the open side and mauling one of the passengers. He was trying to drag the woman out of the vehicle when the driver put his black cap over the leopard's face and to his credit manhandled it back into the wild, leaving the lady scratched and bitten and the passengers badly shaken. But it could have been much worse.

Around the same time another incident reminded me just how careful you have to be in the company of wild animals, especially when you are on foot, and how often accidents occur through human error. In those days Kichwa Tembo offered its guests game walks that started out across the savanna grasslands, then looped back to camp along the Mara River. There are over five hundred species of birds in the Mara and as a keen ornithologist I always enjoyed the opportunity to spot a 'new' one, while keeping a wary eye out for potential trouble in the form of an old bull buffalo or a cow elephant with a young calf. I was far less concerned about encountering a big cat: unless surprised with small cubs, it would probably turn and flee at the first sight of people on foot. If a lion did charge it was unlikely to follow through with such devastating effect as one of the heavyweight herbivores.

The keys to managing a foot safari, I was to learn, are to keep the group small and tightly focused and to have an experienced guide who is familiar with potentially dangerous animals and knows the exact spot to aim for when charged at point-blank range; someone who can be relied upon to stay calm because he has been in similar situations a hundred times before. The rangers who accompanied us on these walks did not fall into that category – they did not have the experience of a professional hunter and, brave as a Maasai warrior might be, with only a spear to defend himself he would be no match for a buffalo or elephant. On one occasion when a buffalo suddenly stood up out of a mud wallow where it had been lying enjoying a cooling bath on the open plains, the ranger accompanying us stumbled backwards as he tried to get his rifle off his shoulder, putting the group between himself and the buffalo. Fortunately, the startled animal careered off in the opposite direction rather than charging us, but I had seen enough to make me decide to lead the group back to camp.

When a large party of American visitors came to stay at Kichwa Tembo with an ex-game warden as their courier, the tour operator asked if I would like to take half of the group on a walk the following afternoon while the courier accompanied the others. The tour operator knew of my interest in ornithology and, having watched an evening presentation I made to his guests, felt that those keen on a spot of birding might like to join me. Knowing how possessive tour leaders can be about their visitors I spoke to the courier to see how he reacted to the idea. He thanked me for the offer, but said he would rather keep his group together.

An unmitigated tragedy unfolded when the party duly set off the following afternoon. On coming to a notoriously dangerous loop in the river, the courier decided to walk into this cul-de-sac of land, despite both the ranger and the Maasai accompanying him telling him they never did that. It was too risky – and all the more so given that there were nearly a dozen people in the group. It was an accident waiting to happen, with patches of dense bush where buffaloes, hippos or lions might lie up, hemmed in on either side by banks with a sheer drop of some five or six metres to the river below.

All hell broke loose when the group surprised an old bull buffalo at the end of the cul-de-sac. With nowhere to go except for a suicidal leap over the steep bank that would guarantee a broken leg, possibly even a shattered spine, the buffalo charged, hooking and ripping into the chest of one of the women and into the groin of another. The ranger's gun either jammed or misfired, with the result that the only shot to hit the enraged bull grazed its lower leg without in any way incapacitating it. The courier grabbed the buffalo by the tail as it gored the women and was tossed into a bush for his bravery. The enormity of the situation quickly became apparent. It was dark by the time a plane managed to evacuate the wounded and, despite every effort, the woman who had been gored in the chest died on the flight back to Nairobi.

The following day the Senior Game Warden, Simon ole Makallah, who was an old friend of mine (and who would be charged with the still unsolved murder of the young Englishwoman Julie Ward in the Mara in 1988, a crime of which he was acquitted and of which I never for a minute believed he was guilty) came into camp and asked if I would drive him to the place where the incident had happened. I knew it well, having ventured in on my own to check it out years earlier. A second vehicle bristling with heavily armed rangers had accompanied Simon into camp, including the sergeant I had testified against some five years earlier over the forged entrance tickets. Simon told me the sergeant was a crack shot and it crossed my mind momentarily that if he were a vengeful man – well, who knew?

When we walked into the cul-de-sac no words were necessary: the grass and bushes had been flattened as if a whirlwind had ripped through them. A square of checked bush shirt, torn from the guide's back when he was tossed into the thornbush, fluttered in the wind. A blood-stained safari vest and a pair of mangled sunglasses trampled by the buffalo lay on the ground. Weighing in at three-quarters of a tonne, a bull buffalo is a wrecking machine once provoked, easily capable of tossing his victim high into the air or knocking them to the ground, using the massive boss on the top of his head to smash and pile-drive them into the earth, hooking with the shiny polished tips of his down-swept horns and trampling with heavy hooves.

Simon told the sergeant and a couple of the rangers to beat a path through the bushes along the river and to shoot any old buffalo they came across. As I waited with Simon, a volley of shots rang out, followed almost instantly by the sound of a heavy animal crashing through the undergrowth close by. A bull came thundering on a tangent past us, followed at the double by the sergeant and rangers. That thought of revenge ran through my mind again, but no further shots were fired. One buffalo had been killed but the one that had run past us escaped, albeit wounded. Simon decided it was time to go back to headquarters as visitors would soon be passing this way on their game drives, making it too dangerous to continue; he promised to return later to track down the wounded bull.

Myles Turner, who had seen duty as a professional hunter before becoming a warden in the Serengeti and who was retired and living at Kichwa Tembo at the time of the incident, had been concerned about the idea of walking safaris from the beginning; he cited the inexperience of the rangers and the calibre of their rifles, which did not have sufficient stopping power for this kind of work – you need the .375 or .458 rifles favoured by professional hunters for big game. But even with an armed guard it pays to be cautious and to heed warnings when living in the bush. Angie and I have had more friends gored or killed by buffalo than by any other large African animal, though statistically my old friend the hippo is the deadliest of all the herbivores.

Life was certainly never dull. On one occasion as I drove towards Mara Buffalo Rocks well before dawn, I came upon a Land Rover broken down by the side of the road. In the passenger seat was Jock Dawson's wife Enid. Jock had retired after a long and distinguished career in the Game Department and as a professional hunter and was now the manager of Mara Buffalo, located a few kilometres upstream from Mara River Camp. I quickly realised that this was an emergency. Enid could barely speak due to a large splinter of bone that had lodged in her throat during dinner the previous evening. Jock was upcountry, so I bundled Enid into my vehicle, leaving her driver to attend to the stricken Land Rover. The drive over rough roads to reach Nairobi can feel like an eternity at the best of times, but now I was aware of every pothole and gravel embankment as I drove as fast as I could while gripping Enid's arm to reassure her that it was going to be OK. I don't know how she managed to stifle the urge to swallow or cough for fear of convulsing, but if she had done either of those things I can only imagine the outcome. Five hours later I delivered her to the duty doctor at Casualty, returning the following morning to find her sitting up in bed with a broad smile on her face and a bone splinter the size of a toothpick sitting in a glass bottle on the bedside cabinet.

Given the uncertainties of the weather and the condition of the roads, you might wonder why anyone would ever drive when they can fly to the Mara in relative comfort in under an hour. But there was one occasion in the late 1990s when I would have given anything to have been driving that road, even if it took all day. I had just arrived at Wilson Airport for my flight to the Mara when much to my delight I spotted the impressive figure of Jimmy Owino striding down the corridor towards me. Jimmy was an old friend from rugby days and Kenya's answer to Jonah Lomu at well over 1.8 metres and close to 110 kilograms. He was built like a steam truck and ate up the ground with an effortless stride; there had been many a time when as a flanker on the opposing team I tried to stop him in his tracks, usually hanging on to one mighty thigh as he dragged me over the pitch until help arrived or he scored a try. I hadn't seen Jimmy since we toured Zambia together with a Chairman's XV some twenty years earlier, so after much back-slapping and high fives my heart sank when he announced that he was my pilot, insisting that I sit next to him in the cockpit. Under other circumstances that would have been a pleasure, but remembering our first training session on tour, when Jimmy suddenly collapsed as if struck by a bolt of lightning (he had forgotten to take his epilepsy medication in all the excitement), I now had visions of trying to restrain him mid-air if something similar were to occur. Jimmy laughed all the way to Mara while I mopped my brow and prayed for a safe landing on the longest flight of my life.

Watching Chui provided me with the opportunity to play the scientist, to live the life I would have done if I had been conducting fieldwork for a Masters or PhD. I took meticulous notes, recording every detail of the lives of Chui and her cubs during that four-month period: how often the cubs suckled and at what times of day, what prey species Chui hunted, the impact of other predators on her life, particularly the lions and hyenas that were such a threat to her cubs and her kills. I plotted the extent of her territory, the distances she moved and how much time she spent with her cubs, along with her behaviour any time that I or anyone else saw her encounter another leopard.

Ever since I started focusing on the Marsh Lions all those years ago, I have filled countless notebooks with data of this kind, in addition to accumulating sketches and photographs. I try wherever possible to

write up my projects in the form of a popular article for magazines such as *BBC Wildlife* and *Swara* to ensure that any tangible results reach as wide an audience as possible. And sometimes Angie and I work with scientists in the field of big cat biology, such as Dr Luke Hunter of the Panthera Fund, providing data that can be incorporated into a larger study. We have helped answer questions such as whether or not leopards breed seasonally (they do in the Mara, it seems – and in Londolozi – at the time of greatest suitable prey abundance) or how successful particular leopard females are in raising young. In areas where there are large numbers of lions and hyenas, a leopard often struggles to raise even twenty per cent of her cubs over the course of a lifetime.

I have derived great pride from playing a part in furthering our understanding of these extraordinary creatures, putting to good use all those obsessive details I recorded – though this prompted our editor of the past thirty years, the peerless Caroline Taggart, to point out to me in an early draft of *The Leopard's Tale* that we probably did not need to know each and every time Chui allowed her cubs to suckle. That might be interesting for scientists to process, but would simply bore the pants off the public.

Within four months of arriving back in the Mara in September 1983 I had sufficient photographs of Chui and her cubs to illustrate a story – six years in the making – to produce a book handsome enough to stand comparison with *The Marsh Lions*. Thank goodness I did, because in January 1984 the three leopards suddenly disappeared. Light and Dark were about six months old, strong enough and mobile enough to follow their mother wherever she chose to take them. I never saw the cubs again, but feel sure they survived because two years later my old friends Warren and Ginny Garst told me they had discovered a leopard with three small cubs in Leopard Gorge. As I watched that mother and cubs I failed to recognise that this was the same creature who had filled my life with such joy and meaning, but imagine my elation some months later when I was checking my photographs and established for certain that it was Chui. Much as I would have loved to see more of her, I knew at least that she had survived. What we know of leopard behaviour convinces me that, if Light and Dark had perished, Chui would almost certainly have mated again and produced more cubs earlier than she did. The fact that she was not seen with cubs for two years after I lost track of her makes it overwhelmingly likely that she had raised her previous litter to independence.

I continued to follow the Mara Buffalo Female and her cubs until they became independent. That meant I was able to document the whole life cycle of these extraordinary creatures. But could I transform my passion into words, having struggled to understand the most basic grammar and barely scraped a pass in English O Level? I knew I had learnt a huge amount about storytelling from Brian Jackman. We had disagreed at times when I felt his prose might be a shade too purple, and about the need to avoid anthropomorphism, though I accepted Brian's view that when writing a book where one tries to see the world through the eyes of a lion some anthropomorphism inevitably creeps in. But as lion biologist G L Smuts commented when reviewing *The Marsh Lions*, 'Since the book is not a scientific account of lion population dynamics this [anthropomorphism] can hardly be regarded as a weakness, but rather – and especially to the unconverted – as an advantage.'

Another person who played a pivotal role in making me believe I could become a writer was Harold Hayes, who for seventeen years wrote for *Esquire* magazine, ten of them as editor. My friend Boris Tismimiezky was once again the catalyst for this life-changing introduction – he had been Hayes' guide on his first visit to Africa. They became good friends and Hayes asked Boris to join him on a safari through Uganda while collecting material for what became his classic book, *The Last Place on Earth*. In this, Hayes followed in the wake of Dr Bernhard Grzimek of *Serengeti Shall Not Die* fame as he cut a brisk pace across East Africa, searching for answers as to how man and beast can survive in a world where humans demand ever more space. He was a masterly storyteller, deftly juggling the different strands and balancing his own personal journey of discovery with details of his day-to-day existence, all the while unravelling the mysteries of science and cajoling sound bites from his human subjects. He made the story of the Serengeti a parable of life on earth, a catalyst encouraging me to try to see the bigger picture – the whole landscape, the one visible to the human eye as well as the landscape within.

I first met Hayes in Nairobi and then on one of his visits to the Maasai Mara while I was working on *The Leopard's Tale*. He was full of encouragement, saying that all I really needed to do was to write as I talked, with emotion as the essential ingredient binding the words together. He knew that I had a unique story unfolding right before my eyes. Listening each evening as we chatted around the campfire, witness to the excitement in my voice as I recounted what I had seen, he assured me that there was no reason to ask someone else to write the book for me. 'This is your story as much as it is the leopards'. Draw on all your passion and love for your subject – own it.' And so I did.

Some while later Boris brought me a copy of Harold Hayes' sequel to *The Last Place On Earth*, *Three Levels of Time*. In it the author had kindly inscribed the words: 'For Jonathan, Who is living the life all the rest of us would like to lead. With admiration and affection

– Harold Hayes, 1987.' I regret never having the chance to talk to him again: he died of a brain tumour in 1989, but not before writing the feature on the murder of Dian Fossey that appeared in *Life* magazine and formed the basis for the film of her life and death, *Gorillas in the Mist*.

While I was working on *The Leopard's Tale* I tried to track down Dr Ted Bailey to find out the results of his research on leopards in the Kruger. I came across the odd mention of the study and Warren and Ginny Garst showed me some dramatic footage that *Wild Kingdom* had recorded of Bailey capturing leopards to fit radio collars and then releasing them – one of the leopards immediately leapt back up on to the release truck to attack the cage it had been incarcerated in, displaying the kind of speed and ferocity that professional trophy hunters are so wary of. But I could find nothing of a scientific nature in the literature.

The Garsts later discovered that Bailey was working in Alaska with the US Fish and Wildlife Services and, fifteen years after I had written to him asking if I could become his research assistant, he published *The African Leopard: Ecology and Behaviour of a Solitary Felid*, based on more than 100 visual observations, 2,500 radio telemetry locations and 112 live captures. His book proved a valuable synthesis of twenty-five years of literature on leopards and their status, as well as offering suggestions on ways to conserve the species. I found myself pondering my choice not to follow a more strictly scientific approach. But the answer was clear to see. The independence I had enjoyed while watching and photographing leopards at close quarters, writing up my findings on their behaviour *and* connecting with the general public had been the right career path for me. Each of us had served a purpose in bringing to light the results of our very different studies on leopards. They complemented each other.

The years spent gradually getting to know Chui and her mother and particularly following Chui with Light and Dark were some of the happiest and most satisfying of my life. When all the noisy vehicles had headed back to camp I could spend a few peaceful moments alone in Chui's company, watching as she emerged from Dik Dik Lugga where she had sought sanctuary during the day, now totally relaxed, calling to the cubs with that guttural *augh* or the quieter, more intimate *pff, pff, pff* sound known as chuffling or prusten, inviting them to join her in the grass. She would lie there, allowing the cubs to suckle, keeping a watchful eye on the surrounding plains for any hint of danger – or for an easy meal.

Those times will live with me forever. But why was it that leopards had always held such a fascination for me? Perhaps it was that in observing them so intimately I caught a glimpse of myself, the part of me that loves to be on my own, to absorb the silence and clear my thoughts, to be self-sufficient in whatever my quest may be. Like the leopard I wanted to step away from the crowd. I needed to follow my own path in life without fear of being judged for not always being one of the boys, to be ruthless in pursuit of my dreams, forsaking the partying and another drink if there was a chance to see those leopard cubs one more time – bad dose of malaria or not.

When *The Leopard's Tale* was published in 1985, Kodak sponsored an exhibition of my photographs and drawings at the Natural History Museum in London which then toured the UK for two years. For me, the museum holds fond memories of school and university holidays. I would wander its august corridors searching for insight and inspiration, hoping to find scraps of interesting information beyond the curriculum to weave into my essays in the hope of garnering a few precious extra marks. Julian Pettifer, with whom I had worked on *Nature Watch*, kindly agreed to open the exhibition and say a few words at the launch, and I was thrilled when I happened upon Sir Peter Scott carefully scrutinising my photographs and drawings. Scott was of my father's generation, a giant in the world of natural history who had been largely responsible for inspiring my childhood interest in wildlife. And not only mine: David Attenborough once called him his hero. Scott knew only too well from his own travels through Africa just how hard it was to photograph a leopard in any kind of detail: a good portrait would usually be considered the fruits of a generous sighting, so to capture anything of its behaviour was a real achievement. I sent him a copy of my book and he kindly responded with a personal note, saying how much he had enjoyed our chat and congratulating me on, in his words, my 'superlative photography'. I can think of no greater accolade from a man of Sir Peter Scott's standing. It was as if my father had spoken.

I was beginning to feel that I was repaying people's belief in me. There were still plenty of folks out there wondering when I was going to settle down and get a proper job, with a good deal of fatherly concern from uncles and godparents who were yet to be convinced that this wasn't all going to end in tears. Meanwhile my mother simply reminded me that, as long as I was doing what I loved and not expecting anyone else to foot the bill, I should press on. Did I sometimes stop and worry about the future? Yes, I did. Was I free of my deeper concerns? No.

CHAPTER

06

THE
GREAT
MIGRATION

There are two Africas…

the green, lush, bright country

when the sap is running and the

earth is wet; or the dry, brown-gold

wastes of the drought, when the sky

closes down… and the sun is

copper-coloured and distorted.

Doris Lessing

GOING HOME

Though Brian Jackman and I had written about cheetahs in *The Marsh Lions* and I had made mention of these elegant cats in *The Leopard's Tale*, I didn't want to make them my next 'project'. I was more interested in another, entirely different predator – the African wild dog.

Wild dogs or hunting dogs are the polar opposite in terms of character and social behaviour to the solitary leopards that had consumed my very being over the past few years. Brindled hunters whose scientific name *Lycaon pictus* means painted wolf, they are formidable predators, adopting the hunting tactics of the courser and perfectly designed for the long chase. Their approach is a stark contrast to stalking and ambushing their prey, then dispatching it with a single killing bite as cats do.

It is not a pretty sight to see a pack of wild dogs ripping into the soft underbelly of their prey while wolfing down the abdominal contents and vital organs in a frenzied competition to consume as much of the carcass as possible in the minimum amount of time. Though this is a very efficient way of feeding, it is no surprise that wild dogs have historically suffered a bad press with farmers and professional hunters – and even some game rangers and park wardens. As recently as the 1960s and '70s wild dogs were often shot on sight, whether on private land or as part of official policy in certain parks and game reserves in East and Southern Africa.

But in the 1970s the Dutch aristocrat turned photographer and filmmaker Hugo van Lawick had somewhat redeemed the 'painted wolves' in the eyes of the world, capturing people's imagination with his touching story about a pup called Solo. I had met Hugo through Brian Jackman and knew that the Serengeti Plains, where he had filmed, were still generally thought of as the easiest place in Africa to observe the dogs. Despite their unjustified reputation as wanton killers and a menace to prey populations, I found their social way of life fascinating. I was eager to make them an integral part of my next book, which I had decided was to fulfil a long-held ambition: following the annual cycle of the great migration's wanderings through the Mara and Serengeti.

I had watched year after year as this army of animals – well over a million wildebeest in total, accompanied by hundreds of thousands of zebras – flooded into the Mara in early June. I marvelled at their tenacity and the way they were so superbly adapted to their migratory lifestyle. I had stood on the banks of the Mara River each August and September when tourism in the Mara was in its infancy, sometimes creeping closer through the undergrowth or hiding down at water level on Paradise Plain to try to capture this epic among wildlife spectacles. Witnessing a river crossing ranks alongside the thrill of seeing coastal brown bears feasting on salmon in Alaska or a breeding colony of emperor penguins tending their chicks in remotest Antarctica, except that this last great migration is played out on the most dramatic stage of all, the dust rising for kilometres around, the throng of animals bellowing and grunting as the drum roll of millions of hooves beats a tattoo on the dry earth.

I have photographed the river crossings from every angle, through the roof hatch of my vehicle or from beneath it – on foot, even, in the early days when the best crossing sites were a well-kept secret. On one occasion I lay buried in the long red oat grass at the mouth of one of the exit channels carved into the steep bank by the hippos. With wildebeest emerging in a press of heaving black bodies, I suddenly found myself looking into the amber eyes of a full-grown lioness through my wide-angle zoom. She was barely two metres away as she rode up on to the flank of a bull wildebeest, biting into the hump of its muscular shoulders and dragging it back down the trail. She stood with one massive tawny paw wrapped around the bull's face, her jaws locked over its nose and mouth as she suffocated the life from it, never for a moment taking her eyes off the place where I crouched behind a veil of grass. Stunned, I crept back to my vehicle with a renewed sense of awe and wonder – it had been so immediate, so intense that I felt as if I could literally touch that experience. It had also been foolhardy and not to be repeated.

And the darkness in my mind? Up until now I had struggled to find answers to the wrong questions, dwelling on all manner of 'symptoms' that to me were proof that I was suffering from some life-threatening disease. My brother, always loving and compassionate, tried to convince me that I was fit and healthy and that my worries were just that – worries. But when my sister, who had studied sociology and psychology at university, mentioned the word hypochondriac for the first time, it filled me with shame. I simply would not countenance the idea that it might be true and that it was my head that needed fixing!

So it was a relief of sorts when I began to focus on something that was both significant and *visible*. I tended to cut and bruise more easily than most – and in this instance I wasn't imagining it, other people could see it too. In my early teens it was of little consequence – a black eye of slightly more extreme proportions than usual from boxing or rugby, swellings to my fingers due to broken blood vessels when playing fives. But as I headed for adulthood the bruising and cutting became more pronounced and troublesome, given my love of physical sport and disregard for my personal safety. In my final year at school, by which time I was experiencing my first bouts of dissociation, I had torn ligaments in my ankle playing rugby and the swelling was so alarming that the doctor was sure I had broken it; that same year I tore a cartilage in my knee – unusual for someone of my age and something that would require surgery not long after I went to university.

Unknown to me, I suffered from an obscure syndrome called Ehlers-Danlos (EDS), whose features were first described by Hippocrates, the Ancient Greek 'father of medicine', in 400BC. EDS is an inherited connective tissue defect for which there is no cure. It shows itself in a bewildering array of features, among which can be a tendency to easy bruising and cutting, with poor wound healing. My mother had always been an easy bruiser – she could break a blood vessel in her finger just turning on a tap. This and the numerous miscarriages she had suffered pointed to her having EDS, though nobody ever put a name to it and neither of my siblings showed any signs of having inherited it. The severity of the condition can vary from mild to life-threatening due to vascular accidents and aneurisms. But in the 1980s I didn't know any of this. Having no idea of the cause of my symptoms helped perpetuate my darkest fears a while longer. They would be my unwitting companions on my forays south to the Serengeti.

The Serengeti lies entirely in Tanzania but forms by far the larger part of the same ecosystem as the Mara in Kenya. It is the refuge and dispersal area for the migratory wildebeest and zebras throughout the rainy season, which typically lasts from November through to early June in northern Tanzania, with a lull in the downpours during January and February. But the climate is increasingly fickle all over Africa and the age-old timings for the onset of our two rainy seasons are no longer so precise. When I first arrived in Kenya the short rains really did begin in mid-October and end in December, as surely as the build-up of massive storm clouds towards the end of March heralded the advent of the long rainy season, with the rain lashing down for much of April and May before gradually withering away in early June.

The wildebeest read the nuances of the weather with far greater accuracy than the weathermen, forever monitoring the pattern of rainfall and gathering in areas with the best grazing: they prefer to feed on short green grass with a high leaf-to-stem ratio, when protein levels are at their highest. With their bulging brown eyes, large ears and long sensitive noses wildebeest are superbly adapted to gauge where the rain is coming from and when. They respond to the thunderstorms at the double, propelled along by their extraordinarily efficient lolloping gait, which allows them to cover the ground at a gallop at no more cost in terms of energy than if they were walking, helping to ensure they are in the right place at the right time. Ox-like heads swinging from side to side, long black tails streaming behind them may well make them look like the clowns of the plains as they skitter along, kicking up their legs and tossing their horns: some say the *gnu* (a Hottentot word) is God's joke, created from the leftovers of his miracle of creation. Maybe, but the one thing we can be certain of is that the wildebeest is a work of art in terms of design and function. The herds literally eat up the ground as they surge over the hills and across the plains, fording any river that stands in their way, sometimes retracing their steps to mow the grass afresh if rain has fallen since they first passed through.

Whether seen from a distant hill top or from up close, the migration resembles a massive black army, devouring the grass from under its feet while fertilising the pastures with piles of steaming black droppings, trampling the acacia seedlings as it passes through. This, along with fire and elephants, helps to keep the woodlands from regenerating and the grasslands intact. The wildebeest *are* the Serengeti as we know it.

Having seen the seasonal massing of the wildebeest in the Mara, I wanted to witness the great migration from birth to death, to follow in the animals' footsteps – though not as my publishers envisioned when they enquired if I could track the journey of a single mother and calf throughout their circuitous 3,000-kilometre wanderings around the Mara-Serengeti. Today it is possible to do just that, using satellite collars and computers to log an animal's position every minute of the day and night – something now being done with wildebeest in the Kajiado district of Kenya. Each study animal is named by children living in the region who map their progress on the school's computer. But that was unheard of thirty years ago.

What it *was* possible for me to witness was the broad brushstrokes of the migration's nomadic wanderings, to see the herds spread out across the Serengeti's short-grass plains, an area of 10,000 square kilometres that spills over into the Ngorongoro Conservation Area to the south and east of the park. The best time to do this would be January through March when, within a frenetic but carefully synchronised six-week period, the cow wildebeest drop half a million buff-brown calves on mineral-rich soils derived over millions of years from ash blown on easterly winds from the Ngorongoro Crater Highlands. The plains erupt in a tide of green in response to the rains, making them both the ancestral home of the migration and its birthplace.

ABOVE More people are killed by hippos than by any other large herbivore; never get between a hippo and the water. FOLLOWING PAGE 1982. I have never taken a better photograph of a wildebeest crossing. The light was perfect and so was the setting along the Mara River.

ABOVE One of the three cheetah brothers known as Honey's Boys
in hot pursuit of a wildebeest calf.

ABOVE Wildebeest crossing the Talek River and exiting through a hippo trail.
Animals sometimes sustain serious injury in the pandemonium of a large crossing..

ABOVE Maasai women singing and dancing to welcome visitors to their village.

ABOVE Maasai men leaping high in the air to prove their endurance and athleticism to their age mates and families. Our friend William ole Pere is the man in the middle.

ABOVE Wild dog in pursuit of wildebeest, Serengeti National Park, 1987.
Wild dogs are coursers, running their prey to the point of exhaustion before pulling it apart.

ABOVE A wild dog immobilises a wildebeest by grabbing it by the nose and upper lip,
allowing other members of the pack to pull it down. This is the shot that won me
the Wildlife Photographer of the Year Award in 1987.

ABOVE Members of the Naabi Pack investigate my Toyota Landcruiser.
They routinely trashed the electrical wiring under the vehicle.

ABOVE Puppies of the Aitong Pack, 1988. Only a few thousand wild dogs survive in Africa:
they are victims of persecution and epidemic diseases such as rabies and
distemper spread by domestic dogs.

LEFT Angie and her older brother David in 1963: as children they were inseparable.
RIGHT One of my favourite pictures of Angie – at Lake Nakuru,
during the filming of *Flamingo Watch* in 1995.

ABOVE Angie is never happier than within view of the ocean.
She was born in Alexandria in Egypt and spent her childhood in Dar es Salaam in Tanzania.

I wanted to accompany the great herds as the wind picked up from the east towards the end of May, sucking the last of the moisture from the land and heralding the onset of the dry season. As the muddy pools and intermittent watercourses evaporate it forces the herds of wildebeest, zebras and gazelles to the north and west. The grass stems on the short-grass plains quickly wither until the next rainy season in November, when the carpet of green erupts all over again. The Serengeti is like a living jigsaw: climate, soil, plants and animals locked together in the magic circle of life, death and rebirth, with the wildebeest the architects of the plains.

My plan was to seek permission to camp out on the short-grass plains in my vehicle, to enable me to live among the wildebeest and zebras over the next few seasons so that I could soak up every element of their existence. I would follow as they headed towards the centre of the park to an area known as the Western Corridor, through whose

black cotton soils our overland trucks had navigated a path ten years earlier, tracing the course of the Seronera River where the wildebeest could always find water in the dry season and where I had seen my first leopard. To achieve this objective I wanted to undertake a recce of the area to find out what permits I would need to work in the Serengeti and to establish contact with the scientists at the Serengeti Wildlife Research Centre so that I could hear their stories and learn about the results of their studies on every aspect of the ecology of the park. Given the historical antipathy between Tanzania and Kenya in terms of political and economic philosophies, I knew that this might not be easy for a Kenya resident.

By good fortune, shortly before *The Leopard's Tale* was published an American couple called Neil and Joyce Silverman were staying at Kichwa Tembo. They had a copy of *The Marsh Lions* with them and asked if I ever took people on safari. Though I had sometimes acted as a guide, I had just finished my last programme with *Wild Kingdom* and signed a contract with Elm Tree Books for *The Great Migration*. With my board and lodging taken care of as the in-house naturalist at Kichwa Tembo, and my drawings and prints earning me sufficient money to pay for my fuel and film, I was able to concentrate on my work, rather than worry where the next dollar was coming from. But as my plans evolved I wrote to the Silvermans about my intention to visit the Serengeti. I was proposing a six-week safari to photograph the calving of the wildebeest and asked if Neil would like to join me. He would.

We set off by road from Nairobi in January 1986 to cross from the Mara into the Serengeti via the Sand River Gate in Kenya and the Bologonja Border Post in Tanzania. Primed by Barbie Allen (who acted as Mother Goose to the scientists working in the Serengeti, providing them with a *poste restante* service and purchasing spare parts for vehicles and difficult-to-obtain food supplies), we arrived at the border crossing armed with the basics of life: toothpaste, toilet paper, soap, sugar, washing powder, light bulbs, newspapers and a crate of beer – not for the scientists but for the Tanzanian customs, immigration and police officers.

As we entered each bleak office to complete the paperwork we could feel the eyes of the officials checking us out, assessing what they could shake us down for. I thought back to my overland trip and our team leader Keith Miller, who always cautioned us to keep it simple: don't say more than you have to, keep it polite and friendly, don't be intimidated – and always keep some 'goodies' in reserve. At first the idea of having to part with *kitu kidogo* (Swahili for 'something small') rankled, but as one Tanzanian safari guide advised me a year or so later, 'Twenty shillings is the price of a cup of tea and can save you a lot of time and grief. Don't make a big fuss about it, think of it as being polite, like leaving a tip before receiving service or taking someone out for lunch to clinch a business deal. Don't wait to be asked for *kitu kidogo*, just put your hand in your pocket and forget about it.' Nonetheless, giving money seemed a step too far at this point, an acknowledgement that we didn't have the proper paperwork when we did.

One man stood out at Bologonja, Senior Immigration Officer Francis Magigi. Urbane, friendly and chatty, he was someone I knew immediately that I would need to keep on side if I was to complete my work. For now everything went smoothly and we headed down the road towards Seronera, a two-hour drive away, with that wonderful feeling of expectation as to what might lie ahead. We had decided to base ourselves at Ndutu Lodge, close to the shores of Lake Lagarja and just inside the Ngorongoro Conservation Area, where Hugo van Lawick had set up a tented camp for himself and his film crews. The lodge would give us easy access to the plains, where the wildebeest would soon be calving.

Hugo had always set the standards when it came to stills photography. I remember standing in a Nairobi bookshop not long after I had started living in the Mara, leafing through a copy of his epic work *Savage Paradise*. I felt both overwhelmed and hugely motivated by his images, thinking how much I would love to see the things he had so beautifully translated to film, let alone photograph them – particularly the leopards. His understanding of light and ability to capture thrilling action shots as well as stunning landscapes made him the complete wildlife photographer. Added to this Hugo was a keen naturalist who was fascinated by animal behaviour, the essence of my own love affair with wildlife. His book *Innocent Killers*, co-authored with his then wife, the primatologist Jane Goodall, featured wild dogs, hyenas and jackals, creatures that the authors came to know as individuals. It was a landmark in communicating insights into the behaviour of their subjects in evocative words and images, and had been an inspiration for my own work on leopards.

The camp at Ndutu was known as 'Hugo's Hilton', a fitting name given his aristocratic heritage. I counted myself fortunate to sample Hugo's menu one evening, gorging myself on roast beef and all the trimmings (including a full-bodied red wine) followed by a chocolate mousse that was so sublimely rich and creamy I wanted it to

last forever, and a glass of fine cognac served around the campfire. It was made all the sweeter by the thought of the endless tins of corned beef and baked beans awaiting me in my own mobile larder. When we finally retired to bed in the early hours of the following morning I felt as if I was travelling on a gently rolling ship as I slept off the effects of that marathon meal in my safari wagon.

As well as being a highly successful options trader with seats on the New York and Chicago Stock Exchanges, Neil Silverman was a keen photographer with all the latest Canon cameras and telephoto lenses; in fact he was much better equipped than I was. The deal was that he would come along for free and cover my expenses on the understanding that this was primarily a recce for *The Great Migration* – not a bespoke private safari. Joyce assured me that her husband had plenty of books to read to see him through six weeks out on the plains and that everything would be just fine as long as we had plenty of Coca Cola (indeed, Neil had crates flown in to Ndutu when they ran out).

But it soon became apparent that Neil's idea of being a wildlife photographer had not taken into account just how much time you have to sit waiting for that leopard to descend from the tree in which it is resting or for the wildebeest and zebras to move close enough for lions to strike. Not long after we arrived in the Serengeti I explained to him how things worked. Early one morning, having established a good position to watch a pride of lions resting up on one of the ancient granite outcrops in the middle of the plains known as *kopjes* (the Afrikaans word for rock head), I switched off the engine. Now we must wait. In the meantime we could make some coffee and snack on some biscuits; Neil immersed himself in the first of his books while I typed up my notes on my laptop and kept a careful eye on the lions. All was fine for the first hour or so, but then Neil asked, 'But what if the lions don't do anything, what if nothing happens?' To which I responded, 'Then we come back tomorrow and try again.'

Suddenly it dawned on Neil what he had got himself into, that capturing the kind of images he had seen in *The Marsh Lions* takes time – days, weeks, years even, depending on what you are trying to photograph. I told him how I had waited six years to finish *The Leopard's Tale* and that one thing I knew for certain was that signing up for a three-day safari where you race against the clock to see as many animals as you can was very different from trying to capture photographs that had an edge to them, that showed their subject in a new or unusual way. That took time and patience. To which Neil responded, 'Well, I can tell you one thing – if those lions don't do anything I am going to be mightily pissed off come six o'clock.' It was only day two and I knew we had a problem.

First I needed to get straight with myself. Why would I think for one minute that an options trader used to thinking fast on his feet would easily settle for hours on end in a hot tin box marooned in the vastness of the Serengeti Plains? Neil was used to being in control, to making things happen, not having to sit quietly waiting hour after hour for lions to strike, almost beside himself with tension and boredom. On one occasion he said he wanted to lie in, proclaiming his disappointment with what we had been seeing. When the time came for us to depart for our regular early-morning game drive, I left him in bed: he could rest if he wanted to, but I wasn't going to miss a moment. But once I softened my position and embraced the gulf that separated our worlds, things became a lot easier.

The turning point for Neil was hastened the day he picked up one of my books – Tony Sinclair and Mike Norton-Griffiths' *Serengeti: Dynamics of an Ecosystem*, the Bible of all things Serengeti, with details of the various findings compiled over many years by scientists working at the Serengeti Wildlife Research Institute. Once Neil started to examine the data – the numbers – he was flying, revelling in the fact that the 35,000 vultures soaring over the Mara-Serengeti were estimated to consume twelve million kilograms of meat and offal annually, a massive clean-up exercise that these giant birds of prey are superbly adapted to execute. I also knew that our planned visit to Ngorongoro, where we would stay in one of the best hotels overlooking the Crater rim, would help make the next stage of our safari a more comfortable and varied adventure for Neil.

From the outset, part of the attraction of the Serengeti for both Neil and myself had been the possibility of seeing wild dogs, a creature that Neil had never set eyes on despite previous travels in East Africa, Zambia and Zimbabwe. After years of absence due to the devastating effects of rabies and distemper transmitted by both wild and domestic animals, wild dogs were being seen again in the Serengeti – just as they had reappeared at Aitong in the Mara. This exciting news was conveyed to me one evening in Nairobi by a talented artist and outstanding ornithologist by the name of John Fanshawe. John and his girlfriend Clare FitzGibbon, who was studying cheetahs in the Serengeti, were trying to piece together what had happened to the wild dog population since George and Lory Frame studied it in the 1970s and early '80s. John and Clare estimated that there could be as few as eighty dogs in the entire park – an area of 14,630 square kilometres.

Neil and I had set our hearts on seeing wild dogs, particularly as we had heard that there was a pack hunting in the area we were searching, a beautiful stretch of country between Naabi Hill and the Gol Kopjes. If we could find the Naabi Pack, then our Serengeti safari would take on a completely different complexion, and so would my book on the great migration. It would be like finding a leopard in the old days.

Hard as we searched, we could find no signs of the dogs. I knew our chances were slim, as it would be some months before the dogs denned – March to April is their peak denning season on the Serengeti Plains, timed to coincide with the maximum amount of easy prey to feed both puppies and adults at the time of their greatest need. With wildebeest accompanied by young calves spread thickly across the short-grass plains, it was easy pickings for the wild dogs. Their success rate when targeting young calves was almost one hundred per cent and wherever they chose to den they were virtually assured of finding the herds within a few kilometres. For the rest of the year wild dogs lead an itinerant life, putting 20 kilometres between themselves and their last resting place at an easy trot.

When Neil mentioned in passing 'strange-looking, small, black hyena creatures' as we headed towards Seronera Lodge I carried on, eager to be back well before nightfall, as I had promised to give a talk to a group of American visitors there. 'Hyenas,' I thought to myself, knowing how they loved to lie in puddles of water or at the mouth of burrows alongside the roads. But when the American guests mentioned that during their game drive they had seen nine wild dogs lying up in hyena dens within metres of the main road my heart sank. Neil was generous enough not to rub it in, but having invested so much in the hope of catching his first glimpse of these rare and fascinating predators, to have me drive right by them was more than a little frustrating. I was mortified. Next morning we set off back down the road at first light, but despite searching the surrounding plains and all the likely resting places, nothing. Imagine our frustration – with less than a week before our safari was due to come to an end – to hear that the dogs were seen on two out of the next three days.

A few days later we found a different pack of thirteen dogs to the east of Ndutu in an area called the Triangle. This pack was known as the

Peddlers and we felt fortunate to be able to spend our last three days with them, watching as friends from the Serengeti Cheetah Project immobilised one of the adult males and fitted it with a radio collar, a procedure that was being carried out with each pack of wild dogs discovered in the Serengeti. When the scientists headed back to Seronera we waited with the male until it had fully recovered from the drugs. It was fortunate we did, as it took many hours for it to get to its feet and longer still before it could safely wander off in search of its relatives, uttering the plaintive *hoo, hoo, hoo* contact call that I remembered so well from the days when I worked for Jack Bousfield in Botswana and all but one of the five wild dogs incarcerated at the capture centre were exported to Frankfurt Zoo. The zoo had only wanted males, leaving the lone female a forlorn figure. Each evening she would call into the still of the night for her siblings, the mournful bell-like sound audible from my house a kilometre away, a call that I knew would never be answered.

Neil and I spent a chilly night on the plains in the vehicle, chasing off the spotted hyenas who soon arrived to investigate the rich scent of the pack and who would certainly have killed the comatose male. But who cared about the cold now? Neil was overjoyed at having seen his first 'painted wolf' and finding out more about the newly founded Serengeti Wild Dog Project. Over the next few years the Silvermans became great friends of our family and their generosity provided funding for vehicles and tracking equipment, fuel and spares, helping to ensure that the wild dog project remained financially secure. The goodwill Neil and Joyce created in the Serengeti helped me get permission to work there, including the privileges of driving off road and sleeping in my vehicle.

Ironically, the head of Tanzania National Parks at this time was the impressive David Babu, who had been the feared and respected Warden of the Serengeti when I passed though the park on my overland trip ten years earlier – the same man that the ranger had been so concerned might catch us and discipline him if we went off road. Babu now gave his blessing to my work. If only there were more wardens like him – a dedicated single-minded individual can make such a difference.

When I returned to Tanzania a few months after my recce with Neil, inspired by Harold Hayes' books, I found myself embarking on a different journey to the one I had first imagined. If there was one place on Earth where I could find peace of mind, then perhaps it might be here. This was an opportunity to explore my own sense of reality. Certainly I would never be more alone.

Given time, maybe I could untangle my irrational view of life and death and think myself back to wellness? With the help of the Nairobi physiotherapist Hilary Ahluwalia, who had treated me for haematomas when I tore a calf muscle and then ankle ligaments, I had finally been able to put a name to my tendency to cut and bruise more easily than other people. Like it or not, Ehlers-Danlos Syndrome was my destiny and at least I could now abandon any ideas that I was suffering from Cushing's Disease (caused by a pituitary or adrenal tumour) with all its life-threatening complications – the latest of my obsessions. But would I simply find something else to obsess over as I had in the past, unable to silence the incessant doubt?

Besides Harold Hayes' stimulating work, two other books had a profound impact on my way of thinking while I was in the Serengeti. One was *Awakenings* by the late Dr Oliver Sacks, the other *The Turning Point* by Fritjof Capra. *Awakenings* was a revelation, particularly given my altered sense of awareness precipitated by dissociation. The book – later filmed with Robin Williams and Robert de Niro – documented the remarkable story of a group of patients in a Bronx hospital who became transfixed, motionless, in a decades-long trance after contacting encephalitis lethargica or 'sleepy sickness', a disease that left more than a million people dead. Nothing to do with the 'sleeping sickness' transmitted by tsetse flies in Africa, this is a disease of the brain which swept the world during and after the First World WarF in the wake of the 1918 Spanish flu epidemic that killed an estimated fifty million people worldwide. These men and women were given up as lost causes, doomed eventually to die bed-ridden and virtually comatose until in 1969 Dr Sacks gave them L-DOPA, a newly discovered drug that literally awakened his patients in an astonishing transformative manner. *Awakenings* is a tale of health and disease, suffering and care – the human condition in all its many manifestations.

What fascinated me was how Sacks viewed all his patients as living entities, not as 'the kidney patient in bed 12'. In so doing he shone a bright and compassionate light on his patients' state of mind and the nature of illness in general. As Doris Lessing (another of my favourite writers) noted, 'It makes you aware of the knife-edge we live on.' Sacks never played 'God in a white coat' with his patients; he opened the door to a two-way dialogue. He listened and empathised with their suffering, taking a holistic approach to health and disease, acknowledging that mind and body were one – something that I needed to embrace if I was to find inner peace. At the time of my childhood fall I had, in an instant, created a new reality, littered with false beliefs that were driven by fear and expressed through obsessions and compulsions.

Fritjof Capra's *The Turning Point* was pivotal in helping me order the thoughts that I was grappling with when it came to understanding the science of life and its implications for spirituality. His writing turned many of my ideas on their head. I had lived my life firmly rooted in the certainties of science – that $1 + 2 = 3$ – and in particular that maths and physics were 'hard' sciences, illuminating our world and the cosmos by measuring and quantifying it in an

irrefutable manner. I had until now believed that they represented the truth, while admitting that this posed a problem for me, as both subjects had always taxed my intellect. If the new physics – quantum physics – informed us that the nature of matter was not what we had believed it to be, then what did that actually tell us? That there were no certainties, perhaps? And as for 'infinity', how do you visualise that?

Capra's writings drew parallels between modern physics and mysticism, in particular Oriental and Greek mystical traditions. He noted a merging of the findings of the social sciences and hard sciences that was more open and inclusive in its attempts to give us a unified view both of ourselves and of our place in this world. This was the opposite of traditional Western culture that encouraged conventional linear thought. Capra called for a holistic approach, rather than clinging to the 'reductionist' view that everything could be understood by breaking it down into its constituent parts – a belief that saw man as a machine. Instead he argued that in order to illuminate the character of the whole we needed to understand the relationship among all the parts, emphasising their interconnectedness and the web-like structure of all systems, whether describing the nature of human life or the environment we live in. He pointed out the unsustainability of materialism and the endless search for 'growth', while holding out hope for future generations by quoting Lester Brown of the Worldwatch Institute, who said, 'A sustainable society is one that satisfies its needs without diminishing the prospects of future generations.'

At university I had willingly embraced Darwin's theory of natural selection and evolution. Doing so seemed to rule out any possibility of a belief in God – certainly not the conventional Christian God I had been exposed to as a child. Until now I had felt no deep void or angst based on what I did or did not believe. I had been so busy loving life that I put the big questions to one side. Living close to nature meant that the idea of birth, life and death had taken on a beautiful and finite simplicity that surely needed no further explanation. This was the sum of it: the physical manifestation of existence broke down to its constituent parts at death, becoming once more one with the wind and the soil. Did one need to believe in anything more?

The certainties that the eminent scientist Richard Dawkins espouses leave me cold in their attempt to articulate the validity of his beliefs. I believe that the only thing we can be certain of about scientific knowledge is that whatever we think we know will inevitably be transformed into new 'truths' as old ones are revised under the microscope of greater wisdom. The findings of science can never be more than part of a grand thesis – a work in progress, not the full story. Surely this should encourage caution lest we rob life of its mystical properties, extinguishing the sense of spirituality that is such a nourishing part of being human. Language, art and music provide each individual with ways to inspire and enrich their journey through life that at times can only be described as transcendent. Suffering from dissociation had certainly pushed me to redefine my own sense of reality and to acknowledge how fragile and changeable that could be – that my ways of seeing and sensing my world might not be as reliable as I thought. I also came to realise that our senses are only attuned to a very limited part of the whole, that we create our world by what we see and feel and that this is only a very thin slither of the ultimate reality.

It has been said, in rebuttal of Dawkins, that needing to believe in something is part of being human. For me, to dream is to soar like a bird. Who would wish to deny people a sense of faith in the sacred in a world defined by creativity of a greater order than science can ever quantify? Prayer sustained my mother throughout her life – for her it was a powerful form of meditation and therapy. Regardless of whether or not she would ever truly be reunited with my father in the way she hoped for, those moments of stillness and reverence were vital to her well being and the source of her strength.

The American astrologer Carl Sagan did a brilliant job of exploring some of these ideas in his landmark television series *Cosmos* that even today, thirty years after it was first aired, is a remarkably coherent work. Sagan was a member of a group of sceptics who espoused scientific sceptical enquiry – as is Richard Dawkins. Nonetheless he was always willing to leave the door open while seeking to lock out the charlatans who live off the fears of the sick and vulnerable, motivated by greed to manipulate people's inherent need to cling to hope when facing the travails of life.

While Sagan was a sceptic and agnostic he believed in spirituality, noting, 'Science is not only compatible with spirituality: it is a profound source of spirituality. When we recognise our place in the immensity of light-years and in the passage of ages, when we grasp the intricacy, beauty, and subtlety of life, then the soaring feeling, that sense of elation and humility combined, is surely spiritual.' I was beginning to realise that not believing in a conventional God could mean more than simply closing the door on more traditional beliefs; for me at least, it could be the beginning of a new and exciting journey in search of enlightenment.

CHAPTER

07

PAINTED
WOLVES

If the great beasts are gone,

man will surely die of a great

loneliness of spirit.

Chief Seattle of the Nez Perce

If ever there was a place demonstrating the unity of all life, then that place was Serengeti, Harold Hayes' 'last place on Earth'. Hayes was right. There is nowhere on Earth quite like this, nowhere with such a broad sweep of landscape filled with so many animals. It is nothing short of a miracle that it has survived relatively intact. This is in no small measure due to the traditional ways of the Maasai pastoralists, who for centuries lived side by side with the wild animals on the savanna grasslands, long before the Serengeti or Maasai Mara was given any form of official protection.

Thinking these thoughts rekindled memories of the year I spent working in America in 1973, of another great migration and another culture with close ties to the land. My time there provided me with the opportunity to explore my fascination with Native American culture and the wild open plains country those indigenous people shared with the bison. I made a point of visiting as many of the famous historical landmarks as I could. These were brought alive by the work of artists of the old American West, none more evocative than that of Charles Russell and Frederick Remington, both of whom captured the energy of their subjects in rough-hewn works of art, whether a sweeping canvas depicting 'Indians' galloping across the plains in pursuit of bison or a bronze masterpiece of a cowboy trying to stay aboard a bucking bronco.

Remington's views on the indigenous peoples were far from charitable, even though they represented the norm in those days. While he regarded the cowboy and soldier under attack as brave and noble, he characterised the Indian as unfathomable, fearless, superstitious, ignorant and pitiless. Both Russell and Remington were still alive on the fateful day, 29th December 1890, when troops of the US 7th Cavalry marched 350 Oglala Sioux Indians (who had earlier surrendered to the soldiers) into camp at Pine Ridge Creek, their intention being to escort them to the Indian Agency the following day. While witnesses disagreed on what sparked the shooting, the tragic outcome is not subject to debate. The soldiers opened fire, killing two hundred men, women and children, cut down without mercy.

Black Elk, an Oglala sage and medicine man, was wounded that day but survived. His words offer eloquent testimony to the pain and suffering of his people:

> I did not know then how much was ended. When I look back now from this high hill of my old age, I can still see the butchered women and children lying heaped and scattered all along the crooked gulch as plain as when I saw them with eyes young. And I can see that something else died there in the bloody mud, and was buried in the blizzard. A people's dream died there. It was a beautiful dream... the nation's hope is broken and scattered. There is no centre any longer, and the sacred tree is dead.

More than eighty years after the massacre, in late February 1973, Wounded Knee was the site of a seventy-one-day standoff between militants of the American Indian Movement and federal law enforcement officials in which two people were killed, twelve wounded and one thousand two hundred arrested. It was with these events fresh in my mind that later that same year I headed for the Pine Ridge Reservation to pay my respects to those who had been killed at Wounded Knee.

Entering the Reservation I soon found the dark underbelly of the American Dream: South Dakota contains two of the poorest counties in the country. The poverty and desolation were overwhelming, with running water and electricity in short supply. Alcoholism and drug use were rampant, as were domestic violence and corruption in

tribal government; unemployment was running at eighty per cent. Not surprisingly, life expectancy was low and there were high rates of infant mortality. Suicides among young people were ten times the national average and tensions were still running high; drunk driving was a major issue, with young Indians sometimes forcing people off the road. There were stories of beatings and murder.

On reaching Wounded Knee I parked my car and walked up to the monument, a simple arrangement featuring a rectangle of white plinths and a memorial stone set against a bleak stretch of open country. As I stood there, a group of tough-looking young Native American men approached me and asked what I was doing. I told them that I had always been interested in their culture and that I meant no offence; I was a visitor. One of them – whose scarred face and broken nose told the story of a hundred bar-room brawls – took a hunting knife from his friend's belt and asked me why he shouldn't just cut my balls off right there and then and be done with it. Fortunately a thickset man with shaven head and the air of a leader about him seemed content to let me be, telling the others that it was time to go, a welcome voice of reason from deep within this cultural wilderness. But when they got into their vehicle it refused to start, prompting my ugly friend and his sidekick to head back towards me. Just as it looked certain that I was going to lose my car and take a kicking, their vehicle spluttered to life and they careered off down the road in a cloud of dust.

I sat for a moment thinking how lucky I had been to have the myth of the hero – my father – so strongly implanted in my imagination. The unconditional love of my family, coupled to a sense of pride and duty instilled by my years at Christ's Hospital, was integral to my being. By contrast, those young men were struggling to connect to their own sense of identity, passed down in olden times through tradition and legend, reinforced by rituals that allowed young people to test themselves and find their place in society, to be proud of who they were and what their past represented. Much of that had been torn from their grasp with the coming of the white man and the passing of the bison.

The Shaman Black Elk spoke of the Seven Rites of the Oglala Sioux, including the Sun Dance, a ritual of renewal and the most important major communal religious ceremony celebrated by Plains Indians. The Sun Dance emphasised the continuity between life and death, that there is no end to life but a cycle of symbolic and true deaths and rebirths, that all of nature is intertwined and interdependent, acknowledging equal standing to everything on the Earth. The ceremony involved sacrifice and supplication to promote harmony between all living beings, celebrating the spiritual rebirth of participants and their relatives as well as the regeneration of the living Earth and all its components, not least the bison. This unified concept of life and death resonates strongly with the Buddhist ideas of impermanence and reverence for all forms of life, inspiring a sense of wonder and respect for the Earth that I find both moving and thought-provoking.

The Sun Dance ritual involved extreme pain to warriors who endured it. Each of the young men presented himself to a medicine man, who took a fold of the loose skin of their breast, then ran a knife through the skin, inserting a skewer of bone through each breast and fastening it to a long skin rope suspended from the sun pole in the centre of the arena. The devotees then danced around the pole as they attempted to break loose by tearing the skewers through the skin, something that even the bravest and most resolute might take many hours to achieve. Today the only rituals that meant anything to some of the young men I encountered that day were gang initiations, often fuelled by drugs and alcohol and glorifying guns and violence.

I continued on my travels across the vast expanse of the Great Plains, once home to the largest and most spectacular animal migration known to history. Before the coming of the white people the American bison roamed these grasslands as a single population of migratory herds that stretched almost from one side of the continent to the other, a distance of some 3,000 kilometres. Estimates of between twenty to thirty million bison make East Africa's great migration, with its one and a half million wildebeest and quarter of a million zebras, seem tame by comparison. By the mid-1880s the great herds of bison had been reduced to just a few thousand animals – in little less than a century. The dramatic decline was the result of the expansion of ranching and farming; increased hunting pressure due to the demand for bison hides and meat; and attempts to protect the railroad. But most reprehensible of all was the deliberate slaughter of the bison to starve the indigenous peoples from their land. Soon all that remained of the great herds were mountains of bleached bones, the animals' massive skulls ground into fertiliser.

The buffalo had symbolised far more than mere food to the Plains Indians. The giant animals were life itself: people relied on them for clothing, shelter and most of their utensils, from fly swatters to children's toys. With the fabric of their society and economy in tatters, the Plains Indians were forced on to reservations, their pride and dignity destroyed. Now, as I contemplated the future of the Mara-Serengeti, I could see parallels in the challenges that faced the nomadic Maasai pastoralists who shared the last great open spaces in East Africa with the wild animals. As the Maasai become more sedentary and their land is subdivided, they find themselves drawn into a cash-based economy rather than relying on cattle for nearly all their needs. Their traditional way of life and distinctive culture will surely wither away as it becomes obsolete in a more urban environment. And what of the wild animals? Who would vote for them?

Though I had come to the Serengeti to follow the journey of the great migration with the wild dogs as bit players, I soon realised that theirs was another story begging to be told. Instead of seeing the wild dogs as part of 'life on the plains', with their breeding synchronised to coincide with the calving season of the wildebeest, I quickly found myself riveted by the character of these extraordinary social predators. Part of what made them so fascinating was their accessibility: they were so visible and easy to follow when anchored to a den, and the fact that they were active mainly during daylight meant that I could follow them on the hunt. Once their puppies emerged, the social dynamic of the pack became even more visible and when the Naabi Pack denned near Gol Kopjes in 1986 and then at Barafu Kopjes in 1987 I spent long periods of time with them.

Exploring the kopjes on foot reminded me of how our early ancestors had roamed these animal-rich plains long ago, sheltering in caves and making fires to cook, to keep themselves warm and the predators at bay, their social way of life continually evolving through language and culture. This was a very different kind of life experience for me after all the time I had spent exploring the mysterious and secretive world of the leopard among the forests and acacia thickets in the Mara. The leopard represented the individual, the pack a social alternative to a life alone, promoting altruistic or 'helping' behaviour. Professor E O Wilson writes of the facet of human life that reflects the selfish imperative of the individual – Richard Dawkins' 'selfish gene' – paired with the altruistic behaviour of individuals living in groups, where 'helping' pays dividends for both the individual and the group in competing with neighbouring clans. Understanding the conflict between our selfish and altruistic tendencies can help us to find peace with the drama of being human. It also shows how cooperation has allowed us to conquer the planet.

It was easy to see how wolves had evolved into man's best friend – how their intelligent and inquisitive nature enabled them to cross the gulf between predator and ally, becoming both guard dog and pet in return for scraps from around the campfire, offering security and companionship in equal measure. We humans tend to think of this process as being all about us, but it seems likely that the domestication of wild creatures such as the wolf and the cat was driven by their needs as much as ours. Spending time with the wild dogs also allowed me to understand just how different they are from big cats and why domestic dogs are so attractive and endearing to us; why 'the wolf in your kitchen' wants to lick your face (because you are one of the pack; to greet you; to solicit food) or defers to its human master as it would to an alpha male or female. Just as fascinating was understanding how the solitary nature of cats helps ensure that they forever retain an air of mystery, of other-worldliness, walking alone much of the time and revealing a self-sufficiency that I have always loved. A dog is much easier to read; the feline air of subtlety and complexity is missing.

The wild dogs allowed me to connect to a vibrant energy that was quite different to that of the massed herds of wildebeest. The great migration is a phenomenon: it has a life of its own, an identity greater than its parts. A single wildebeest is undoubtedly unique, but I found it far harder to connect emotionally to a wildebeest than I did to a member of the Naabi Pack, where each individual was revealed as a well-defined character. A wildebeest's closest relationship is between mother and calf, a bond that gradually weakens and dies by the time the next calf arrives a year later. So I found a certain impatience creeping in as I hurried to complete *The Great Migration*, eager to dedicate my time fully to the pack rather than the herd.

Marooned in the solitude of the short-grass plains, I waited anxiously for the large courier package to arrive from my publishers in England. They had dispatched the colour proofs of *The Great Migration* to a UK film crew visiting the Serengeti to deliver to me. There is no greater joy or despair for a writer or photographer than poring over the first proofs of his or her work. In this instance there was the intense pleasure of seeing some of my best images jump off the pages, mixed with the disappointment of a badly cropped or poorly reproduced photograph. I quickly realised that there was still a lot of work to be done by the repro house, along with some glaring errors in the text that needed correcting. Imagine then my dismay when I glanced at the covering letter stating that any changes needed to be transmitted to the publishers by – last week! It was a Friday and I knew that I had to drive back to Arusha immediately. There, my friends at Abercrombie & Kent could pass a message to their Nairobi office for onward transmission to the UK. But it meant a nine-hour journey even if the road stayed dry.

I set off from Seronera, belting cross-country as fast as my Toyota could manage. An hour or so later I realised that the disturbing noise coming from somewhere under my car was demanding immediate attention. I had long since learnt that if you hear a strange noise it is no good praying it's nothing serious – stop and investigate and don't continue until you have identified the problem. If possible, fix it; otherwise, bandage it up sufficiently to enable you to continue. Otherwise be ready for a wheel to fall off because the nuts have come loose or your engine to seize because your radiator is leaking. In this instance it was the universal joint on the front propshaft that had come adrift and would have to be removed. I knew that I could still drive the vehicle using the other prop shaft – but without four-wheel drive.

Having sorted the problem I was soon haring down the road again, noting just how black and brooding the sky ahead was looking. Sure enough as I climbed towards the Crater Highlands the heavens opened, unleashing the mother of all storms. I could barely see through the windscreen, let alone keep the vehicle from slipping off the road. But I knew that I had to keep going if I was to have any chance of getting to Arusha in time.

With these thoughts spinning around my head, I barely saw the sign that suddenly loomed into view – DIVERSION. Too late I found myself on a murram road with a surface as slick as a skating rink and a camber that dipped steeply on either side into a slurry of cloying mud. My Toyota was a heavily laden tank, full of supplies and equipment, with a rear end that weighed a tonne, making it a nightmare to keep straight on a slippery road. Without four-wheel drive to help keep the back end from slewing down into those valleys of mud, I lurched sideways along the road, desperately trying to force the vehicle up on to the grass. I came tantalisingly close before wedging my front wheels up on the verge with the back wheels still on the road. Now what? The high-lift jack would be of little use in all that mud.

My trusty winch had saved me on many occasion in the past, so spotting a small acacia tree just within reach of the cable I set to work. Soaked to the skin within seconds I engaged the winch. Inch by inch the vehicle edged forwards on to relatively firm ground until – BANG – out popped the tree by its roots and the vehicle settled back into the mud. Exhausted, I boiled up some soup and decided to grab some sleep. When I woke a few hours later, refreshed and ready to dig myself out of trouble, I found that I had an audience of half a dozen fit and muscular-looking Maasai warriors armed with long glistening spears and red-holstered *simis* (short stabbing swords). The warriors were accompanied by a wizened old greybeard with long ear lobes and a sparkle in his brown eyes.

It quickly became apparent that the old man was not only partial to a few beers but was adamant that the acacia tree that now lay torn and bedraggled on the grass close to my vehicle was his property. I was stuck on his land and was in effect a trespasser. He was insistent that not only would I have to pay handsomely for the tree, but that we would have to go through protracted negotiations with the warriors as his witnesses, given that it was the only tree of any description for as far as the eye could see – and apparently one of his favourites. The young warriors seemed to be enjoying the entertainment, happy to lean against my vehicle and compete with one another for a view of themselves in the side mirrors, carefully touching up the red ochre on their long braided locks and elegant faces while admiring their dazzling white teeth. The last thing they wanted to do right now was to get spattered in mud attempting to push my overladen vehicle out of the quagmire. Once their half-hearted attempts proved futile the only answer was to have another go with the winch.

With no tree as anchor I would have to dig a channel at 90 degrees to the vehicle and slot my spare wheel in the trench to brace the winch cable against. I had done this before on the Serengeti Plains, digging for hours on rock-hard ground during the dry season to extricate myself from the only mud wallow for kilometres around. Out came my trusty shovels and a pickaxe, a couple of *jembes* (similar to broad-bladed hoes) and crow bars as I set to work. Meanwhile the old man directed operations, nearly strangling himself on the winch cable when he tripped and fell flat on his face in the mud as he tried to attach it to my spare wheel. Eventually the young morani decided to join in, turning it into a competition witnessed by a gathering crowd of curious villagers, with young maidens and children to impress. An hour later, covered in mud, I was back on dry ground and ready to depart, the warriors dancing and singing in celebration of a job well done.

By this time the old man had been off to the nearest boma for another tot or three of the potent honey beer that the Maasai so love, and was no doubt hallucinating about the size and value of the tree that I had felled from his ancestral land. Before I could lock the door the old boy was sitting proudly in the passenger seat next to me, provoking visions of us driving all the way to Arusha as we negotiated over his tree. Fortunately he agreed to settle for my remaining handful of local currency along with my prized sheath knife before I got too far down the road, the warriors cheering and whooping me on my way as I headed for town.

The good news was that I managed to get a fax through to the publishers listing all the corrections. The bad news was almost worse than if I had never been in contact. I had been particularly careful to scrutinise the maps – an essential part of the book in that they showed the general pattern of the wildebeest's and zebras' migratory wanderings both past and present. The maps highlighted three distinct locations and timings – the southern plains (November-May), Western Corridor (June-July) and the Mara (June-October). At the last minute it was decided to use a colour code to differentiate the three zones – but to my horror when the book was printed the key showed the wildebeest as being in the Mara from November to May and on the southern plains from June to October – the reverse of what actually happens. In changing from graphic patterns to a three-colour code the artist had muddled it up. I was distraught. The publishers promised to correct the map for the American edition and any reprints, but when an enthusiastic tour operator congratulated me one morning at Kichwa Tembo on how my new book had solved a longstanding problem – she could now send photocopies of my migration map to all her clients so they could decide exactly when to travel to view the herds – I knew just what a potentially embarrassing disaster I had to contend with. Fortunately nobody ever mentioned it again.

The Great Migration was published in 1988. Meanwhile I continued to monitor the various wild dog packs in both the Serengeti and the Mara, which gave me the chance to see first hand just how different Tanzania and Kenya were in terms of both their politics and their economic goals. Kenya's traditional approach to wildlife-based tourism has always involved low cost but high numbers, while Tanzania had taken a more restrictive view of how many tourist facilities they were prepared to allow in and around their parks and reserves. In the late 1980s and '90s the Serengeti (which is almost ten times the size of the Mara) had around 800 beds, compared to the Mara's 2,000, meaning that you saw a lot fewer visitors in the Serengeti and the impact of their 'footprint' was minimal by comparison. As the Tanzanians used to like to remind Kenyans, theirs was a Ministry of Wildlife and Tourism – in other words, the priority in Tanzania was taking care of wildlife, rather than allowing the tourist industry to dictate policy. Warden David Babu was testament to that.

However, just how important tourism revenue is to conservation and the economies of both countries is illustrated by what happened when Tanzania closed its border with Kenya in 1977, and kept it closed for six years. As visitor numbers to Tanzania plummeted, poaching spun out of control – the black rhinos (estimated at over five hundred in the 1960s) disappeared, elephant numbers halved and meat poaching increased dramatically. Park vehicles were soon in short supply, with fuel and spare parts either unavailable or at a premium. Meanwhile the Mara, which had previously been little more than a stopover for visitors returning from a safari through northern Tanzania, quickly established itself in its own right, and Kenya benefited from increased interest in all its tourism products.

With Tanzania's tourism still in the doldrums while I was in the Serengeti, my main companions out on the plains were the scientists working at the Serengeti Wildlife Research Institute, along with the upmarket private safari operators. They tended to frequent the more remote parts of the park and Ngorongoro Conservation Area, often setting up mobile camps near to the spectacular granite kopjes. It was always nice to catch up on news from Kenya, though I well remember the frustration I felt after a few days of being alone at the Barafu Kopjes with the Naabi Pack and their latest litter of puppies, on waking to the voice of a friend from Kenya who had spotted my vehicle as I took a nap one morning while feeling grim from a particularly nasty bout of malaria. I could hear him excitedly telling another safari vehicle that he had found the wild dog den – quickly making amends by offering me some welcome supplies of fresh food.

The highlight of my time during those years in Serengeti was when the Ndoha Pack denned at Handajega, deep in the Western Corridor, in May 1987. This was a very different experience from being out on the plains with the Naabi Pack. No tourists visited Handajega in those days. I had never known solitude like this before, never felt so totally isolated from everything that previously had made me feel human – the sense of quiet in my brain was palpable. Surrounded by a landscape of palm-fringed watercourses and dense thickets opening into wide open spaces, I was able to immerse myself in the life of the pack in an even more intimate way than I had done while watching Chui and her cubs. It was just me and the dogs – dogs that I did not know well and that would take time to settle to my presence. I needed to start with a clean slate, to identify individuals, become one of the pack while I waited for the magical moment when the puppies first emerged from the den.

When I arrived, the alpha female immediately started to move her month-old pups to a new den close to the original burrow, carrying them one by one in her mouth. There were twelve in all. I retreated, watching through binoculars to sense the pack's mood, and soon enough some of the adults came trotting over to my vehicle to investigate. Within a day or so they began peeing against the tyres, sniffing the underbelly of the car and ferreting out any lose wires, latching on to anything that they could bite or chew – just as the Naabi Pack had done. The whole vehicle would rock as the dogs braced their back legs and leaned into the task, clamping their powerful jaws firmly on to the canvas covering my winch and high-lift jack, yanking and tugging until they shredded it or got bored. Meanwhile I would be brewing up the first cup of tea of the day on my gas cooker.

The majority of my food came out of a tin; plenty of corned beef and baked beans, which I found endless ways of preparing – beef and beans served cold, one cold the other hot, the corned beef fried to a crisp and served with or without mango chutney or English mustard. This was familiar territory for me, the same basic fare my family endured for a time when I was little so that I could have that Davy Crockett raccoon-tail hat, the reward for collecting a dozen or more wrappers off corned beef tins. At least it was edible. Working on a tight budget, I stocked up with some dirt-cheap tins of Kenya Meat Commission tripe and other fairly awful-sounding delicacies, the gut-churning smell of which remained with me for weeks afterwards – as did the repercussions they had on my stomach. When the Silvermans visited that year they resupplied my vehicle with luxuries such as sachets of Swiss Mist hot chocolate, double chocolate chip cookies and, heaven upon heaven, pots of Nutella spread which I rationed so they lasted for weeks.

The wild dogs' greeting ceremony was always one of my favourite moments of the morning and evening, the time when the rag-tag assortment of individuals was transformed into a single entity – the pack. Each of these dogs was an individual, its destiny dictated to a large degree by its own nature: some equal, some subordinate, some top of the hierarchy as alpha male or female, some destined always to follow and never to breed. But what I found so fascinating was that each of them was also a vital part of something larger than themselves. Different agendas played out within the pack, sometimes subtly hidden, at other times transparent, as for instance when some of the dogs were biding their time before breaking away from the pack. Subadults of the same age and sex do this, setting out in search of members of the opposite sex with whom to form a new pack. Wild dogs on their own struggle to survive, but as part of a pack they take on a collective power, intelligence and energy that is wonderful to behold.

Waiting for the dogs to stir towards the end of the day was like being with a pride of lions or a leopard as the heat of the sun dissipated and a gentle breeze swept towards them. The dogs would stretch out their long slender legs and yawn, each gently jolted from its slumber by the same silent wake-up call coursing through their veins. While a leopard might sit and contemplate its next move or a lion get up and then flop down again alongside a fellow pride member until the light had faded from the sky, the dogs would rise and run around. They greeted their own age mates, responding to subtle nuances of body language, ears either cocked or laid back, eyes staring or downcast. Then as a subgroup they would run to younger or older dogs, brothers or sisters, parents or uncles and aunts, yearlings or puppies who would already be going through the same ritual with their own age mates, uttering high-pitched wittering calls like hungry pups, licking into each other's mouths, peeing and crapping with unbridled excitement. If they were hungry, and they generally were – they often hunted morning and evening when they had pups – they would trot off in single file into the thickets in search of impalas, or out on to the plains in pursuit of the fleet-footed Thomson's gazelles. And if there were wildebeest in the area they would search for the young calves that were the mainstay of their hunting forays at this time of year.

I would follow in their wake so as not to disturb them unduly, the tail-end Charlie of the pack. If I tarried a while a dog might run back towards my vehicle, almost as if to see if I was joining them

or not. When the dogs spotted suitable prey they slowed to a walk, bunching up shoulder to shoulder, their large bat ears cocked with intent and anticipation, then folded back to reduce their silhouette as they stalked as close to their quarry as possible. You could feel the tension rippling through their lean frames, every muscle and sinew gathering for the charge forward that I knew was coming. The minute the wildebeest or gazelles turned and began to flee, the dogs would be after them like a pack of hounds hunting a hare or stag, racing flat out to close the distance on the animal they had targeted, constantly watching for signs of weakness or disadvantage – an injury to a leg or a disease such as mange. They homed in on the young and vulnerable, old and infirm, with the pack sometimes splitting up to hunt more than one animal when they were particularly hungry or had a lot of mouths to feed. All the while I could feel my own heart rate rising, the adrenaline coursing through my veins with the excitement of the chase.

The dogs would gallop along for kilometre after kilometre until their prey tired sufficiently for them to pull it to a halt or they realised that they had been outrun or outmanoeuvred. It was like watching great athletes: the dogs are long-distance runners with the kick of a sprinter. A hunt always seemed to have a touch of joyful abandon to it, as if they were straining at the leash to be off, long pink tongues lolling out of the sides of their mouths, revelling in the chase and the prospect of food. But there was also a sense of utter determination, an urgency to keep on going until the prey began to weary. Then it was just a matter of time and sometimes the end came mercifully quickly.

Occasionally on a moonlit night the dogs would hunt when the wildebeest herds tarried close by. I would hear the pounding of hoofs, the herds coughing and spluttering in the dust, and the occasional high-pitched yipping of the dogs. The commotion often brought hyenas at the double to try to steal any kill the dogs had made. A hyena might linger, nonchalantly chewing on the metal valve of one of my tyres, prompting me to open the window to tell it to 'bugger off'. Woken from a deep sleep one night by the incessant rocking of the vehicle, I eventually shot out of bed, scrambling over the seat and through the door, yelling at the top of my voice as I sprinted naked across the plains in pursuit of the startled hyena. I then managed to trip over the entrance to a warthog burrow and pitched head first to the ground. Not a pretty sight, but it seemed to do the trick – for a while at least.

Emotionally I was always with the pack, never the prey, feeling the hunter stirring deep within me. Yes, of course I hated to see an animal suffering. And I wasn't always convinced by the idea that the prey animal was in deep shock and felt no pain while being torn to pieces. Were the wildebeest calf's cries of distress a forlorn call for help in the hope that its mother might round on the pack and chase it away? (Occasionally this happened if there were only one or two dogs.) Or were they the sounds of an animal in terrible but usually brief pain? Perhaps both.

Knowing how hamstrung the rangers were for vehicles, spare parts and fuel, I would sometimes drive to the ranger post at Handajega and offer to take them on an anti-poaching patrol. Corporal Abnel Mwampondele was a remarkable young man. Despite being in an isolated outpost with no transport and little supervision or support, nothing would have stopped him from being up each morning before dawn, his boots and kit immaculate – indeed sparkling – revelling in the chance to get out into the bush to try to make a dent in the meat poaching that was prevalent in the area. Hundreds of wire snares were set among the thornbushes and game trails. At times – particularly during the middle of the day, when the Ndoha Pack were flat out in the shade of a lugga – I would check out the pathways snaking through the bush to where the animals could still find water during the dry season, removing any snares I found along the way. Sometimes I would discover a freshly butchered carcass just minutes after the poachers had departed with their spoils; at other times the impala or wildebeest might still be alive, its dark eyes bulging in terror as it yanked and pulled the wire snare ever tighter around its neck or leg.

The poachers knew I was out there with the wild dogs and I would wonder sometimes as I drove into a village bordering the park to buy fresh fruit which of the men hanging around the open doorways and bars were working the snare lines. On one occasion driving from Seronera back to Handajega late in the afternoon I spotted a large white lump some distance from the road that I had not remembered being there before. I had packed away my binoculars, so drove off the road to investigate. As I drew closer men stood up from what I could now see was the skinned carcass of a bull giraffe that they had tried to conceal with branches while they butchered it. One of the men had a rifle, the others knives and pangas. They turned and sprinted for the distant lugga, fortunately without firing off a shot.

I had seen Abnel in action in this kind of situation and knew he would have relished being here. One morning we came across a gang of young villagers with dogs who had cornered a huge male warthog at a burrow in the middle of an open plain and speared it. Abnel shouted for me to chase them, firing off a round from the open roof hatch as we quickly ran them to a halt: all except the biggest and surliest of the gang, who was reluctant at first to get into the car. With the men huddled in the back of my vehicle together with their spears and pangas and the warthog's tusked head as evidence, we headed back to Handejega, but not before Abnel had clouted the gang leader with the butt of his rifle to let him know who was boss – and shot dead one of the dogs that ran over to the vehicle looking for its master. While I felt great sympathy for people living in abject poverty, Abnel was having none of it. He was adamant that the soil surrounding the park was fertile; that there was plenty of forage for people's livestock; and that maize and potatoes grew in abundance. Meat poaching was a business like any other – people made money from it. As far as Abnel was concerned they had better not think they could get away with it on his watch or bring their cows into the park. That kind of unflinching dedication and conviction was hugely powerful and inspiring to observe.

Sometimes at night I would see lights flickering out on the plains or hear the occasional gun shot, but I never felt in any real danger sleeping out in my car. In fact I enjoyed the tension it added to life. Not long after I left the Serengeti, Abnel and his rangers mounted a major anti-poaching initiative in the Handajega area, ambushing a large gang of armed poachers who opened fire on them. After a fierce battle in which seventeen of the poachers were arrested and three wounded, some of them were convicted and given three years in prison. This was victory indeed for the rangers in circumstances where local magistrates were often sympathetic to the poachers and reluctant to impose heavy fines or prison sentences. Abnel told me that the poachers wanted to know who the *mzungu* (white man) from Kenya was living out on the plains in his vehicle (I had Kenya licence plates on my Toyota); apparently they thought I was armed, though the only 'cannons' I possessed were my long Canon telephoto lenses which, impressive as they might look, would have offered no protection in a tight corner with armed men. Interestingly, while the level of meat poaching in the Serengeti has long been of concern for fear that it might precipitate a sudden collapse in the migration, the wildebeest population has remained remarkably stable at around 1.2 to 1.5 million with around 200,000 zebras, held in check by the vagaries of the rainfall and consequent availability of grass and water in the dry season.

During my third season in the Serengeti I was invited by Geoff and Jorie Kent to join His Royal Highness the Prince of Wales during his private tented safari to the Serengeti. Geoff served as captain of the Windsor Park polo team and invited Prince Charles to become Patron of Friends of Conservation, the charity which he and Jorie had founded a year or two earlier with the help of Myles Turner and his wife Kay, and with myself as a member of the Conservation Committee. Prince Charles is a keen artist and passionate outdoorsman with a deep affinity for nature. He loves to spend time in wilderness areas and was keen to see the pack of wild dogs that I had been watching.

Sure enough, he witnessed the Naabi Pack hunting the night I joined him in camp. As sometimes happens, the calf the dogs were pursuing raced towards the nearest vehicle as they caught up with it – it happened to be the one the Prince was travelling in. The calf turned to face its attackers with its vulnerable rump pressed protectively against the side of the car. The dogs were so habituated to vehicles that they had little hesitation in pulling the calf down and killing it, much to the Prince's anguish. When he returned to camp I thought he was probably wondering why I wanted to write a book about creatures such as these. But as the pioneering conservationist George Schaller maintained, 'Nature has neither cruelty nor compassion. The ethics of man are irrelevant to the world of other animals. Dogs kill out of necessity, in innocence not in anger, hardly a situation to engender revulsion on the part of man.'

While you could feel Prince Charles's interest and compassion, he knew how to have fun, too. At the end of the final dinner he was presented with a farewell cake and suffered the initial embarrassment of being unable to cut it, as tradition demanded. The maître d' expressed mock surprise, then summoned the chef, scolding him for baking such a seemingly unpalatable cake and instructing him to bring a sharper knife. A panga was duly produced, which the Prince wielded with a cry of royal relish as he demolished the 'cake' – which turned out to be a suitably large elephant dropping camouflaged with lashings of white icing. The roar of approval was shortly followed by the appearance of the real cake.

When *The Great Migration* was published later that year I sent Prince Charles a copy to which he generously responded:

> A thousand thanks for sending me a copy of your fascinating and beautifully photographed book. I shall treasure it as a marvellous reminder of those very special days in the Serengeti this year and of the pleasure of meeting someone as committed and enthusiastic as you are to the conservation and continuance of that unique natural phenomenon of the migration. I felt so privileged to have seen it all when I did. God knows how we are going to ensure it all goes on without being destroyed by the obvious pressures building up on all sides. I will try to play what part I can and I know you will in more ways than one. Yours sincerely, Charles.

My dear old Mum – beside herself with pride – had the letter framed and hung prominently in her hallway, not least because it stopped visitors in their tracks before they could ask, 'When is that boy of yours going to settle down and get a proper job?'

By good fortune, on the flight into the Prince's camp I found myself sitting next to the Principal Immigration Officer who was being flown in to oversee the paperwork for the royal visit. How lucky, I thought to myself: who better to settle once and for all the fix I now found myself in? Francis Magigi, the Immigration Officer at Bologonja Border Post, had decided that unless I applied for a work permit he would bar me from entering the Serengeti. I explained my predicament to the officer, telling him that I had the blessing of David Babu, of Professor Karim Hirji, Director of the Serengeti Wildlife Research Institute, and of Bernard Maregesi, the Chief Park Warden, but that despite being told by the relevant authorities that I could collect material for my books while on a visitor's visa, Magigi was saying no to any further visits.

Reassured by the Principal Immigration Officer's offer to sort things out, I headed back to Nairobi to replenish my supplies before returning to Arusha, where I was issued with a new visa. But Magigi was having none of it. When I next passed him on the road he asked for my passport. With great relish he crossed through my three-month entry permit and gave me a week to finalise my stay, telling me what I now knew – that when it came to the Serengeti, his word was law.

Nature now intervened. Rabies and distemper once more took their deadly toll on the wild dogs, wiping out most of the packs in the ecosystem and in the process sparking an ugly war of words. 'Experts' disagreed over whether or not radio-collaring might have in some way stressed the dogs sufficiently to compromise their immune system. This would make individuals more prone to disease, with deadly consequences for the whole pack. A thorough review of the matter seemed to prove that this was not the case, though it did serve to remind everyone involved just how precious the life of every wild animal is, endangered or not. While this was far from the final chapter I had envisaged in the lives of the wild dogs I had been privileged to study up close, it marked the end to my time in the Serengeti, hastened by Francis Magigi's intransigence. It also meant a welcome return to the Mara.

As I write this some twenty-five years later, the most recent estimate for Africa's wild dog population revealed 6,600 dogs (only 1,400 of which were mature animals). Over half of these were located in Tanzania and Mozambique, with the 45,000-square-kilometre Selous Game Reserve in southern Tanzania home to 800 of them. Key locations further south are northern Botswana, western Zimbabwe, eastern Namibia and western Zambia, with habitat fragmentation, conflict with human activities and infectious diseases ensuring the continued decline of this fascinating species.

The good news is that wild dogs are once again to be seen on occasion in the Serengeti and the Greater Mara, albeit in low numbers, not least due to the large numbers of lions and hyenas in the region.

Painted Wolves proved to be one of my most satisfying books to work on, with a number of strong characters to build a story around and the chance to examine how competition and disease impacted on the lives of the wild dogs. I worked hard to make the drawings perfect and, armed with longer and faster telephoto lenses and a greater understanding of light, I was confident that my photographs were beginning to display a more moody and professional feel. In fact in 1987, four years before *Painted Wolves* was published, I had won the overall award in the prestigious Wildlife Photographer of the Year Competition, an accolade that all aspiring and professional wildlife photographers dream of. My winning shot had been a striking photograph of one of the Naabi Pack grabbing a wildebeest by the nose and upper lip. Another of my wild dog images had won a runner-up award and I had a handful of 'highly commendeds' featuring other subjects. The competition manager Helen Gilks wrote to me with the news, commenting:

> I do think the overall standard of the photos you submitted this year was superb! I can remember seeing the pictures you sent in three years ago [I had won the Animal Portraits category in 1984] and thinking how interesting they were, if not always perfect, and then year by year they have got better and better.

She went on to say that the competition had attracted more entries than ever that year – in excess of 10,000 photos, from some forty different countries. I was overjoyed.

Prior to the publication of *Painted Wolves* I went to see Sir David Attenborough at his home in Richmond to show him the drawings I had created for the book and to ask if he might do me the honour of writing a quote for the cover, which he generously agreed to do. We discussed the fact that my publishers were reluctant for me to call the book *Painted Wolves*, arguing that people's perception of 'wolves' might put them off buying it. David chuckled and told me to stick to my guns – and I did.

David has a great love of art, and visiting his home was like entering a museum with paintings and artefacts from around the world, leading to a magnificent upstairs library that he cheerfully confided his book royalties from *Life on Earth* had paid for. David's infectious enthusiasm has no bounds. It was endearing to see him pull out old and very valuable handwritten letters by early explorers, displaying not a hint of preciousness in the way he shared and handled them – he wanted you to feel the paper in your hands, soak up the words, live in the moment.

However, my most vivid memory of David stems from a time some weeks later, when he invited me to join him and his wife Jane for dinner, along with the author and adventurer Anthony Smith, a former presenter of the long-running BBC series *Tomorrow's World*. Smith had led the *Sunday Telegraph* balloon safari expedition in 1962, flying a hydrogen balloon from Zanzibar to the East African mainland with Alan Root as cameraman to document his adventure. We had plenty to talk about that night – so much so that when I looked at my watch I realised I had missed the last train home to Berkshire. Mortified, I explained my predicament, upon which, without fuss or formality, David headed off to the spare room to prepare my bed. I was up at the crack of dawn next morning, but not early enough to prevent him from bringing me a mug of tea in bed.

With my time in Serengeti drawing to a close, I had the opportunity for reflection. There was a sense of life having come full circle. I was nearly forty – two years younger than my father had been when he died – and had achieved many of my most cherished ambitions. I had written books about the creatures that fascinated me most – the lions, leopards and wild dogs – and documented the epic journey of the great migration through the place I considered the most spectacular wildlife region on earth. I had experienced the challenges and exhilaration of working as a television presenter on *Wild Kingdom* and known the joy of winning the Wildlife Photographer of the Year Competition. I had made the acquaintance of two of my childhood heroes, Sir Peter Scott and Sir David Attenborough, both of whom had been a major influence in my choice of career and the life I wanted to live.

More than anything, I was as passionate and enthusiastic about working with wildlife as I had been that day ten years earlier, when Joseph Rotich had spotted two Marsh Pride males standing tall and proud in the long golden grass at the edge of Musiara Marsh and asked casually if I would like to drive down to take a closer look at them. I wondered now if he realised just how much I had wanted to connect with those lions, to spend time getting to know them as individuals, and how significant a milestone that moment was.

CHAPTER

08

ANGIE

…the scale and depth of the metaphors the mind is capable of manufacturing as it grapples with the universe, stand in stunning contrast to the belief that there is only one reality, which is man's…

Barry Holstun Lopez
OF WOLVES AND MEN

It was while I was at this crossroads in my life that I met Angela Bellamy – Angie, the woman with the long blonde hair and two beautiful children, who would transform my life through her gentle acceptance and ability to listen and not judge. She not only gave me reason to live another kind of life, she helped me to accept my past and envisage a different kind of future.

My need to describe with words whatever I am experiencing elevates and liberates my mood, providing a kind of release – words bring my world alive. This is the very opposite of the contemplation and quiet that come naturally to Angie. She finds peace and understanding through meditation and yoga, and her approach helped me to understand my thought processes more clearly and to find a new kind of clarity and discipline. Until I met her I had been committed to pursuing the life of my choice. I had lived a relatively uncomplicated existence in the bush at Mara River Camp: a tent with a bed and a hot shower; plenty of fresh food cooked over an open fire; the freedom to take visitors out each day on game drives in the Reserve. That was my kind of heaven, with the campfire the focal point each evening, a time to relax and relive the highlights of the day's game viewing before falling into bed, with or without female companionship.

After five years I graduated to a room in a rustic thatched house at Kichwa Tembo, but it was still very much a life of threadbare simplicity. The bonus was that I was now free to spend my days in a vehicle of my own, following the lions, leopards and wild dogs that so enthralled me, while earning my board and lodging by giving slide presentations of my work to guests most evenings and running a drivers' training programme – a first in the Mara at that time.

I found life so fulfilling alone that if relationships weren't to my liking I simply walked away. Unrealistic, perhaps, but the life I was living hardly lent itself to commitment. Most of my girlfriends after Hilary were airline stewardesses from Europe, who loved safari and the romance of Africa well enough, but who weren't from Africa. What kind of future could we have fashioned together, with me living in a tent or sleeping in my car, while they were thinking of building a permanent home and raising a family?

That all changed when I met Angie. She was working as the buyer and manager for a chain of curio shops owned by Jorie Kent. On one of my irregular visits to Nairobi a friend mentioned that Angie was having problems sourcing copies of my books. She had left her telephone number, so I rang her. I fell in love with her soothing voice long before I set eyes on her.

We agreed to meet for lunch. Angie had been married twice before and had no wish to repeat the experience; the last thing she was looking for was another relationship. She is shy to the point of sometimes seeming reserved, but with a gentle way about her that people find reassuring. In stark contrast to me, she has a wisdom that comes from her extraordinary gift of listening intently to what people have to say. A strong, independent woman who has always rolled up her sleeves and got on with life, she commits herself to

whatever project she is working on: organised, disciplined and dedicated. Most important of all, if Angie is your friend then you are blessed.

Whatever reservations Angie might have had about relationships, allied to my own fear of commitment, soon evaporated when we realised just how much we had in common – not least a love of family and children, and a passion for wild places, photography and drawing. It reminded me of a passage in *Sunset on the Manyatta* by Kenyan author Kenneth Watene:

> Have you ever stopped to wonder why it was that we felt so free with each other? I suppose... It would seem as if you were a spirit that originally belonged to the same realm with my spirit, and our meeting was the rejoining of a splintered one.

Talented artist that she is, Angie also has that wonderful gift of making wherever she settles into a home, of being able to convert mere bricks and mortar – soulless entities in themselves – into a repository for a rich tapestry of quilts and cushions, carpets and sofas, photographs and paintings; a place that breathes life, warmth and love. Trinkets and keepsakes are scattered like seashells on the beach of life, reminding one of the wonder of this world and the comfort of home.

Angie was born in Alexandria in Egypt, where her father was a cotton buyer. The family had been torn from their roots when Colonel Nasser sent the expatriate community packing during the Suez Crisis of the 1950s. The Bellamys settled in Dar es Salaam in Tanzania, providing four-year-old Angie and her older brother David with an oceanside upbringing that nurtured Angie's abiding love of the sea.

The best things that had come from Angie's two marriages were her children, Alia and David, who were fourteen and five when I first met them. I could not have asked for more different and special young people to be father to. Alia bears a striking similarity to Angie with her blue eyes and blonde hair; she radiates a joie de vivre that you can feel almost bursting from every pore of her beautiful being, while David is tall and handsome, with a generosity of spirit and a strength of character that are a joy to behold.

At the time I met them, Angie lived with the children on a ramshackle property at the end of Ololua Ridge, with the garden of their rented tin-roofed house backing on to a forest in the leafy Nairobi suburb of Karen. Bringing up two children on her own meant that money was tight. The house was always abuzz with activity, a place of laughter filled with friends, but security was non-existent – and even in those days Nairobi was regarded by many as a dangerous city, earning itself the nickname 'Nairobbery'. The walls of the house were as soft as putty, the flimsy windows an invitation to thieves, a break-in waiting to happen. Angie had recently put in a steel gate to secure a safe zone for her and the children at one end of the house, with bars on the windows, but we both knew that these would be of little deterrent to a determined gang of thieves armed with bolt cutters or door-wrecking boulders and brute force.

It hardly boosted our confidence to find that Ololua Forest was notorious as the dumping ground for car-jacking victims. One night shortly after I moved in, our nightwatchman Boniface heard cries for help echoing from the forest. They came from a businessman who had been hijacked, robbed and then driven to the forest. His assailants had stripped him naked and tied him to a tree, giving themselves plenty of time to escape while adding further to his suffering. Boniface found the man shivering from fear and cold, terrified that hyenas would eat him alive before anyone discovered him.

Until then the forest had been a magical place, somewhere to escape from the hustle and bustle of the city, a place of tranquillity and mystery, the dappled light filtering through to the rich damp earth. But it was a place of sadness too. I remember walking the narrow pathways one evening in search of Angie's beloved Sam – the blackest of black cats, more human than cat. Sam was Angie's best friend, her confidant and faithful companion. They had an extraordinary empathy and bond. Sam always seemed to know when Angie was feeling low and needed cheering up, appearing from nowhere to be with her, sitting or lying stretched out as only a cat can, his deep rumbling purr soothing and calming. One day he simply vanished. A new tenant had taken over the guest cottage on the plot, bringing with her two small and feisty dogs. Our cook told us that one of the dogs had chased Sam, perhaps injuring him. We called and searched in vain, hour after hour, the agony of knowing that Sam might be injured or sick and have dragged himself off somewhere urging us on; the thought of him waiting to be discovered gnawing at our hearts. We were devastated never to find him.

For the most part, though, the Ololua house was perfect. The rent was affordable, the garden wild, the sound of children playing echoing through the forest. I was loving the opportunity to be a father to Angie's children, glowing at the sound of that magic word 'Dad', a word I had never uttered. I did all the things that I had longed to share with my own father, being there for David on Father's Day and visiting Alia at boarding school in England as often as I could. My memories of this time are filled with joy: from seeing Alia blossom at university to witnessing the delight on David's face when I returned from overseas with a remote-control car; the thrill of catapulting his first model aeroplane high into the sky, only to watch as it crashed back to earth into the thorny embrace of the acacia bushes at the edge of the forest. No matter.

Scratched and torn – us and the plane – we launched it again and again. The sand pit in the garden became the venue for high-jump contests, with games of rugby played out in the pouring rain. Muddy and exhausted we would charge up and down the pitch, winning and losing the World Cup for England or playing in the final of the All Africa Football Championship for Kenya.

How different these Kenya children were from me at that age. As a youngster on a torturous journey I would be the first to ask my Mum, 'Are we nearly there yet?' Not David. He would settle down in the back of the safari wagon for the six-hour drive over rough dusty roads to the Mara, building a room of his own with fold-up canvas safari seats and mattresses, and settling into a world of make-believe: dumper trucks, green ninja turtles, WWF wrestlers his companions; playing one-on-one combat with an army of soldiers. The vehicle would reverberate with his squeals of delight and cries of triumph, mimicking the sounds of gunfire and explosions as some poor soul bit the dust.

He would remain in this fantasy land until we found the Kichwa Tembo Pride or Half-Tail the leopard – then he would quickly re-enter the natural world and engage totally, photographing the animals or drawing them in his notebook (both he and Alia have inherited their mother's artistic talent). The children came to know the big cat characters that defined our lives as well as we did – Chuchu the grandmother of the Kichwa Tembo Pride, Queen the car-climbing cheetah, Half-Tail the Mara's star leopard – though I am sure they appeared different in the clear-eyed minds of children.

When he was older, David confided to us how intimidating it had been, trapped in the back of the vehicle with two wildlife photographers, one of them particularly single-minded and manic in his approach. Alia found it difficult too. It could be hard for me to remember to give quality time to the children when some amazing photographic opportunity presented itself. 'Getting the shot', especially when one of the big cats threatened to explode into action, required all-consuming concentration. In those moments it was as if my life depended upon it, the vehicle lurching across the plains as I tried to secure the best position for us to record what was going on. The adrenaline rush can be unhealthily addictive; it's what the long days – even weeks – spent cooped up in the vehicle are all about.

Angie was always quick to rebalance the situation when this happened, explaining to the children that this was how we earned our living – that photography wasn't just a pastime. David tried to comprehend that this was 'work', but at the same time found it scary in its intensity, the do-or-die element that for a young child meant a disturbing loss of control. It was a reflection of what one underwater photographer described as the 'I'd put my head in the shark's mouth' moment: a kind of madness when nothing else matters – not even your own safety.

But even my madness had to be reined in once I acquired a family. After a while I embraced the fact that being Dad meant sometimes setting my own priorities aside and spending more time in Nairobi than ever before. I was willingly moving away from the all-consuming desire to prove myself, make a successful career in

my field of choice, live up to expectations; ready to surrender those ambitions for the sake of a more balanced existence.

For David there were other, less fraught moments to soothe away the bedlam: the hikes through wild country up the 300-metre Siria Escarpment that overlooked our base at Kichwa Tembo were a welcome respite from the confines of the vehicle (though we were always alert to the possibility of stumbling on to an old bull buffalo snoozing in the long grass); and we savoured our picnics along the Mara River, when David would get out the camping gear, help to collect the wood and light the fire to celebrate the most spectacular Big Breakfast you could imagine. He loved the climbs up the Escarpment, where we would find a suitably tricky gully or overhang to test our rock-climbing skills, taking it as seriously as if we were scaling Mount Everest. Best of all was rafting through the white water along the shallows of the river in an inflatable tyre-tube anchored to a long rope, the thought of crocodiles and hippos adding an edge to the proceedings for David and his school chum Tom Aveling. Pitching the boys' tent in the heart of Marsh Pride territory, where the sound of lions roaring or fighting often came thundering across the plains after dark, was another adventure to test their nerve.

Having a family of my own was undoubtedly the final step in my healing process. I had been gifted a new and exhilarating way of being and in taking this on found freedom from the remnants of my darkest thoughts. Now my focus was Angie, Alia and David, their wellbeing my overriding concern. They were the priority, not me. This allowed me to see more clearly than ever before that the belief I had clung to with such unyielding tenacity – that I was going to die as a consequence of that fall thirty years earlier – simply wasn't true. I had been in a giddy race to outlive my father as the only unequivocal proof that I wasn't dying. My tendency to cut and bruise easily was no more than a frustrating inconvenience, despite the fact that in time I would require surgery to remedy excessive wear on my joints, exacerbated by the condition. More importantly, I was coming to terms with the fact that anxiety and depression – along with a touch of mania and obsessive compulsion – were part of who I was. It sounds so simple, yet it had taken me half a lifetime to break free of my demons.

Proposing to Angie seemed the most natural thing in the world. We were married in 1992 in a beautiful ceremony atop the Siria Escarpment, with eagles soaring above the animal-stippled plains. My mother and Colonel Connor – both in their eighties – were there to witness our joy, along with our children and friends from the safari community and surrounding tented camps. We celebrated with lunch beside the Mara River and later, when we had returned to Kichwa Tembo and were relaxing around the campfire, a Maasai elder and his wife approached from out of the shadows. They had been waiting all evening to honour us as elders, with a beautiful beaded necklace for Angie and an ornate *rungu* (a wooden club) for me. The following day we took my mother, the Colonel and the children to the village to celebrate as our Maasai friends sang and danced in welcome.

As an expat living in Africa it is all too easy to survive with one foot out the door, never committing yourself sufficiently to transform a residence into a home. In failing to put down roots you risk existing in a state of permanent limbo. Expats tend to keep their options open, to have a Plan B in case they have to leave in a hurry, an eventuality that can rob today of any sense of tomorrow. This is one reason why Europeans and Asians who take Kenya citizenship are often referred to as 'paper citizens', hinting at the fact that if the going gets tough they are likely to pack up and leave. Friends who had worked in Mugabe's Zimbabwe or had relatives there recounted tales of families clinging on in the face of hostility and anger, subject to robberies or beatings, eventually losing their properties, even their lives. While that never seemed likely in Kenya, it was a sobering thought, and security is of concern to everyone who lives here. Having made the Mara my home for so many years I had rejoiced in the freedom of having little by way of possessions. A few books and some clothes in a tin trunk at the Colonel's house in Nairobi were the sum of my life's journey – anything else of value was stored in England with my sister and brother.

But now all that was changing. A year after we were married we decided to look for a property in Nairobi to call our own. Angie reminded me that Kenya was our home and the 'what ifs' that can so easily colour an expat's view of life in Africa must be set aside. Having a proper home would please our children, who lived in the moment and whose minds were uncluttered by worries about security, health insurance and pensions. We were fortunate that I earned foreign exchange from sales of my books and photographs. In those days most people who had a desirable property for sale wanted to be paid in hard currency: Kenya still had exchange control and people were anxious to build a nest egg outside the country in case they felt the need to make a hasty departure. Travelling overseas meant applying for an allowance to buy your airline ticket and fund your stay: it did not stretch far.

Consequently the black market for forex was rife. Nairobi was awash with sleazy-looking, sharp-eyed men with scruffy clothes and nimble feet who would sidle up to you to enquire if you wanted to change money – or purchase an elephant-hair bracelet or ivory carving, both of which were illegal. The price for the incautious would be a furtive meeting down a dimly lit alley where the vendor's accomplices would quickly gather. Then the heat was really on. A bit of haggling, a lot of jostling, and the shout would go up,

'The police are coming – run.' The punter would be left clutching a brown paper bag whose contents were ninety nine per cent waste paper and a few Kenya shillings, with not a policeman in sight.

One of Angie's great loves is plants in all their varied guises, from the tiniest garden blossom to a towering indigenous tree. So one of our requirements for a property was a plot with trees. We focused our attentions on Karen and Langata, which have always been Nairobi's 'green' suburbs.

At the time, the local newspapers were full of doom-laden stories about Nairobi's dwindling indigenous forests. Greedy politicians were intent on plundering the last of the city's undeveloped forested landscapes, including Karura and the Ololua Forest, where we were still living. Parcels of public land would be sold on to a third party with the identity of the corrupt official shielded by a dodgy 'shell' company and some crafty accounting.

But the crooks hadn't reckoned with the steely determination of Professor Wangari Maathai, the environmental activist who founded the Kenyan Green Belt Movement; she was someone whom Angie had met and always held in the highest esteem. Almost single-handedly the charismatic professor led a grass-roots campaign to stem the looting of public land and address the worrying loss of trees throughout Kenya, encouraging people to plant a million trees to reverse the tide, while all the time lobbying for greater rights for women.

According to the IUCN – the International Union for Conservation of Nature – a forest cover of ten per cent is the minimum required for sustainable sources of water in any country. Kenya has less than one and a half per cent. Whenever the bully boys came with staves and clubs to impose their will in raping the forests, they would find Wangari Maathai standing in their way, defying them to move her and her brave band of protesters. But move them they did. Pictures of Maathai, her head swaddled in bandages, made front-page news, though they never broke her spirit. Many years later she was rewarded for her bravery and foresight in the realms of both conservation and empowering women by becoming Africa's first female recipient of the Nobel Peace Prize – a richly deserved accolade. As she always maintained, we would do well to nurture the environment, because it will be disputes over the ownership of land, trees and water that fuel the wars of the future.

Professor Maathai died of cancer in 2011 and in 2014 Karura Forest was back in the news, with talk that a developer had been illegally allocated seven hectares of land in its heart to build a six-star multi-storey hotel. As Chair of the Greenbelt Movement, Wangari Maathai's daughter Wanjiru has vowed to support on-going efforts to stop any attempts to put up a hotel. She will need all the courage and determination of her formidable mother to fulfil that pledge.

All this meant that, even back in the 1990s, properties with trees were as scarce as an abundant source of fresh water in Nairobi. Most people who bought land wanted to clear it when they moved in – either for security or to farm it. Those with the most attractive properties were often reluctant to sell, happy to sit and wait for a better deal, with the most sought-after homes purchased by word of mouth before they even hit the market.

But one day while I was on safari in the Mara, Angie rang to say she had found somewhere – not just anywhere, but a house with land begging to be bought. The owner was Frank Howitt, a road engineer who was built like a solid English oak and could turn his ample hands to anything, as happy living out of a truck on the dusty road to Lokichoggio near the Sudanese border as he was tuning up a grader or earthmover in the back yard of his property in Langata. He had a voice like gravel and a cratered moonscape of a face that you could only describe as lived in. Big and genial, with a twinkle in his blue eyes, Frank was loved by everyone who knew him, as was his half-sister Dolcie Spencer, with whom he lived. You would have sworn that they were an old married couple, presiding over a house full of mongrel dogs and couch-potato cats, with a pot of steaming tea forever on the go and the smell of fresh pancakes and chocolate sponge baking in the oven. Typical of Kenya's charm and hospitality, their door was always open to a steady throng of visitors from every corner of the country and overseas.

Angie had been tipped off that Frank and Dolcie had a plot of land for sale – eight hectares along the Mukoma Road in Langata. I knew the area well: it was home to the wildlife sculptor Rob Glen. Each year at Christmas time the locals would gather at Rob's gallery to admire his latest bronzes and to drink, the evening turning progressively noisier and busier as the alcohol kicked in. It was like a Kenyan wedding: a great way for me to catch up

on gossip during a visit to Nairobi. There was always a gathering of old safari hands and ex-professional hunters with a yarn to tell, stories of narrow escapes from dangerous wild creatures: invariably someone had been gored by an irate buffalo or mauled by a leopard since we last met.

Everyone knew everyone, the up-country folks played as hard as they worked and we all fancied ourselves as art critics. On one occasion I had tarried to the last and, with a few too many glasses of wine and a couple of beers under my belt, had dug deep into my pocket to acquire one of Rob's bronzes, a massive chunk of metal depicting a bull buffalo tangling with a male lion. It was an imposing piece of work that for years found an uneasy home on my mother's dining-room table. The buffalo was bent forward with shiny down-swept horns attempting to pound the lion into the ground, guaranteeing at least half my mother's dinner guests a prime view of the bronze's most eye-catching feature – the bull's enormous knackers. Rob had depicted them in all their considerable glory, and they made for some animated and at times embarrassed conversation around the table, much to my mother's delight.

I had met Frank and Dolcie at one of Rob's boozy evenings and knew that over the years Frank had bought parcels of land in various districts in Kenya, but bided his time in developing them. There was always some new project on the go – a gold mine in Uganda was just one of them. Strapped for cash, he continually juggled his assets, selling off a plot every so often to fund his ventures. Land in Kenya had proved as good an investment as any. Prices kept climbing regardless of the uncertainties, though when I mentioned to a tax consultant friend that I was thinking of buying land he gave me a quizzical look that said I must be mad. Fortunately, other more adventurous souls such as Alan Root and Allan Earnshaw of Ker & Downey Safaris advised me to buy as much as I could afford.

The eight hectares Frank wanted to sell consisted of two plots – one a treeless wasteland of poorly drained black cotton soil that has since been developed as a gated community with ten houses on it, aptly named Giraffe View. The other was a paradise of rich red soil, with trees aplenty and an old double-storey stone house planted smack in the middle with no concession to future development of the land. The most enticing aspect of the deal was that the plot boasted its own borehole. The only downside was that in those days Langata was considered Karen's poor relative. The fact that so many of the plots were large – four hectares or more – might be seductive to romantics like us looking for a touch of wilderness, but the isolation made security a real issue (and still does – not so long ago a botched carjacking at the gates of Giraffe View left one of the passengers dead).

I could hear the excitement in Angie's voice as she described the property to me and I agreed to drive up to Nairobi the following day. For some reason I needed to pay a visit to the hospital, probably due to a dose of one of those familiar safari companions bilharzia, giardia or some other amoeba-type parasite that I frequently played host to. I stopped off at Casualty for a blood test and as I waited for the results I could feel something was wrong. Outside, a convoy of vehicles was pulling up and people were running about with anxious faces and raised voices. I thought at first that a politician or minister had arrived, but apparently a young American woman had just been carjacked at the nearby shopping centre in Hurlingham. When she hesitated in handing over the keys to her vehicle she was shot dead.

As I drove to meet Angie my mood was coloured by the events that I had just witnessed. All the negative thoughts about the wisdom of investing in Kenya came flooding back. I tried to stay positive, to share Angie's enthusiasm for the beautiful piece of wild land she now showed me, but I couldn't see it through her eyes. Where she saw dreams and potential I saw a property that had been neglected and fallen on hard times, with flat concrete roofs that leaked on to the beautiful wood parquet floors. Tree hyraxes had found a way into the house and used it as a latrine; the stench of ammonia was suffocating. The land was an unfenced mishmash of trees and tangled undergrowth that people used as a picnic site, a thoroughfare for evening walks. To Angie this was a secret wild garden with jacaranda and olive trees, yellow-barked acacias and wild gum, a maze of rock terraces decorated with aloes overlooking the forest at the bottom of the property where wild creatures made their home. It just shows how circumstances and mood can colour everything for better or worse.

It didn't take long for my natural optimism to resurface. Buying rather than renting was one of the best decisions we ever made. We have always said that we bought a view with a house. And what a view. From our bedroom veranda you look out over the distinctive blue, knuckle-shaped Ngong Hills immortalised in Karen Blixen's lyrical book *Out of Africa* – her house is barely

ABOVE Wedding day on the top of the Siria Escarpment, 26 March 1992. Never knowingly without our Canon cameras – and the rare occasion I willingly put on my only suit.

ABOVE A real family at last. FOLLOWING PAGE More painterly than photograph. The moment the grey heron flew into the frame Angie knew she had a winning shot. It won her the accolade of Wildlife Photographer of the Year in 2002.

LEFT TOP The joys of fatherhood on safari to the Mara. LEFT BELOW Angie with Alia and David. RIGHT Having the time of our lives on safari in our beloved Maasai Mara.

ABOVE Life in the bush is all about cameras and computers.

ABOVE One of Notch's Boys surveys his territory at dawn
on a rise overlooking the Talek River.

ABOVE A newborn elephant calf is encouraged across a river with a reassuring nudge of its
mother's giant leg. FOLLOWING PAGE King penguin colony, South Georgia. South Georgia is
often described as the Serengeti of the Southern Ocean – it is a wildlife paradise.

ABOVE Emperor penguin chicks. Only a third of juvenile emperor penguins survive their first year; many of them fall victim to seabirds such as giant petrels and skuas.

ten minutes from ours. It is a glimpse of Eden, with the stand of tall trees at the bottom of our property shielding us from the sight of other houses. Professor E O Wilson noted that, given the choice, people across the world's cultures want three features in their environment:

> They want to be on a height looking down, they prefer open savanna-like terrain with scattered trees and copses, and they want to be close to a body of water, such as a river, lake or ocean. Even if all these elements are purely aesthetic and not functional, home buyers pay any affordable price to have such a view. People, in other words, prefer to live in those environments in which humans evolved over millions of years in Africa.

These are precisely our thoughts – and if there are animals in sight all the better, even if they are only represented by sculpture and the water is a beautifully landscaped swimming pool. We had bought just that.

Having fallen in love with that pristine view we set about restoring the house. Flat roofs were torn down and replaced with pitched ones; a guest wing emerged where before there had been a storeroom, and we created an upstairs master bedroom and bathroom overlooking the hills. We reclaimed the property from the tree hyraxes and their pungent droppings – though their ear-splitting contact calls still remind us that we live in a wilderness, albeit on the outskirts of a city of four million inhabitants.

Our neighbours across the murram road to our south are the African Foundation for Endangered Wildlife, a breeding sanctuary for the endangered Rothschild's giraffe and home of Giraffe Manor. Its inhabitants sometimes knocked down the telephone wires before the city council decided to bury them under the ground – a small price to pay for the giraffes' elegant presence. A leopard occasionally ventured on to our land from the sanctuary and Frank Howitt regaled us with tales of his own encounters. Leopards are particularly partial to dogs and one evening a leopard bushwhacked Frank's pack on their afternoon walk through the sanctuary. But it had reckoned without Frank's heavyweight intervention. With a furious grunt of protest and a defiant shout of 'No bloody wild animal is going to kill my dog', Frank forced the leopard to turn tail, though it left the dog torn, bloodied and needing to be stitched back together like an old patchwork quilt. These days we sometimes wake to the whoop of a lone hyena and on occasion have a lioness – or two – padding through the neighbourhood, keeping the spirit of the wilderness very much alive while helping to deter human 'predators'.

Given the fact that Nairobi is perceived as a dangerous and intimidating place, you might well ask why we choose to live here, ensconced behind our reinforced doors and barred windows, encircled by electric fences and metal grilles, our living rooms and bedrooms fitted with intruder alarms and panic buttons, nightwatchmen and dogs patrolling the garden and security vehicles crisscrossing the neighbourhood 24/7. But Africa has always been home for Angie, and now it feels like home to me too. Being sent away to boarding school in England when she was eight years old made Angie realise just how much she loved the sense of freedom, the warmth of the people and the climate, the privilege of being able to head out on safari during school holidays or take a dip among the coral reefs of the Indian Ocean.

Having done what we can to make ourselves safe in our home we throw open the windows with relish, letting the African sun seep into our being. We sit on the veranda and feel the breeze on our faces. We take time to walk around our beautiful property, to marvel at the trees, revel in the sight of the long-crested eagle flying low overhead and glory in the sound of a hundred different bird songs. Never a day goes by without our wandering down to the bottom of the plot to the spot that Angie has made her own, where everything that is important to her – water, the myriad birds, the rolling view back up to our house, the trees that she has planted and nurtured – help to reinforce the natural harmony that is the heartbeat of her existence.

As E O Wilson implied, Africa is in the blood of each and every one of us – black and white – creating a resonance dating back a million or more years to the time when our ancestors emerged from the forests on to the sunlit savannas. This is where it all began. It is all of this, the sense of place, of home, that makes us feel part of this remarkable land.

CHAPTER

09

AFRICA
TO
ANTARCTICA

I go among the fields and catch

a glimpse of a stoat or a fieldmouse

peeping out of the withered grass –

the creature hath a purpose and its

eyes are bright with it.

John Keats

Letter

Though I have always loved spending time in the company of wild animals it was inevitable that at some point Angie and I would feel ready to focus on the lives of our friends among the Maasai community. Over the years we have camped out in our vehicle to celebrate the colourful rites that mark important transitions in the life of each Maasai man and woman. We have shared the carefree days of their childhood, borne witness to the test of character and maturity that circumcision represents, shared their pride in becoming warriors and respected elders of their community, and their joy at marriage and the birth of children.

Those ancient rituals stir the heart and soul like nothing else we have witnessed. To awaken to the singing of warriors an hour before dawn, their breath smoke-like in the chill air as the young men gather to drive a bull to slaughter, streaming backlit down the hillside against the rising sun, is to step back in time to a very different existence, filled with myths and legends to fire the imagination. We have watched in silence as a dozen red-robed warriors from Tanzania sought the counsel of the Laibon (the spiritual leader of the Maasai) on the forested slopes of Kenya's Loita Hills, having travelled many kilometres through wild country to earn his blessing. The Laibon spread a cowhide before us and threw a collection of stones passed down through generations of shamans so that he might commune with the spirit world. He rose tall against the blue sky and showered the warriors with fresh milk spat from a long-necked gourd to speed them on their way home. Energised by the ritual, the warriors raced alongside our vehicle as others clung to the sides, running and laughing with the sheer joy of being alive as we headed for the border, leaving a cloud of dust in our wake.

In the summer of 1989 the BBC decided to break new ground with a series of live broadcasts from the Maasai Mara during the wildebeest migration. I was asked to join Julian Pettifer (with whom I had worked on *Nature Watch* years earlier) as co-presenter and resident naturalist. Everyone loves lions and my in-depth knowledge of the Marsh Pride would help make them the key animal characters for the series. The BBC had perfected the art of mounting massive outside broadcasts for sports and lifestyle events in the UK, but *Africa Watch* would be a different kind of challenge. Given the vagaries of the weather, would the wildebeest turn up on time – and, more importantly, would the satellite links prove reliable enough to broadcast live for ten days from the heart of Africa to the UK, Spain, America and Japan?

My old friend Jock Anderson set up a tented camp for us among the riverine forest bordering Musiara Marsh, the dry-season focus of the Marsh Pride's activity. The live hub of the show, housing tonnes of electrical cable, satellite dishes and banks of television monitors, was located in a tent on the rocky ridge overlooking the Marsh. We had a week to prepare and practise before transmission day and were relieved when tens of thousands of wildebeest and zebras poured into the area on cue.

It wasn't long before the mischievous subadult lions in the Marsh Pride made their presence felt. Emboldened by the darkness, they cavorted through the production tents, chewing on the precious cables responsible for the live feed and clawing and gnawing their way into boxes of supplies. This was enough for some of the armed rangers responsible for the crew's safety to be redeployed to guard the production tents and keep the lions at bay. It reminded me of the time during the making of *Ambush at Maasai Mara* when one of the hugely impressive pride males came striding into our sleeping quarters early one evening, while we were still out filming. Terrified for his life, Jock's cook sought refuge high in one of the trees. The male sniffed around the makeshift kitchen and marked it with squirts of pungent urine, letting everyone know that this was his place too. Then he strode away again. When we arrived back in camp shortly after dark we were surprised to hear a voice calling from the treetops enquiring if it was safe to come down.

There were other dramas, too, of a more human kind. The Kenya government was very sensitive about the media and about security in general, and it had been a long and convoluted process to get the necessary permissions to broadcast live. The simplest thing would have been for us to beam images directly from a satellite dish in the Mara, but the Ministry of Communications was not prepared to allow this. The signal would have to be routed via the main satellite station at Longonot in the Rift Valley, in the shadow of the extinct volcano of the same name. The Kenyan engineers were adamant that everything was in order and that they did not need anyone from the BBC looking over their shoulders.

As the stirring music and titles cascaded into my earpiece and on to the monitor in front of me I sensed the unique thrill of going live – I could feel the mania rising. Julian introduced the new series

in his normal polished fashion and then we began our commentary, linking live footage with clips of videotape recorded earlier. Everything seemed to be going according to plan and we were elated as we came to the end of the first segment. But our euphoria soon gave way to huge disappointment when our American co-producers at the Discovery Channel told us that the footage was coming through in black and white rather than colour. Worse still, it was breaking up. The problem was immediately diagnosed as being due to the links at Longonot. Somehow the BBC engineers had to gain access to the station.

Fortunately Richard Leakey, by this time head of the Kenya Wildlife Service, was due to arrive in camp later that morning for an interview with Julian. When he heard what had happened he immediately phoned the head of the satellite station and told him to allow the BBC engineers to diagnose the problem and fix it. He returned assuring us that everything was going to be just fine. When we asked him how he could be so sure he said, 'I told the boss to sort it out now or the next phone call would be to the President.' Nobody wanted to incur the wrath of President Moi – and very few people had the kind of access granted to Leakey.

For me, one of the highlights of *Africa Watch* was meeting the Japanese photographer Mitsuaki Iwago, who co-presented the Japanese version of the programme. Iwago was one of my heroes. Unhindered by any preconceptions of biology or behaviour in the way he saw and photographed animals, he was an artist who wanted to get inside the head of his subject – to become a member of the pride of lions or pack of wild dogs. His technique was to get in close, the lower the better: preferably out of his car, better still underneath it. On one occasion while working in the Ngorongoro Crater he told me he felt a rough sensation on his forearm and turned to find a lioness licking the salty sweat off it. In Serengeti he came to know a mother cheetah with large cubs so intimately that he was able to sit among them. People questioned this breach of protocol, but his images spoke for themselves.

Iwago reveals nature in all its savage beauty. Backlight and sidelight imbue his images with drama and emotion, something Angie encouraged me to embrace – to be more imaginative in my approach. Iwago was also fastidious about the printing of his work. For the production of his first major book – a large-format treatment of the Serengeti – he had slept on the sofa at the printers, fortified by endless shots of espresso to ensure he was wide awake when each new sheet of photographs came off the press. He liked his images highly saturated with brooding plum-coloured skies, sparkling emerald-green plains and vivid blood-red carcasses. Years later I would adopt the same approach when working with printers in Singapore, snatching a few fitful hours of sleep at a nearby hotel between print runs. It was exhausting, but worth the effort.

Iwago owned a copy of *The Marsh Lions* and was kind enough to tell me that he had been inspired by what he saw – though I think what he meant was that he was inspired by the possibilities inherent in what I had seen. When I asked him how I could improve my photography he replied, 'Be more adventurous, cover every angle, move out of your comfort zone, challenge yourself.' The key would be how to do it without disturbing the animals.

Before we broke camp Julian raised the question of the next step in my television career. Two of the producers on the series, Alastair Fothergill and Keith Scholey (both of whom would later serve as distinguished heads of the BBC Natural History Unit), had recognised my on-camera potential and set about finding me a series of my own to present. The main problem was that very few of the BBC's wildlife shows involved presenters – except of course for those hosted by David Attenborough, whose blue-chip series such as *Life on Earth* were the NHU's flagship programmes. Long-running series such as *Wildlife on One* and *The Natural World* were narrated by the great man, but did not use presenters. Consequently, it would be five years before my next role in front of the television cameras. In the meantime I was happy to continue writing and photographing and doing what I loved best – watching wildlife and making a new life for myself with Angie and the children.

In the early 1990s I had just completed a book called *Kingdom of Lions*, a reprise of all that had happened to the animal characters I had followed since the publication of *The Marsh Lions*, when an opportunity presented itself that would open up a totally different world for Angie and me, expanding our horizons both visually and cerebrally in a way that we could never have imagined: Antarctica. Abercrombie & Kent, who owned Kichwa Tembo Camp, had recently taken over the marketing of a ship called the MS *Explorer*, an expeditionary vessel that had made a name for itself as the 'Little Red Ship'. It was the brain child of Lars-Eric Lindblad, a pioneering travel specialist who had thrown down the gauntlet to other operators by offering his guests the ultimate in adventure travel, from Galapagos to the ends of the earth. His speciality was cruises to the place alluded to on maps of old as Terra Incognita – 'the great unknown land' dreamed of by explorers and potentates. I already knew all about the Little Red Ship because one of its guest lecturers for many years was Sir Peter Scott, son of 'Scott of the Antarctic'.

Being a Scott by name I could hardly have failed to be intrigued by the story of Captain Robert Falcon Scott. With four companions he famously achieved his ambition of reaching the South Pole in January 1912, only to find that the Norwegian Roald Amundsen had arrived a month earlier, on 15th December 1911. Scott and his men were crushed by the sight of Amundsen's tent and Norwegian flag marking the spot where they had calculated the South Pole to be. The British party stood marooned and despondent among the great expanse of whiteness that had been their bitter companion for the past seventy-seven days. It had been 1,200 kilometres of leg-weary misery as they battled the elements on foot and on skis, and in the very British tradition 'man-hauling' their own equipment on reaching the polar plateau – unlike Amundsen, who used dog teams for this arduous task. Scott noted in his diary, 'Great God! This is an awful place and terrible enough for us to have laboured to it without the reward of priority.'

Scott and his companions perished on a return journey blighted by deteriorating weather, frostbite, snow blindness, hunger and exhaustion. They pitched their final camp on 19th March 1912, barely eighteen kilometres short of One Ton Depot, which should have been their salvation. Starving and further weakened by scurvy, they remained pinned down by blizzards and swirling snowstorms as life ebbed from their bodies. Scott's diary and his letters to King and Country became the stuff of legend, creating a heartrending tale of honour and stoicism in defeat that made Amundsen's triumph almost a footnote in history by comparison. Scott ended his 'Message to the Public' thus:

> We took risks, we knew we took them; things have come out against us, and therefore we have no cause for complaint, but bow to the will of Providence, determined still to do our best to the last...Had we lived, I should have had a tale to tell of the hardihood, endurance, and courage of my companions which would have stirred the heart of every Englishman. These rough notes and our dead bodies must tell the tale, but surely, surely, a great rich country like ours will see that those who are dependent on us are properly provided for.

Their bodies were discovered by a search party eight months later, on 12th November 1912. Scott in death seemed finally to conquer the doubts and the feelings of inadequacy that dogged his innermost thoughts. Others criticised his judgement and leadership, maintaining that he should not have taken ponies; that he should have killed and eaten his dogs one by one as they tired; that manhauling might have nourished the spirit and sense of honest labour, but knowing how to ski and use dog teams to the best of their ability was the way to win; that to come second, however valiant the journey or effort, was to lose.

While my father was the most influential figure in my youth, Captain Scott was a *Boy's Own* hero whose story was to become a myth to live by. It made me aware of the importance of serving a cause – the concept of duty as represented by the Christ's Hospital ethos of service to something bigger than oneself.

The fact that my father was an ardent countryman who had always loved wildlife paintings created another connection to these other Scotts. Signed prints of Peter Scott's artwork hung prominently in our living room and when I passed the entrance exam for CH my mother gave a magnificent framed print of waterfowl rising from water at sunset to my primary school, Challow Court, honouring the link that my father had felt too.

I was fascinated by the life that Peter Scott had created for himself, founding what is now the Wildfowl and Wetlands Trust (WWT). At its headquarters at Slimbridge, Gloucestershire, a wide window looks out over a lake where wild swans and myriad species of waterfowl gather seasonally. Peter Scott was two years old when he lost his father, the same age as I was when it happened to me, and Robert wrote in his final letter to his wife, the sculptor and artist Kathleen Scott, 'Make the boy interested in natural history; it is better than games.' That idea of a connection to wilderness and wild creatures, of living an outdoor life and being hardy resonated with me growing up on the farm – though my love of games never diminished, and nor did that of Peter Scott, who was a champion figure skater, yachtsman and glider pilot. He went on

to become the most influential conservationist of the twentieth century, overseeing a national network of WWT centres across the UK as well as being pivotal in the creation of the World Wildlife Fund (now the World Wide Fund for Nature). I felt truly honoured to make his acquaintance and feel the glow of his approval for my work in East Africa.

Angie and I needed Antarctica as a counterbalance to Africa; we were ready for a new challenge as photographers. If anything was going to rival the sheer expanse of the Serengeti or abundance of the Mara's wild animals in our affections, it was always going to have to be somewhere of indescribable beauty, defined by its vastness yet embellished by a different palette of colours. Where Africa is predominantly earth browns and yellows imprinted with the dark and beautiful silhouettes of acacia trees, Antarctica is ice-cool blues and greens, with towering icebergs and a dazzling whiteness that is as much a state of the imagination as it is a colour. Antarctica is minimalist in character, pared right down to the essentials of rock and ice, snow and water. You can hear the silence – unless you are in the midst of a penguin rookery or fur seal colony, where the noise is deafening. In Antarctica there are far fewer species than in Africa, but those that do occur are found in unbelievable numbers, with millions of penguins and fur seals to rival the wildebeest migration in the sheer drama of the way they dominate the landscape.

Arriving at the tip of South America at short notice for my first expedition south I was completely unprepared for what I might find, noting that many of the passengers on the boat wore circular patches of sticking plaster behind their ears. It had never occurred to me that sea sickness might be an issue. Until then I had never heard of the Drake Passage, the immense expanse of ocean that spans the globe at this southerly latitude. With no landmasses to block their path, the winds and currents whip up a fury that can transform the Drake into a nightmare of a crossing with mountainous waves.

One thing you can be sure of when taking a cruise to Antarctica is that the food will be a significant part of the onboard experience. The first night at sea the five-course menu was ripe with lavish French cuisine, creamy sauces and lashings of fine wine. Having sampled all of this I fell asleep in my cabin to the gentle swaying of the ship. A few hours later I awoke to a sensation similar to being caught in a spin dryer, rocking and rolling in tandem with the swell of the ocean. I clung to my bunk, strapped myself on to it at one point, determined not to give in to the nausea that consumed me. Finally at around six o'clock I rose from the dead, prompting the inevitable – and not for the last time that morning. As fate would have it I was due to give the first talk in the lecture theatre on top deck after breakfast. I grabbed a couple of the sea-sickness pills prominently displayed in a basket at reception, along with a dry cracker and a glass of water, and headed upstairs. Looking green and feeling as if I was drunk, I clung on to the lectern as I shared with those guests who weren't hunkered down in their cabins my thoughts on wildlife photography and how it might apply in the ocean of whiteness we were headed for. Fortunately I soon found my sea legs and that hideous experience was never repeated.

The minute we reached the ice I knew that I had to return with Angie so that we could experience this exquisitely sculpted place together. Nothing in your everyday reality prepares you for Antarctica. It has that same blend of wilderness and adventure that we have always gone in search of. Just as a safari is much more than a holiday, a journey to Antarctica is an expedition of the body and the soul, an adventure with a special edge to it. Antarctica never leaves you. It is glimpsed wherever you might be; when the wind turns chilly or snow is falling you see its essence reflected in the clouds and the water. It is a land beyond reality that I knew Angie would find achingly beautiful.

Friends among the expeditionary crew told me to be sure that my next trip south included South Georgia, the sub-Antarctic island that is biologically part of Antarctica and often described as the 'Serengeti of the Southern Ocean'. The following year I was back with Angie, and when we stood on deck on a grey and windy morning as we approached South Georgia's Salisbury Plain, rendered speechless at the sight of 10,000 king penguins stippling the tussock-clad hillsides, we knew what our friends had meant.

There were times on landing at places like this – Gold Harbour and St Andrew's Bay among them – when our senses were so overwhelmed that we simply did not know where to start photographing. Elephant seals sprawled at our feet in such numbers that we could barely find a path through them, a thick blubbery mass of snorting, bellowing bodies covering the beach. Further along the shore would be throngs of young king penguins stacked up ten rows deep, all in a thick fluffy down of brown feathers that made them look like bag ladies in old fur coats. Curious and unafraid, they would press closer, forcing us to wade into the ocean to pass them, while their magnificently attired parents, with faces washed gold, slalomed and tobogganed through the boiling surf. Angie would find a quiet spot and sit watching and waiting for the moment to present itself, moving deftly through the wildlife like the dancer she once was to find the right angle for the shot she had in mind. Meanwhile I would strip down to my T-shirt, invigorated by the crispness of a sunny morning and the sensory overload, as I raced around trying to see and photograph as much as possible. We talked and laughed and gloried in those days of overwhelming joy and beauty, always aware of the connections that bound us together.

It was from this desolate windswept chunk of mountainous rock that Scott's great rival Sir Ernest Shackleton set out in 1914, hoping to be the first to cross the continent via the South Pole. But the triumph that Shackleton dreamed of was to elude him. His expedition ship the *Endurance* became trapped in the ice, forcing the party to camp out on the floes for more than five months. Shackleton then left most of his men on Elephant Island and set out with five companions in a six-metre boat called the *James Caird* – one of three lifeboats salvaged from the *Endurance*. This time his aim was to cross seven hundred and twenty nautical miles of open ocean to seek help from the whalers at South Georgia. After sixteen storm-tossed days at sea the men reached the island. The 'small boat journey', as it became known, and the group's subsequent crossing of South Georgia on foot (they landed on the opposite side of the island to the whaling station at Stomness) remain in the annals of Antarctic explorations as Shackleton's finest hour. They have also been an inspiration for my journey through life, to try to live with courage and confront my fears head on.

In the preface to his 1922 book *The Worst Journey in the World*, Apsley Cherry-Garrard, one of the party who discovered the bodies of Scott, Wilson and Bowers in 1912, wrote, 'For a joint scientific and geographical piece of organisation, give me Scott; for a Winter Journey, Wilson; for a dash to the Pole and nothing else, Amundsen: and if I am in the devil of a hole and want to get out of it, give me Shackleton every time.' Or as another put it, 'Get down on your knees and pray for Shackleton.'

This visit to Antarctica was the beginning of a twenty-year love affair that Angie and I have shared at the bottom of the world, made all the more meaningful by the fact that the starting point for many of our journeys south was Argentina, where Angie's mother Joy Backhouse was born. It was here, in the hill country of Cordoba, that her larger-than-life grandfather Hugo Backhouse (who wrote an autobiography called *Among the Gauchos*) ranched cattle and bred and trained polo ponies. More than that – he rode alongside Lawrence of Arabia during the First World War, captained the Argentine polo team in 1936 and spied for Britain in both world wars.

In one of life's wonderfully moving chance encounters, we were staying at a polo ranch in Cordoba when Angie mentioned her family's connection to Argentina. The manager held up his hand and said, 'I know your grandfather's name. Hugo Backhouse was a great friend of my own grandfather, in fact my father used to talk about this wild, crazy 'gringo' who spoke our language and rode like a gaucho. They shared the joys and sorrows of life with my grandparents, celebrated the birth of their children and death of loved ones. Hugo was like family.'

Angie had tears in her eyes as we decided to try to find the ranch where her mother was born. With the benefit of some inside information and the help of a friendly taxi driver we did just that, tarrying long enough to be welcomed by the head gaucho, who allowed us to walk around the beautiful old stone building overlooking a broad stretch of wild country. We stood and soaked up the ambience of the place where Angie's mother and her brother had ridden bareback and dived naked into the gushing waterfall in the meadow below, a place where mountain lions roamed and eagles soared.

What made travelling on the Little Red Ship so special was the sense of family. Sitting out on the prow chatting to the crew as we sailed along the Lemaire Channel or 'Kodachrome Alley' as it is known (a tribute to how much film has been exposed trying to capture the beauty of its snow-capped mountains and fractured pack ice), we were in heaven. We loved the energy and enthusiasm of the expedition team, which comprised scientists, explorers and naturalists, many of whom had lived extraordinary lives. We felt privileged to have known people such as Sir Wally Herbert, who in the 1960s became the first man to walk to the North Pole, prompting Prince Charles to salute Herbert for having 'determination and courage of such great proportions that his country should mark his achievements eventually by having him stuffed and put on display!'

When AK sold the Little Red Ship, she was bought by GAP Expeditions, but after a few more years of sailing she had her own *Titanic* moment when she foundered amid the ice off the South Shetland Islands and sank. Fortunately, conditions were mild by Antarctic standards and the passengers had to endure only a few hours in the lifeboats before they were rescued.

We then began to travel with Exodus and Quark Expeditions on a number of their ships, including an unforgettable semi-circumnavigation of Antarctica, from Ushuaia in Tierra del Fuego to Christchurch in New Zealand, on the fabled *Kapitan Khlebnikov*, a Russian icebreaker outfitted with helicopters to help find a way through the ice. We also made two pilgrimages to emperor penguin rookeries at Snow Hill Island in the Weddell Sea. Temperatures of −20°C were no deterrent when it came to spending time in the company of emperor chicks that could only be reached with the help of helicopters and a two-kilometre slog through knee-high snow. It really did feel as if we had travelled to the ends of the earth in our quest for evocative wildlife photographs and adventure.

Despite Antarctica's remoteness and the international pledge that it remain a place of science and not exploitation, if the day ever dawns when its mineral wealth can be accessed at an attractive price some nations may wish to challenge or ignore the spirit of the Antarctic Treaty. After all, it is not as if man's bloody footprint is not clearly visible on the continent already, with millions of seals slaughtered for their fur and oil in the nineteenth century, followed by the demise of the great whales in the twentieth. While the fur seal population has made a remarkable recovery, abandoned whaling stations on the shores of South Georgia and along the Antarctic Peninsula are bleak testament to those times, as are the rotting fuel drums and refuse that litter the backyards of some of the scientific bases, reason enough for caution in how we treat this sacred place. Even in the relatively short time that we have been visiting Antarctica the impact of global warming on the pack ice has been significant – Western Antarctica is warming faster than any other place on earth, with midwinter temperatures rising 6°C in the past sixty years. The ice is literally melting beneath the feet of some penguin colonies, spelling disaster for species such as the Adelies that rely on the pack ice for food. Emperors, largest of all penguins at up to 45 kilograms and 1.2 metres tall, breed on the fast ice (sea ice attached to land), predominantly at locations around the Ross Sea. They incubate their single egg on their feet to keep it warm, and if the ice melts too early then the chicks do not yet have their waterproof adult plumage to protect them from the icy seas. Our love and concern for the frozen south prompted us to write *Antarctica: Exploring a Fragile Eden*, published by Collins in 2007.

As Angie and I have both lived a life defined by adventure, it is hardly surprising that people always want to hear stories of our most dangerous and frightening moments among wild creatures. Angie was born in Africa and grew up on safari, her soulmates bush babies and mongooses. As a child she was living the life I dreamed of.

She tamed all manner of wild creatures, befriending a dwarf mongoose called Mong who would sleep between her feet and nip her toes if she moved, and a mischievous vervet monkey called Bingo. If Bingo hadn't been put to bed by dinner time he would race around the house swinging from the chandeliers and peeing on the guests. There was a genet cat called Spots, and Sam the dormouse who during the daytime loved nothing better than to snuggle up under Angie's plait of long blonde hair, curled behind her ear.

This was rich fare compared to the domestic cats and dogs that were my companions in England, though the sudden emergence of a ferret or two – all fiery-eyed, wraithlike suppleness – from the deep pockets of the local gamekeeper's greatcoat certainly added a bit of spice to life on Cuba Farm. When I graduated to hamsters and guinea pigs, then slow worms and grass snakes, I thought that was pretty exciting, but nothing to compare with the time Angie discovered a 4.5-metre python as thick as her thigh curled up under her baby son's cot down on the Kenya coast. It made for an eye-catching headline in the local newspaper, but it could have been a tragedy: three-month-old David would have provided a tasty snack for a python that size.

Talking of snakes, I did wonder what on earth was going on early one morning in the Serengeti as I got out of my safari wagon to stretch my legs and a puff adder fell from the sky and landed at my feet, very much alive. I looked into the sun to see a bird of prey wheeling overhead: obviously disturbed by my sudden emergence from my vehicle, it had dropped its breakfast.

Tales of 'derring-do', particularly when played out among beguiling creatures in the world's wild places, have always found a ready audience, but if Angie and I have learned anything from living among large and potentially dangerous animals in Africa, it's that

when trouble strikes it is invariably due to ignorance, complacency or incaution on the part of the people involved. This is what ignites the animals' natural defensive response in protecting themselves or their young from real or perceived harm. A leopard wounded by a trophy hunter, a cow elephant anxious for the safety of her young calf or a buffalo surprised in thick bush can all be terrifyingly unforgiving adversaries. A bull elephant called Tyson charged us while we were filming *Elephant Diaries*, trashing $30,000 of camera equipment as we ran for our lives. Angie once nearly sat on a puff adder during a tea break in the bush in the Mara, and then there was the time I unintentionally shared the back seat of our safari vehicle with a large male baboon with canines the size of my thumb intent on stealing my treasured bag of crisps. When he lunged towards me with fangs bared in response to my attempts to intimidate him, the crisps were all his. Incidents like this are guaranteed to get the adrenaline pumping – and in the main thoroughly avoidable.

The reality is that the little creatures you never see – except perhaps in a biology class or under a microscope in a Tropical Diseases Hospital – are the most likely to put you in hospital: mosquitoes, tsetse flies, assassin bugs and freshwater snails all act as vectors for tiny parasites that can kill. A million people die of malaria in Africa each year – mostly children under the age of five – making it the number-one killer, with human assassins not far behind, followed by snakes and man's best friend, the domestic dog. The most sensible defence against malaria is to forgo the more comfortable shorts and sandals for long trousers and socks in the evening; smother yourself with insect repellent and sleep under a well-secured mosquito net treated with repellent. Living in Africa, we don't take antimalarials unless we are visiting the coast. It's better for both your eyesight and your liver to be vigilant about the symptoms (fever, headache, chills) and simply to have a blood test when you feel below par. If it's positive, take the cure.

Mind you, the delight I saw spread across the pasty face of the specialist at the Tropical Diseases Hospital in London on finding *Plasmodium vivax* (a recurrent form of the malaria parasite) in my highly anaemic blood slide was almost worth the blinding headache. So joyfully enthusiastic was his reaction that it momentarily distracted me from how lousy I was feeling. He then admonished me with: 'Africa? White man's grave, you know – takes its toll. My advice would be to leave while you're still relatively young and fit.' After a few days on a quinine drip at St Pancras, wedged into a bed alongside patients suffering from all manner of ailments and parasites, I knew what he meant. There's another world riding the tropical air currents and lurking in the undergrowth: far less charismatic than lions and elephants, it's far more dangerous to your health. But no amount of parasites was going to persuade me to give up my life in Africa.

Ironically, one of the most frightening incidents Angie and I have faced wasn't in Africa at all, it was in Antarctica. The beauty of the frozen south is that most of the creatures you encounter on land are completely unafraid of humans. Elephant seals may weigh up to four tonnes and look pretty fearsome, but they mostly slumber like giant slabs of lard along the pebble beaches, while penguins wander up to you confident that you mean them no harm.

The one creature that everyone tells you to be wary of is the Antarctic fur seal, particularly during the breeding season when the testosterone-fuelled males are at their most aggressive. You only have to watch the rival 'beachmasters', as the mature dominant males are known, charging across the beaches to compete for the right to mate with females (barely a week after they have given birth) to know that these are animals to be avoided. Thanks to their ability to direct their hind flippers forwards, they can launch themselves towards you at a startling gallop. Add to that a set of teeth to rival a leopard's and you have a 110-kilogram running machine that can tear through human flesh and leave a nasty infected wound. But by listening to sound advice we had always managed to avoid trouble. That is, until we came face to face with a Hooker's sea lion – a species also known as the New Zealand sea lion that looks and acts like a fur seal, but is even bigger.

We were on our semi-circumnavigation of Antarctica on the *Kapitan Khlebnikov*. Our expedition had included the opportunity to pay our respects to Ernest Shackleton's hut at Cape Royds, from where he reached within 160 kilometres of the South Pole in 1907. Most moving of all had been our pilgrimage to Scott's *Terra Nova* hut at Cape Evans on Ross Island – the hut that he never returned to. But now our final excursion ashore would be at Campbell Island, with the chance of photographing the handful of royal albatrosses that breed there during the summer months.

As we stepped off the ship, Shane, our expedition leader, reminded us to give any Hooker's sea lions that we encountered a wide berth. Angie and I nevertheless set off at a gallop, anxious to spend as much time with the albatrosses as we could. The vegetation reminded us

of the stunted treescape from *Lord of the Rings*, straggly trees and bushes forming an interlocking tapestry of vegetation, with a maze of tunnels and pathways created by the sea lions as they crossed between the beaches and higher ground.

I walked ahead of Angie, carrying a large rucksack full of camera gear and a heavy tripod in one hand. Halfway along the trail a large male sea lion trundled into view, flip-flopping down the boardwalk leading to the albatross breeding site. Shane's instructions had been to retreat in orderly fashion towards the ship if this happened. But having slogged this far up the path I was reluctant to head back. All we needed to do was to step off the walkway into the vegetation and the sea lion would surely continue on its way. I told Angie to stay behind me and stepped into the undergrowth. The sea lion, now moving rapidly towards us, decided that my way was his way.

Animals tend to look even larger seen up close – particularly when you are on foot. Given that the dimensions of an average male Hooker's sea lion are 320–450 kilograms and 2.4–3.5 metres – twice the weight of a male lion and longer – I had every reason to be concerned. As the sea lion lumbered towards me with mouth agape revealing some very impressive teeth, I backed up and instantly fell flat on my backside. I was thankful to be wearing a pair of heavy-duty insulated Antarctic rubber boots that along with my tripod I instinctively thrust towards the sea lion's open mouth, uttering every swear word I have ever dreamed of stringing together. The bull towered over me, looking every inch the heaving, huffing-and-puffing 'mountain of flesh with teeth' that is so intimidating to smaller rivals. Then, much to my relief, my venomous tirade, flailing rubber boots and club-like tripod did the trick and he turned and disappeared into the darkened world beneath the vegetation.

Shaken and barely able to rise from the ground with my heavy rucksack still strapped to my back, I staggered to my feet, double-checking that all my toes were intact. I turned to look for Angie, expecting to be told what an idiot I was. But there was no sign of her. Then to my horror I heard yelling.

The sea lion had left me to go and challenge Angie, who had taken a tumble down the slope and was now desperately trying to scramble up and over shrubs and bushes, pursued by a wave of moving vegetation that I knew could only be the sea lion. I lumbered towards her, shouting and screaming at the top of my voice, desperately trying to reach her before the sea lion could bite her. At that moment she fell over again with her pursuer barely a metre away. It felt as if I was running over an obstacle course as stunted trees collapsed under my headlong charge, a hundred fibrous arms reaching out to snag and trip my every step. When I reached Angie we both felt a sense of utter relief as we realised the sea lion had vanished. Only later did we discover that she had damaged a disc in her lower back as she twisted and fell while trying to escape.

We hobbled back to the pathway and, as we did so, for an awful moment the vegetation below us began to ripple and swirl again. The sea lion was back to haunt us one last time, exhibiting the same dogged persistence that makes these males such formidable foes in their battle for supremacy against others of their own kind. Then he was gone.

In 1995 I teamed up with Simon King and Chris Packham on another live series called *Flamingo Watch*, broadcast from the Rift Valley's soda lakes. Sadly, compared to *Africa Watch* it felt rather dull and one-paced. Flamingos are dramatic when seen in their hundreds of thousands, but given that it was not the breeding season there was only a limited amount of behaviour to concentrate on. Footage of the colony feeding on the microscopic aquatic algae Spirulina that abounds in the lakes or of the birds flying en masse was punctuated by only the occasional dramatic moment when a fish eagle or marabou stork swooped to snatch up a flamingo and spice things up a bit. That works fine within the confines of a single programme, but not when you are broadcasting daily. Consequently we had to rely heavily on pre-recorded material to fill in for the lack of live action.

Little did I realise at the time that I was about to hit a purple patch in my BBC career that would last for the next fifteen years. Alastair Fothergill and Keith Scholey had finally got the green light for me to present my own series. Called *Dawn to Dusk*, it would consist of six African adventures, with me travelling through East and Southern Africa in the knowledgeable company of people working with animals in stunning wilderness settings.

The six locations chosen for *Dawn to Dusk* were painstakingly researched to provide safari adventures to rival anything you might find in a bespoke travel brochure. Who wouldn't want to visit the Namib Desert and track endangered black rhinos and desert elephants on foot in the company of Blythe and Rudy Loutit, founders of the Save the Rhino Trust? Or to fly in a hot-air balloon over the Serengeti with Alan Root, who brought along as a filming prop a large puff adder which he kept in a cloth bag in his plane, much to the consternation of his passengers and our producer Sara Ford! Then there was the opportunity to track chimpanzees at Gombe National Park in Tanzania, where Louis Leakey had enabled Jane Goodall to establish her pioneering research project in 1960. For thrills and spills there was white-water rafting and canoeing on the mighty Zambezi with the legendary safari guide John Stevens, who had served in the Parks Service and as a member of an elite tracking unit in the bush war; and for high-priced luxury there was an elephant-back safari with the eccentric and volatile American Randall Moore in Botswana's Okavango Delta, where I had gained my first real experience of living in the bush. In fact we made two shows in the Delta, the second one featuring the Mombo Pack of wild dogs at their den in the Moremi Game Reserve with cameraman Richard Goss, who had earned a name for himself filming brown hyenas.

What was particularly fascinating for me was to listen to the life stories of six very different hosts, each of whom had, like me, followed their love of wild animals and made a career out of their passion through science, filmmaking, wildlife tourism or in the Parks Service. Among the highlights was the opportunity to get close to Randall Moore's elephants. Randall had managed to bring three wild-born circus elephants back to Africa on an epic journey by sea, overcoming every setback the authorities put in his way. He eventually found a permanent home for his gigantic charges in Botswana.

And what a home it was – the Okavango is unique. To be able to view the Delta from the back of an elephant was as exciting for me as looking out from the upper deck of Tim and June Liversedge's houseboat had been twenty years earlier. At night the sound of the Grateful Dead would echo across the water from Randall's tented home. Each morning he would arrive with his hair pulled back in a ponytail, thick black moustache immaculate and a cigar clamped between his teeth. Energetic, entertaining and temperamental, he left you never quite sure which Randall might emerge. What you could be sure of were his love and commitment for his elephants – 'sentient beings', he called them. I was to discover the truth of this for myself ten years later, while filming *Elephant Diaries* in Kenya. One afternoon I found myself surrounded by a group of young elephants that had been orphaned and eventually returned to the wild by the David Sheldrick Wildlife Trust. I rested my head against one of the elephant's temples as the others crowded round me, enveloping me with outstretched trunks and giant flapping ears. At one point they suddenly stopped as one and we stood there in a state of reverie, a connection that I could feel resonating through my whole body.

Then there were the chimpanzees at Gombe, on the placid and inviting shores of Lake Tanganyika. To be honest, I have never been particularly fascinated by our primate cousins. I was far too intrigued by Africa's other large animals to want to spend time in the company of our closest relatives. But who could fail to be inspired by the work of Jane Goodall, who had taken her childhood love of chimps and turned it into a spectacularly successful life of inquiry and adventure? Through painstaking observation and meticulous data collection, allied to the insights that only long-term projects can provide, she confounded the sceptics among the scientific community, who were suspicious of her non-academic background. She went on to enthral a worldwide audience with

Above Emperor and chick, Snow Hill Island.

Above Emperor chick admiring Angie's photographic equipment.

ABOVE The Russian icebreaker *Kapitan Khlebnikov* pauses on fast ice off the Phantom Coast, Amundsen Sea, to allow passengers to meet their first emperor penguin.

ABOVE Angie hanging on to her favourite Canon 500mm telephoto in an Antarctic snow storm.

ABOVE Adelie penguins among a maze of ice, Robertson Bay, Cape Adare.

ABOVE Ice cave, Antarctic Peninsula. The Antarctic ice is melting so fast that the stability of the whole continent could be at risk by 2100, scientists have warned.

ABOVE Novice monks in Bhutan admiring photos of themselves.

ABOVE Is anyone interested in my photographs? On safari in Rajasthan, India.
OPPOSITE Mihir Garh, Sidharth Singh's extraordinary boutique hotel at the edge of the Thar desert, Rajasthan, India.

ABOVE We had ten weeks to film the first series of *Big Cat Diary* in 1996. Up before sunrise and back after dark was the order of the day.

ABOVE Cleaning up after a 'crappy' encounter with Kike the cheetah as Toby Strong records the deed, 2003.

ABOVE There are perhaps only 7,000 wild cheetahs remaining in Africa.

ABOVE Honey's Boys knew no fear – one of them takes a close look
at his reflection in Mark Warham's Canon telephoto lens.

ABOVE *Elephant Diaries*, 2005: taking a stroll with the orphans on their way to a waterhole and feeding site in Tsavo East National Park (photo: LISSA RUBEN).

ABOVE *Big Bear Diary*, 2005. The male known as Ted fends off a female called Audrey to stop her taking the fish he has just caught during the salmon run. Hallo Bay Bear Camp, Katmai National Park, Alaska.

her plea to nurture the planet rather than deplete it, to truly grasp that we are just one highly evolved member of the tree of life. She has made more difference than anyone in demanding better care for captive primates used in medical research and an end to the killing of great apes as an exotic food. How right she is when, in response to worthy sentiments about cherishing Mother Nature for future generations, she points out that our generation has already plundered our children's future.

Thank goodness for the luxury of Lake Tanganyika to dip into each evening after arduous days scrambling through the vines and undergrowth, trying to keep pace with Jane's protégée Charlotte Uhlenbroek. While I looked as if I had been trapped in a sauna Charlotte never even 'glowed', let alone broke into a sweat. Her study group, the Kasakela chimpanzee community, included the legendary female Fifi (who died in 2004 at the remarkable age of forty-two) and her two sons Freud and Frodo, both of whom went on to become alpha males. Frodo was a chimp with the presence of a silverback gorilla. Everyone was wary of him, and not just the other chimpanzees. He had nearly broken Jane's neck on one occasion when he clouted her violently around the head – fortunately Frodo was a thumper rather than a biter.

Looking into the eyes of one of the great apes speaks volumes for their intelligence – you recognise the primate in yourself. Looking into Frodo's dark eyes you also saw something else – not the calm assuredness of his brother Freud, but the awareness of the power to intimidate. At the time of our visit, Freud was the alpha male, but Frodo was the one to watch out for. Our producer Robin Hellier found this out one morning when the huge chimp swaggered down the path in our direction, his long black hair bristling as he performed the equivalent of a drive-by shooting, upending Robin and yanking him along the pathway by the ankle, making it abundantly clear who the real boss of the show was.

The following year Freud was debilitated by sarcoptic mange and Frodo promptly deposed him as alpha male. A year after that he attacked the American cartoonist Gary Larson, leaving him scratched and bruised. Worse was to come. In 2002 Frodo gained even greater notoriety when he killed a fourteen-month-old child whom the niece of a member of the research team had carried into his territory, despite the fact that children under twelve are not permitted to visit the park. Tanzania National Parks officials debated euthanising Frodo, while the research team argued successfully that he had simply been following his predatory instincts in viewing a human infant as prey: chimpanzees are known to hunt down other mammals, notably colobus monkeys, and kill them for fresh meat.

One of my abiding memories of meeting Frodo is when I put my rucksack down while doing a piece to camera with Charlotte. We had been warned to keep our possessions close to us. Next minute my rucksack was surrounded by a scrum of chimps, all eagerly licking the sweat from the back of the bag and webbing. I could see Frodo in the thick of it, sinking his canines into one of the straps – just the kind of television moment producers love. As the chimps began to lose interest I saw the chance to retrieve my precious gear – there were thousands of pounds' worth of cameras and lenses inside. But perhaps sensing my intention, Frodo wrenched the rucksack away from his mother Fifi and swung himself into the nearest tree, flailing the bag around his head and thumping it against the trunk. Fortunately when he became bored with his prize and let it drop back to earth nothing was damaged. Frodo died in 2013, aged thirty-seven, having sired at least eight infants, the second highest number recorded in the Kasakela chimpanzee community.

While we all hoped that *Dawn to Dusk* would lead to a re-commission for a series in North America, I was painfully aware that it was make-or-break time as far as my television career was concerned. Despite good reviews six years earlier for my performance with Julian Pettifer in *Africa Watch* I was pretty green when it came to hosting a programme on my own. The step up from being interviewed or narrating to presenting to camera is enormous. When someone is asking you questions you can relax and enjoy the experience – the onus is on the interviewer to perform to camera; as long as you know what you are talking about, it is like chatting to a friend. When it comes to making the transition to presenting,

some people are naturals, but many find it daunting and for some it is impossible. Their performance becomes wooden rather than animated, their voice a flat monotone rather than full of energy. Today, of course, with everyone taking photographs and videoing every aspect of their lives on their smart phones and iPads, talking to camera and hamming it up is all part of life. But back then it didn't come so easily.

Even though I felt confident talking to the camera while filming *Dawn to Dusk*, I fell into the trap of asking questions that I already knew the answer to, in an attempt to tease more information out of the local experts who were less familiar with television than I was. The trick would have been to ask rhetorical questions – 'A male giraffe can grow up to 5.5 metres tall, right?' rather than 'How tall is a male giraffe?', when I knew the answer. Hardest of all was being with Alan Root in the Serengeti – both of us already knew whatever the other might be able to say about the great migration and the ecology of the area. I was roasted by Christina Odone, the *Daily Telegraph*'s television critic, and even Alan copped some flack in her scathing review entitled 'Hush! It's the sound of an eager beaver'. She accused me of 'imparting irrelevant information from his passenger seat in an airplane, a hot-air balloon – even from his perch upon a rock' and of not letting the awe-inspiring scenery and the majesty of the animals speak for themselves. Then she went on:

> I wouldn't follow a guide like this to the corner shop... But perhaps under the African sun banality becomes contagious, because he [Alan Root] too started issuing some pretty inane lines: 'It's a great time to be a lion,' as the wildebeest migration began. 'Yup, it is a great time to be a lion,' Jonathan Scott agreed. After some more of this, I found myself wishing Scott would become the snap, crackle and pop on the lion's breakfast menu.

Hard as it was to stomach I couldn't help admitting the justice of some of Odone's words: my manic side had got the better of my more considered voice. And you certainly don't want presenters telling you what you can plainly see. It was an important lesson: if you can't add value to the commentary, then keep quiet.

CHAPTER

10

BIG
CAT
DIARY

All charming people have
something to conceal,
usually their total dependence on
the appreciation of others.

Cyril Connolly
Enemies Of Promise

T hat could have been the end of my life as a television presenter. Fortunately the first series of *Big Cat Diary* had been commissioned that same year and was less scripted, relying much more on actuality: a conversation between myself, my fellow presenter Simon King and the television audience, with a minimum of formal pieces to camera. I was back in my comfort zone among the big cats in the Mara, and a lot wiser too.

My old friend Keith Scholey was by now the Head of the BBC Natural History Unit. He saw the sea-change sweeping through television, driven by a hunger for real-life dramas that allowed the audience to empathise with the individual animal characters. We had learned from *Africa Watch* and *Flamingo Watch* that going live wasn't enough to hold our audience's attention – it wasn't like football, where knowing the result was all that mattered. Why not film with presenters to witness the action – but without showing the material live? That would save a huge chunk of money and pre-empt the possible disappointment of nothing much happening on the night. *Animal Hospital* had audiences on the edge of their seats, wondering whether the animal character that was tugging at their heartstrings would survive its ordeal, be it a donkey with a broken leg or a kitten near to death. Translate that idea to Africa's charismatic big cats and you might find you had a massive hit on your hands.

Big Cat Diary was the most significant television opportunity of my career and a major change in style for wildlife programmes produced by the NHU. It was such a simple concept. Go out each day on safari and record what you find, focusing on the big cats. Let their stories unfold in front of your eyes. It was honest – what you saw actually happened – but it was also an animal soap opera, narrated with knowledge and passion. The aim was to use presenters as real people: we wouldn't simply be there to provide carefully scripted links in the way I had done on *Wild Kingdom* in the 1980s. We wanted our audience to connect to us in an emotional way, providing them with the chance to join us on a virtual safari in the most accessible and easy to photograph wildlife paradise on earth. The essence of what we filmed as *Big Cat Diary* was the same thing that Angie and I had been doing on a daily basis for years – in my case dating back to 1977, when I started watching and documenting the life of the Marsh Pride. Now we were going to film it.

While the first series of *Big Cat Diary* wasn't quite as spontaneous stylistically as we had hoped – it was still too formal and lacked the emotional warmth of presenters as real people that would define later series – the big cats provided us with plenty of memorable moments to keep our audience on the edge of their seats, not least the irrepressible Half-Tail and her boisterous cub Zawadi.

We found Half-Tail and Zawadi every single day, which anyone who knows leopards will tell you is testimony to what an extraordinary gift to the programme they were, and to the skill of our dedicated team of spotters from Governors' Camp. In fact, the original concept for *Big Cat Diary* relied on us being able to find leopards with that kind of certainty. Half-Tail made that possible and, having watched her for so many years, I felt incredibly fortunate to be able to tell her story. Sadly, my old mentor Joseph Rotich had passed away before Half-Tail emerged around Fig Tree Ridge and Leopard Gorge. He would have chuckled at the thought of a leopard like this, one that required none of the skills that he had painstakingly tutored me in. Joseph believed that to really appreciate the wonder of watching the ultimate predator you had to earn your sightings.

The year after *Big Cat Diary* first hit the screen on BBC1, Angie and I were invited to present segments for a new American television series called *Wild Things*. Produced by Paramount, it would prove to be just the opportunity I needed to evolve as a presenter. The executive producer was a dynamic American called Bertram van Munster who cut his teeth as a cameraman-producer on the hugely successful actuality series *Cops* for Fox TV and went on to create the reality show *The Amazing Race*. Bert had one piece of advice to his cameramen: 'No tripods, no locked-off shots, shoot from the shoulder, keep it real.' Everything had to have a sense of immediacy, of being in the moment, with the emphasis on action. The field producers on these shows were raw young graduates with only a modicum of experience, eager to make a name for themselves and to impress Bert. They were expected to shoot, too, using small, hand-held digital video cameras to capture the cameraman and soundman at work: all those behind the scenes 'making of' shots that the audience love, built into the shows themselves.

Wild Things filmed for three years (1997–99), after which Paramount had accumulated seventy-two hours of television content for syndication and could sit back and watch the money roll in. Each one-hour show was a composite of six-to-eight-minute segments, featuring a different animal star observed by a photographer, filmmaker, vet or wildlife conservationist. It was similar in some ways to *Nature Watch* back in the 1980s, but with more hype and action to appeal to the American audience. There were echoes of *Wild Kingdom*, too, with the presenter almost as important as the animals, though in general without the heavy manipulation of the story or the wildlife.

This was a wonderful opportunity for Angie and me to travel the world in our true-to-life role as wildlife photographers and naturalists. Each segment was a personal quest in pursuit of great images of charismatic creatures. There were moose – and grizzly bears feasting on salmon – in Alaska (thank goodness those ginormous mosquitoes didn't carry malaria); giant saltwater crocodiles in Australia; and three-metre komodo dragons on Komodo Island in Indonesia. We photographed Asiatic rhinos in Kaziranga National Park in Assam and Bengal tigers in Jaipur's Ranthambhore National Park with legendary forestry officer Fateh Singh Rathore and conservationist Valmik Thapar, meeting the fabled tigress Machli, who at the time of writing is still alive at the age of nineteen.

We also encountered orang utans at Camp Leakey in Kalimantan, Borneo, with Birute Galdikas, the third (along with Jane Goodall and Dian Fossey) of Louis Leakey's famous 'Trimates'. Leakey had been eager to discover what the great apes could tell us about human development, and felt that women were more intuitive observers, so he established what turned out to be three of the most remarkable wildlife studies ever, under the auspices of these three remarkable women. We were keen to observe Galdikas' efforts to help wild-born orangs that had been reared in captivity find sanctuary in their native forests, even as the illegal loggers ferried precious hardwoods out of the parks right in front of our eyes.

Camp Leakey was home at times to the hugely impressive Kusasi, a 110-kilogram male orang who had a tendency to grab hold of you with both his hands and feet, as actress Julia Roberts was to discover. One imprudent Spanish television presenter couldn't resist the photo opportunity of getting up close to Kusasi and was lucky not to be hurt on being pulled to the ground and manhandled. The only way to control Kusasi in those circumstances was to show him 'fire', reminding him of the terror of when he was kept captive and badly abused as he grew ever larger and stronger; rangers carried a cigarette lighter for just that purpose, but for some reason didn't have one on this occasion.

Having worked on *Wild Kingdom*, I was determined to try to prevent anything untoward being done in the thirst for exciting material. So when the field producer on the Asiatic rhino show saw the opportunity to put a mother rhino with a small calf under pressure by surrounding her with the elephants we were filming from, in the hope that she would charge, I immediately called a halt. And when a two and a half-metre komodo dragon charged towards me after a refuse bin disintegrated as I attempted to shift it out of the shot, I was forced to jump to one side and whack the giant reptile on the head with the notebook I was holding as the cameras rolled. I knew that this kind of sequence could easily be used to portray the komodo as a bloodthirsty killer. The truth was that the giant lizard was only interested in the rustling of the litter from the bin, which might indicate prey close by. I asked the cameraman to let me record a sound bite addressed to the producers back in the USA, saying that this footage was not to be used. A while later I received a message asking if they could use it as part of a high-octane promo 'tease' to advertise the new series. I said no – and like to believe that they didn't.

Over the course of filming *Wild Things* the camera became my friend, something to confide in, to communicate with. Presenting started to become fun; there were no formal pieces to camera, just life as it happened, warts and all. If you messed up or something wasn't working you just smiled and started again. Now I was really enjoying myself. It reminded me of the day when Keith Scholey invited me to accompany him on a shoot in the outskirts of Bristol, filming *Life of Plants* with David Attenborough. Keith and I were due to set off for Botswana the following week to film an elephant-back safari with Randall Moore. He was convinced that if I could only be myself on camera we would have a winning formula and that watching David at work would allow me to see how he did it.

The interesting thing for me was to observe that while David had a very natural style, coupled to that unforgettable voice, his presentation did have an element of performance to it – natural, yes, but not the Attenborough I knew on a first-name basis. While working on *Wild Things* I finally got it. It wasn't enough to simply be myself in the way people were telling me – I needed to deliver 'me' along with that subtle extra ingredient that comes from the confidence of being relaxed and in the moment on camera. This allows you to add a little bit of emphasis, to play with your words, relish the pauses, build drama or emotion – to connect to the audience in a way that engages them totally in your story. Once you can do that, you can fly.

My new-found confidence was immediately apparent when *Big Cat Diary* was re-commissioned in 1998. By the time the show had become *Big Cat Week* five years later and I made Kike the cheetah's acquaintance on camera we were going out on five consecutive nights on BBC1 over the course of a single week. Now each of the three presenters – Simon King, Saba Douglas-Hamilton (who joined us in 2000) and myself – had a cameraman in their vehicle, recording everything that happened, whether you spilt your beans in your lap or had a cheetah crap or pee on you. It gave the show a much more contemporary feel and the ratings went through the roof, at one point reaching seven million viewers in the UK alone.

The three of us were very different in our character and style of presentation. I had known Simon since 1990, when I advised on a film he was making on Kali, a lioness from the Marsh Pride, and we had worked together again on *Flamingo Watch* a year before the first series of *Big Cat Diary*. Simon had been on television since he was a child and often worked with his father John King, who was a senior producer at the BBC. Simon is the consummate professional, perfect for live television where you need to be able to juggle lots of ideas, stay calm and pluck the right words out of the stream of thoughts running through your brain. Both he and I are avid naturalists with enquiring minds, always keen to learn more about the behaviour of the animals we are watching. We are also both determined and competitive, which helped drive us to deliver ever more engaging performances without it becoming a major issue.

When Saba Douglas-Hamilton joined us, after *Big Cat* had been on air for six years, her eye-catching charm and confidence gave a new feel to the show. Her popularity with the blokes made for a hilarious encounter with a mob of Liverpool football supporters one evening when I was in London. They were headed for a major away match at Chelsea, a team I used to watch as a teenager. Fans of both clubs had been sinking pints of their favourite ale along Earl's Court Road, where Angie and I were staying. Things looked as if they might get out of hand long before kick-off, so I waited until most of the pubs had emptied and then wandered back down the road to find somewhere to watch the match. Headed towards me was a large contingent of shaven-headed Liverpool lads fresh from the pub and looking very much up for a bit of 'bother' with the rival firm. Thinking it wise to step off the pavement as they drew alongside, I was somewhat taken aback when one of them shouted, 'It's the bloke from *Big Cat Diary*, the one the cheetah crapped on', as if he had just spotted a long-lost friend. But I wasn't nearly as bemused as his mate, who was finding it challenging enough to simply stay upright and clutched on to me as the most convenient 'lamppost' to wrap himself round while virtually asphyxiating me with alcohol fumes. Naturally my new friend wanted to revisit the Kike moment − or should I say 'movement'? − before telling me at some length what a 'fit bird' Saba was. As they headed for the match they shouted, 'You're not a Chelsea supporter, are you?' Which of course I was, but I had the sense to keep quiet about it.

All this was far less disconcerting than the man who stopped me in Oxford Street and, struggling to remember my name, shouted, 'Got it! You're Jonathan King' − an unfortunate amalgam of Jonathan Scott and Simon King, given that the real Jonathan King (a former '60s pop star famous for his hit single *Everyone's Gone to the Moon*) had recently been sentenced to seven years in prison for assaulting teenage boys.

In 2001 Angie and I were commissioned to write three books to accompany *Big Cat Diary* − *Lion*, *Leopard and Cheetah* − to reveal the findings of scientists studying the big cats, along with our personal experiences of each of the three species. This gave us the opportunity to travel around East and Southern Africa in our quest for great images to accompany the text. Travelling and photographing together and working on our own projects − just the two of us – is what we love best. Angie has always been the driving force behind our work, whether encouraging me to believe that we could create the best-selling **CD-ROM** *Safari*, even if it meant her learning how to tape the video clips and record the sound, or taking on the onerous task of completely revising our safari guide books. It was she who embraced the digital technology that was to transform our photography, managing the processing and cataloguing of our images on her computer while cajoling me to join her in what was for me an alien world. Angie is a tireless organiser who loves to find ways of making things happen – she had run her own craft business before we met – while I have a tendency to want to stay in my comfort zone or believe that we are too busy to take on more projects. Her drive and flexibility have allowed us to stay in the field and ride the turbulent waters of earning a living 'doing something with wildlife'.

It was during this period that Angie won the overall award in the Wildlife Photographer of the Year competition. Photography has been a constant in Angie's life, allowing her to express her view of the world – much more artistic and imaginative than mine – without need for fuss or fanfare. I remember admiring the black and white images on her studio wall when we first met, as well as her meticulous scrapbooks filled with photographs and drawings, her writings and poems, pressed flowers and feathers adorning every page in a celebration of life. Angie loves to sit quietly 'in the zone' rather than becoming caught up in the more competitive side of wildlife photography that can seem more like hunting for trophies than the pursuit of art, appealing to the macho instincts that often drive men in these circumstances. Her winning photograph of elephants and a grey heron reflected in the Luangwa River in Zambia combines all the elements that define her work – more painting than photograph. One of the judges said, 'There is something so serene about this picture – and so unusual. It's partly that the elephants are obliviously relaxed, but also that they are perfectly composed and almost perfectly still – hardly a ripple in the water.'

We had travelled to the South Luangwa National Park to photograph leopards – it is one of the best locations in the world to see them. But on this occasion we struggled to find one. Seizing the moment, we realised that there were some wonderful images to be had down at the river each morning, waiting for the elephants to come to drink and cross. I was convinced that the perfect shot was at water level, but Angie was having none of it, telling me to 'hush'. She set up her tripod and favourite 500mm Canon telephoto, added a polariser to enhance the richness of the colours and many hours later captured the shot that she had visualised. The grey heron added that extra element – the luck that you earn by being patient and prepared. There were nearly 20,000 entries the year Angie won – double the number there were when I had won the same award fifteen years earlier.

Angie's success made us the only couple ever to win the top prize as individuals, and that same year our son David (who had already won a prize in a special category of the junior competition) was runner-up for the second time in the juniors with his image of a fur seal pup being mobbed by king penguins on South Georgia. His photograph was featured on the back of the 2002 book of winning entries, with Angie's elephants on the front. Proud wasn't the word for it, though the irony is that, due to my appearances on television, people tend to think of me as the photographer. In fact the majority of our most lyrical and imaginative images are taken by Angie.

There were some wild times filming *Big Cat*. Vehicles rolled, tents were flattened in storms or, worse still, blown into the Mara River, contents and all. One morning an ancient African greenheart crashed on to a tent, fortunately when nobody was asleep inside. Meanwhile it was the hippos, buffaloes and elephants rather than the big cats that were most likely to provide us with scary moments. The lions and leopards were rarely seen as they padded quietly along the footpaths in front of our tents at night. But with the bunch of testosterone-fuelled youngsters that made up most of the *Big Cat* team, on the adventure of a lifetime in the African bush, anything was possible, particularly in the early days when everyone camped in the bush for ten glorious weeks along the banks of the Mara River. Forget online dating. A number of long-term relationships were incubated and sustained, together with some very brief ones.

The fancy-dress parties each Saturday night allowed people to let off steam and were carefully choreographed by our irrepressible production manager, Mandy Knight. Word would go out over the vehicle radio network, dubbed 'Kit Cat Radio', announcing this week's theme. Someone in each vehicle would keep their eye on what the cats were doing while the rest of the crew prepared their outfits from picnic boxes (and sometimes the contents), bunches of red oat grass, acacia pods and whatever else came to hand. Simon's usually involved stripping to the waist to show off a chiselled six-pack or ended with him shinning up a tree Tarzan-style to impress the locals. Others took the opposite tack and covered themselves from head to foot in gaffer tape, mimicking an accident victim swaddled in bandages, or in my case donning a pair of Angie's stunning leopard-skin tights topped off with a pink Miss Piggy wig. Enough!

Filming was relentless, which was how I loved it. When days off became mandatory (as did a four-day mid-shoot break), I viewed them as an opportunity to head back out on safari with Angie,

who worked as one of our ace animal spotters and the stills photographer for the series. It brought home to me how much being in the field had become my life. It made me feel so alive, I just could not get enough of it. It was never a job. But the pressure was on all of us to deliver. Each time the series was re-commissioned the budget was cut by ten per cent and so was the time in the field. Eventually we were producing five half-hour programmes in a month. (By comparison, the BBC are currently working with the Marsh Pride as the stars of one of three fifty-minute programmes for a new series called *Dynasty*, filmed over the course of a year and a half!)

Big Cat Diary combined all the elements of wildlife programme making that I cherish. It was honest, informative and told its stories with passion and enthusiasm. Most rewarding of all, it helped promote Kenya and the Mara as a safari destination like no other to millions of people around the world. Visitors would stop to tell us that *Big Cat* was the reason they were here to witness it for themselves – they still do.

The key to the show's phenomenal success was the strong big cat characters. Though we had names for most of our featured animals, these were never meant to humanise them – simply to make it easier to identify them and communicate with our guides as to their whereabouts. It certainly helped our viewers to connect strongly with the individual cats, something that is at the heart of our own work. Nonetheless we avoided anthropomorphism as much as possible: animals are not surrogate humans, even though we probably know the intimate details of the lives of some of the big cats better than we do those of many of our human friends. We love their essence, a reality that is so obviously different from being human. The thrill of discovering what is happening in their world is what still, after all these years, keeps Angie and me wanting to set out early each morning. Their story has no ending.

So what was our relationship with the big cats? It would be impossible not to feel a very visceral connection when spending long periods of time in the company of creatures such as Kike and Half-Tail. Angie always remembers the day I left her watching over Half-Tail as the leopard enjoyed a catnap in one of her favourite trees along Fig Tree Ridge. I had to head back to camp for a few hours and wanted to be sure I could still find Half-Tail on my return. Later in the afternoon I arrived back to find Angie sitting at exactly the same spot, but with no sign of our star. As I gesticulated with more than a hint of irritation to ask what had happened, Angie smiled, put her finger up to her lips and pointed beneath the open film door of her vehicle. There, sound asleep and as good as gold was our leopard, curled up in the shade cast by the door. At one point Half-Tail looked up at Angie with those liquid golden eyes tinged with green. There was no sign of fear or alarm – just an acknowledgement, perhaps, that all was well in her world. We lived for those moments.

The emotional bond Angie felt with Half-Tail was evident the time we witnessed a young adult male leopard hunting down and killing her month-old cubs, born in Leopard Gorge in October 1997. We were filming with *Wild Things* at the time and television being what it is the cameraman immediately focused on Angie's response to the sight of the young male emerging from the cave with a tiny cub, bloodied and lifeless, hanging from his jaws. Angie's tearful face needed no words to communicate her feelings and we resisted the producer's cajoling for her to say something. Later that morning Half-Tail returned to the Gorge and we watched her defend herself bravely when the male treed her, forcing him to back up and tumble six metres to the ground. She was wide eyed and salivating profusely with the stress of what had happened, searching and calling in vain for her cubs. How could we not be greatly moved by her distress?

However, life and death moments such as these are such an integral part of day-to-day existence on the African savanna that I generally felt very in control of my emotions when confronted by the harshness of nature. I may be an extrovert and a chatterbox, but it went against my instincts to respond on camera in an overly emotional way. I believe deeply that humans should not interfere, that nature's way is best in managing the scheme of things in wilderness areas. Not so television, which thrives on emotion – the endless demand to know 'How did you feel?' We were encouraged by our producers to respond in the way that our audience would expect – to empathise openly so people could sense our concern. On one occasion my producer wanted me to show more sentiment when Kike's three newly independent cubs were mobbed by a troop of baboons. Situations involving relatively inexperienced young adult cats and aggressive adversaries can lead to injury. But on this occasion I felt confident that our cheetahs were in no real danger and refused to over-react simply to please the camera and give an impression of jeopardy I didn't believe existed.

Jeopardy was a word that we would hear a lot of as *Big Cat* grew ever more popular, allied to the fact that since the genesis of *Big Cat Week* in 2003 we were back on BBC1, with its greater emphasis on entertainment. In England there were meetings with producers of the BBC's most popular human soap operas to explore the formula that ensured these shows held the loyalty of their audiences year after year. Three strong characters (a lion, a leopard and a cheetah) would give enough variety to the narrative; add a powerful opening to grab the audience's attention, inject just the right amount of 'jeopardy' and end with a cliff-hanger, leaving viewers panting in anticipation of what might happen next episode. We were told that our commentary should reflect this approach – instead of clans of hyenas, how about 'gangs' of hyenas; for battles, why not 'wars?'

But we all resisted that temptation and as one of our senior executives visiting from the UK said, 'There is absolutely no reason to dumb down the programmes in that kind of way.' Similarly, when my producer asked if I minded the editors using a different end piece to a segment featuring the young cheetah named Duma, I refused. Ever since Duma's mother Shakira had abandoned her (as cheetah mothers do) to negotiate the uncertain path to full independence, we had watched day after day as the youngster tried and failed to make her first kill. It was a fascinating transition to witness, as Duma constantly stopped to call for her mother as she wandered in search of prey. Late one evening, when it was almost too dark to film, Duma finally managed to chase down and kill a young Thomson's gazelle. It was a dramatic moment despite the poor quality of the image, so to my way of thinking using a previous hunting attempt of Duma's shot in good light to cut with the final moments of the real chase was out of the question. We prided ourselves on the legitimacy of the series. This was a slippery slope that I had trodden before with *Wild Kingdom* and one I had no intention of embarking on again.

At one point I felt my role as a presenter on *Big Cat Diary* might be threatened by the pressure to discover new 'talent' and keep the programmes fresh; I was mindful of the damning *Daily Telegraph* review of my presenting on *Dawn to Dusk*. Fortunately *Big Cat Week* proved a turning point for me and the greater informality worked to my advantage. With it came the chance to work on a number of other 'diaries', including narrating *Chimpanzee Diaries*, and co-presenting two series of *Elephant Diaries* in Kenya and *Big Bear Diary* in North America.

Big Bear Diary offered a very different kind of adventure to watching big cats from a vehicle. Tracking coastal brown bears in Katmai National Park in Alaska meant working on foot with a small team. Our producer Adam Chapman contacted me before we left for the first shoot and cautioned me that 'on the recce one of the planes heading out of camp was carrying too much weight and dipped a wing in the sea as they took off from the beach and landed in the drink. Flying can be a bit hairy; pilots cannot use instruments, so visibility has to be good. Expect to get weathered in on every trip.' Adam was certainly right about that – we got 'weathered in' on all three shoots.

His second warning was that we would be filming at Hallo Bay Bear Viewing Camp, just a few kilometres from where American bear enthusiast Timothy Treadwell and his girlfriend had been attacked and eaten by bears less than two years earlier. It was the end of the summer when the deadly attack took place, the toughest time for bears as they struggle to put on every last kilo of fat before burying themselves in their winter den. When Treadwell went outside to investigate the noise of a bear close to camp, the sound of the ensuing attack was unwittingly recorded on a video camera inside the tent. The tape ran for six minutes as first Treadwell and then his girlfriend fought for their lives. If a bear ever thinks of you as food, it does not have a specialised killing bite to incapacitate you first in the manner of a lion or leopard – it just starts eating you.

The darkly brooding film producer Werner Herzog crafted a remarkable and chilling documentary called *Grizzly Man* on Treadwell's life with the bears of Katmai. It describes one man's obsession with a creature that can stand 1.5 metres at the shoulder, weigh up to 680 kilograms and tower 3 metres tall on its hind feet, rivalling the polar bear as the largest land-based predator. At one point in Herzog's film there is ground-zero footage shot by Treadwell of two giant male bears standing and tearing up the soil as they grapple for ascendancy, trading skull-crushing blows and savage bites – a chilling glimpse of what a defenceless man might be up against. On another occasion there are images of Treadwell reaching out to a bear and almost getting bitten. The bravado verges on madness. Treadwell broke all the conventions. He camped close to bear trails, stashed food in his tent at times rather than securing it out of reach and got too close to bears in his attempts to befriend them or call their bluff. Increasingly he found dealing with ordinary life far more taxing than living with bears – the bears asked nothing of him; people held him to account.

Treadwell was bipolar and for a while took medication to try to stabilise his mood swings. But eventually he stopped taking the pills – they helped temper the lows, but what was life without the highs? I could empathise with this – it was part of what drove me, too. The bears gave Treadwell a purpose in life; he believed he was saving them from hunters and poachers, even if that was true only in his imagination.He loved to communicate his passion for bears to young people and savoured the attention he received from the media, though many people questioned his behaviour and were concerned for his safety long before his death. Watching Herzog's film, subtitled *One Man's Descent into Madness*,

I was constantly reminded that we should never mistake the benign tolerance of wild creatures to our presence for any form of friendship. While I love the adrenaline-fuelled rush of living close to the edge, I have never felt the need to make physical contact with wild animals – to pet them, love them or hug them, to view them as surrogate humans.

In September 2006, during filming of the fourth series of *Big Cat Week*, news filtered through to the Mara of the tragic death of Steve Irwin, the Australian 'crocodile hunter', who had been pierced in the chest by a stingray barb while filming an underwater documentary entitled *Ocean's Deadliest*. I remembered watching with fascination when Irwin first appeared on television in 1996, the same year *Big Cat Diary* hit the small screen. I had never seen anything quite like it; it may not have been David Attenborough, but who could fail to be impressed by his original brand of enthusiasm and love of wild creatures? Watching him reminded me of the pressure we all felt at times to satisfy the demand for ever more drama and jeopardy. The challenge is to find the means of exploring the natural world in ways that retain our sense of awe and wonder without putting either animals or humans at risk.

The American naturalist Henry Beston expressed these sentiments to perfection when he said:

> We need another and a wiser and perhaps a more mystical concept of animals. In a world older and more complete than ours they move finished and complete, gifted with extensions of the senses we have lost or never attained, living by voices we shall never hear. They are not brethren, they are not underlings; they are other nations, caught with ourselves in the net of life and time, fellow prisoners of the splendour and travail of the earth.

Two of the best-loved animals over twelve years of *Big Cat Diary* were a three-month-old lion cub from the Ridge Pride called Solo and a cheetah cub named Toto. As the only surviving cubs in their respective litters they were perfect *Big Cat* characters, given how easy they were for our audience to identify. The fact that both cubs were so small and vulnerable added a real sense of poignancy to their story – just them and their mothers against the rest of the animal world. I wasn't at all convinced they would survive the course of filming, so was delighted when we were able to locate Solo again two years later and witness his transformation into a tough, brawny adolescent lion. Our audience loved that kind of continuity and, because the Mara is our second home, Angie and I were able to continue to follow our stories when the time came for the camera crews and production unit to head home to England.

Toto achieved fame on a totally different scale, capturing the hearts of audiences around the world with his never-say-die spirit. He accompanied his mother Honey – another *Big Cat* favourite – as she navigated every obstacle along Rhino Ridge and among the rolling grasslands on Paradise Plain, where the lions and hyenas were a constant threat. Nature could not have written a more enthralling script. With their distinctive black tear marks and the long mantle of grey hair running from the nape of their neck to the root of their tail, nothing in the animal kingdom comes close to a cheetah cub for cuteness and there were endless captivating moments with Honey and Toto playing and grooming. When mother and cub ran into a troop of baboons there was real jeopardy and it made for one of the most memorable moments of *Big Cat Week* 2005.

We were a month into our story with filming drawing to a close when two large male baboons stalked across the grasslands towards Toto, prompting him to race for cover on the open plains. At first

Honey tried to distract them by striding purposefully towards them, her head held low in a threatening manner. But baboons are crafty primates with highly developed colour vision that can pick a spotted cat out from its surroundings: they had no doubt experienced similar scenarios with leopard or cheetah mothers trying to keep cubs out of harm's way. I was not only witnessing a rarely recorded piece of natural history, but I knew it would inject just the kind of drama that television thrives on. One part of me was the observer, quietly watching as the story played out. But my television brain was demanding more. Our producers would be expecting plenty of emotion on my part to validate the concern that we had fostered for little Toto with our audience. I couldn't just sit and watch. I had to say something.

The heart of the matter was addressed as we waited for the situation to resolve itself: Toby Strong, the cameraman tasked with filming me, said, 'Jonny, tell me you're not going to stand by and let little Toto get killed by those baboons?' When I said that was exactly what we would have to do he was outraged, asking me to radio our wildlife cameraman for his thoughts on the matter. When he responded that his job was to film what happened, not to interfere, Toby was shocked at our seeming lack of compassion for Toto's plight. But it had nothing to do with what our hearts might be telling us. We were not there to play God. If we started to do that, where would it stop? Predators by their very nature have to hunt to kill, while baboons react aggressively to a possible threat from predators out of self-interest, forcing them to move on (killing the young of their adversaries helps to keep numbers in check and baboons are known to kill cheetah and leopard cubs on occasion). Are we going to rid our wild places of crocodiles, hyenas, wild dogs and vultures because some people believe them to be distasteful in their habits, rather than viewing them as a natural part of life on the African savanna?

In the end Toto came to no harm and I showed appropriate concern for his plight. That night I lay in bed and thought about my feelings, admitting to myself that compassion is part of what makes us human – there is no need to stifle the inclination to empathise with the plight and possible suffering of other life just because the rules say you cannot interfere. I certainly agree with putting a badly injured animal out of its misery or at least reporting the situation to the Reserve authorities. Wild as the Mara might appear, it is under management and tourism pays a large part of the bill. Consequently the authorities are more likely to intervene when a charismatic lion or cheetah is injured, acknowledging visitors' sentiments. But where possible we should all leave well alone.

Just days before we finished filming, Honey and Toto disappeared. When Honey emerged again there was no sign of Toto and I could only imagine that lions or hyenas had ambushed and killed him.

I felt that we needed to state the obvious and tell our audience that Toto was dead, but in the BBC's desire not to upset people I was asked to soften my approach. 'We'll never know what happened,' I commented, 'but the odds were always stacked against him. It's harsh out there and these are real-life dramas. Inevitably for some of our cats there just can't be a happy ending.' For months – years even – I continued to receive letters asking what had happened to Toto, was he still alive, could people come and help look for him?

The reason that *Big Cat* was loved by millions of viewers around the world was that people became engrossed with the lives of our big cat characters – just as Angie and I have always been. This was all too evident the day the ticket collector at Marylebone Underground Station in London asked me how Half-Tail was doing, years after she had been killed in a wire snare set by herdsmen in retaliation for her taking livestock from one of their thornbush bomas. When I told him of her demise it is no exaggeration to say that he was devastated. There is something both humbling and uplifting in witnessing this deep connection to our animal companions. But if you ever wanted a character to inspire the spirit of survival, to show how precious life is and encourage you to cherish every moment, then Toto embodied that. Of all the cubs we have watched Toto was the one that stole our hearts, even as the memory of Half-Tail and Zawadi endures.

People often ask us if big cats such as Half-Tail and her daughter Zawadi, whom we followed for much of their long lives, recognised us. While some of the big cats undoubtedly became habituated to our vehicles, those same vehicles acted as a mobile hide, masking our human form. What was very apparent was how relaxed some of the cats became around vehicles that treated them with respect – just as Chui had done all those years ago with Dark and Light.

I imagined that, to them, observer and vehicle became one. But whether the leopards sensed my human aura and responded to it in a positive manner I do not know. This is not to say that leopards – and lions and cheetahs – are not capable of recognising individual people or bonding with them. In captivity big cats develop strong attachments to their owners or handlers that one can only describe as 'emotional'. Look at the relationship that George and Joy Adamson forged with the wild-born lioness Elsa. But we must never forget that wild lions and leopards live by their own rules and speak a very different language from our own. And therein lies the fascination and the sense of wonder.

CHAPTER

11

THE NATURE
OF
LIFE

By the vanity of the same
imagination he equals himself
to God, attributes to himself divine
faculties, and withdraws
and separates himself from
all other creatures.

———————————————

Michel de Montaigne
THE DEFENCE OF RAYMOND SEBOND

A way from Africa, life with Angie led me on a spiritual journey to rival the wonder of the natural world. My visual horizon had long been whatever lay directly in front of my face, until she made me aware of the glory of the star-filled sky (an alien place that taxed my imagination) and our planet's place in the cosmos. She opened my eyes too to the wonder of the oceans, with visits to Zanzibar and Kiwayu on the shores of the Indian Ocean, and more recently to the Red Sea in Egypt, where she was born. Here the extensive coral heads and brightly coloured fishes are things of splendour, though rivalled by the stunning whiteness of a windswept beach in Myanmar that we visited with David in 2015 and that made us feel like Robinson Crusoe washed up on a desert island.

India and its magnificent tigers and temples have continued to enthral us ever since we first filmed there in the late 1990s – as has Nepal. While I was filming *Elephant Diaries* Angie sat spellbound listening to His Holiness the Dalai Lama on his visit to Scotland. And twice we have made pilgrimages to the mountain kingdom of Bhutan – the Land of the Thunder Dragon – taking particular pleasure in exploring the stunning temple fortresses known as *dzongs* and talking with the monks and lamas during the annual Paro Festival celebrating the life and work of Lord Buddha.

Just 300 kilometres in length and barely 150 kilometres in breadth, Bhutan may be small, but what other nation measures the wealth of its people in 'happiness' rather than Gross Domestic Product? With a population of just 750,000 people it is the perfect place to reflect on life in the fast lane; the chance to step back in time and reorder one's priorities away from the industrialised world. In 2010 barely 27,000 people visited Bhutan. That's less than the number who journeyed to the icy wastes of Antarctica, and just a fraction of the 300,000 who make a safari to the Maasai Mara in search of big cats each year.

Enthralled as I was by the colour and spectacle of the Paro Festival, Bhutan reminded me of how intrusive photography can be – how getting the shot can rob the moment of meaning. I was everywhere that day, deep among the throng of Bhutanese villagers or crouched at floor level amidst the ranks of dancers and monks, capturing an endless procession of fractured images from the whole. At one point I greeted the lama who had spoken to us at our lodge the previous evening, chuckling to himself at the irony of the English saying 'ignorance is bliss' when 'enlightenment' is the ultimate goal to a Buddhist. I was bursting with excitement at what I had been seeing through my lens. Sensing my somewhat manic euphoria, the lama stopped me in my tracks with his words:

> The festival is not meant as entertainment. This not 'show time'. It is a celebration enacted through the power of song and dance to speak to us of the fears and joys each of us experiences in life. If you do not take time to sit and be present to what is happening here, then you will have lost all sense of meaning inherent in the moment. Your photographs may please the eye, but they won't nourish your inner being. Go and sit with Angela. She understands.

A few years later, while visiting a Zen Master at a monastery in Japan, I felt similarly humbled and enlightened when with radiant face the monk tasked me to look at the world without language, to strip my thoughts clean of words and preconceptions, to look through different eyes at the miracle of our planet, to enlarge my sense of reality.

Yet Africa is in our blood, the thought of the Marsh Pride and the leopards of Leopard Gorge never far away, always drawing us back home to Kenya. In 2009 I narrated *The Secret Leopards* for the BBC/Animal Planet, documenting with footage culled from

Big Cat Diary and locations around the world the life of the most adaptable big cat of all, a cat that even when wild habitat becomes scarce and denuded of prey subsists close to man. There were stories of leopards living in the outskirts of towns, described as the new 'urban fox' – but larger and potentially far more dangerous. Leopards are smart, though; they know to keep to the shadows when people are around, particularly during the daytime. In one instance leopards were discovered resting up in underground sewers in Mumbai, emerging at night to snatch domestic dogs and cats, pigs, goats and poultry. They even sometimes target children, as happened when a rabies epidemic killed off many of the dogs; adults, too, on occasion. However tragic this may be in human terms, it is evidence of the leopard's opportunism and ability to survive.

While the leopard is still locally common in parts of sub-Saharan Africa and tropical Asia, numbering in the hundreds of thousands worldwide, the African lion is in serious trouble. In 2010 I was asked by the BBC to present a two-part series called *The Truth about Lions*, with the Marsh Pride as the main characters. The story would set out to reveal why lions live in groups – the only one of the thirty-six members of the cat family to do so (male cheetahs form groups too, but females do not) – while highlighting the threats to wild lions across Africa. At last I would have an opportunity to discuss the issues. Conservation was a no-go area on *Big Cat Diary*, given that talking about the demise of the natural world was considered depressing and a turn-off. Of course it was – it certainly wasn't meant to be entertaining.

The science for *The Truth about Lions* was provided by Professor Craig Packer of the Serengeti Lion Research Project, which dates back to the 1960s and the pioneering work of Dr George Schaller, who went on to work with governments to protect huge tracts of wild land in Asia and in particular the Tibetan

Plateau, home to snow leopards, rare gazelles and wild goats. Packer, who had studied primates under Jane Goodall at Gombe, arrived in the Serengeti in 1978 believing that he could answer the question as to why lions became social in a couple of years of intense field work. Thirty years later he and his students announced that they had the answer.

One reason it took so long was that lions spend up to twenty hours a day doing very little, preferably resting up in the nearest cover. It is not that they are lazy, just that they are big and powerful and must conserve their energy for the explosive burst of power and pace that will ensure a meal rich in protein. Once they have gorged themselves they can rest again – unlike herbivores, whose vegetable diet, with only a tenth of the nutritional value of meat, means that they must spend the majority of their time feeding. Packer made me chuckle when he said that the word 'lion' should be added to the Periodic Table of inert gases!

By following the Marsh Pride for so many years, Angie and I have been able to gain insights into their behaviour and compare our findings with those of the scientists. We have observed that pride males are not always related; that making friends with a

non-relative may enable a lone nomad to take over a pride and breed, something he would find almost impossible to do alone in prime lion habitat like the Mara-Serengeti. We have seen how incoming male lions kill any small cubs sired by the previous coalition of pride males that they have chased away, sometimes after fierce battles that can leave one or more males dead. Infanticide is well documented in many species of cats – though not cheetahs, who live such itinerant lives it would be difficult for males to know exactly whose cubs they had fathered. It is a natural response from a new male – or males in the case of lions – on claiming a territory: without dependent cubs the females come back into oestrus and are more likely to mate with the incoming males.

We know that lion cubs of a similar age are raised in a crèche and that lionesses will join forces to attack any new males who threaten their young – or run and hide with them if they are large enough to escape. Was this then the reason for lions to live in groups? Or did it simply make it easier to gain a meal? After all, lions acting together can pull down an animal the size of a buffalo that can feed the whole pride. Perhaps it was a combination of these factors?

Apparently not. In the end Packer and his co-workers found that owning the best real estate was what drove lion society to evolve. The largest prides control the best territories, ones with access to shade, water and secure hiding places in which to raise their cubs. Even better if the territory includes a river confluence to funnel prey towards ambush sites. Unfortunately humans covet the same things.

Gone are the days when lions were the most widespread large land mammal on earth after humans. They have vanished from ninety per cent of their historic range and loss of habitat has also lost them their natural prey, bringing them into increased conflict with livestock owners. Meat poaching has also taken its toll, with lions and other predators sometimes caught up in wire snares. A hundred years ago there were perhaps 200,000 wild lions roaming free in Africa. Today there are barely 20,000. The situation is desperate enough to prompt conservationists to swallow an unpalatable truth: that allowing strictly controlled trophy hunting in buffer zones and game-management areas bordering parks and reserves – areas that are unsuitable for photographic tourism – can generate sufficient income for local communities to tolerate predators. Personally, I find killing animals for pleasure under any circumstances anathema and far removed from the ethos of the Bushmen or Native Americans, traditional hunters who revered the animals they killed for food; in the latter case the wolf, the bear and the eagle were powerful totems, incarnate as part of the spirit world. The relationship between hunter and hunted was sacred, nurtured by the hunter's respect for the natural world as sustenance for body and soul. To abuse it risked life itself. That kind of wisdom has long since been abandoned by our leaders.

As a case in point, in 2015 Craig Packer's research permit was cancelled and he was banned from entering Tanzania. He explained:

> I became increasingly concerned about the effects that human pressures were having on [the lions'] conservation: unvaccinated domesticated dogs were spreading distemper into the Serengeti, local people were killing lions in retaliation for eating livestock and loved ones, and trophy hunters were over-harvesting lions in the game reserves. We could work with veterinary agencies to vaccinate dogs and local people to reduce conflicts with rogue lions, but the hunting companies controlled most of the lion habitat and they were failing to conserve the lions.

Their failure largely stemmed from the corruption in the system. I tried to reform the Tanzanian hunting industry, but the forces of corruption were too powerful to defeat. I knew I was risking my research activities, but I felt compelled to try to make a difference. Lions are in such trouble that their conservation is more urgent than extending my research another few years... I felt it was more important to tell the truth about how corrupt the wildlife sector in Tanzania has become. And how a few people with good connections are operating like strip miners, skimming off the remaining wildlife instead of helping to protect it.

At the heart of Marsh Pride territory is the place known as Bila Shaka, meaning 'without fail', recognised by drivers and guides from Governors' Camp as the best place to look for the lions. Bila Shaka was always the traditional birthplace for the pride, a seasonal drainage line marked out from the surrounding plains by patches of woodland, croton thickets and acacia bushes. No longer. Elephants, fire and the passage of safari wagons opening up the thickets – and Maasai cutting down the thornbush for their cattle bomas and firewood – have denuded the area of much of its cover, shrinking the lions' territory and forcing them to seek shelter further to the south and west.

Added to this are the changes in the landscape brought about by the proliferation of camps and lodges in and around the Reserve, plus the impact of cattle grazing inside it, the biggest threat to the lions right now. In recent years cattle have been encroaching into the Reserve on a nightly basis, when visitors are safely back in camp but lions are most active. To the east around Talek Gate hyena researchers estimate as many as 20,000 cattle are driven into a seventy-square-kilometre area within the Reserve each day/night, their tracks visible from outer space as deep scars on a landscape increasingly grazed bare. Given that the Reserve is 1,510 square kilometres in area, it is possible that up to 100,000 cattle are dependent on grazing within the Reserve, eating the grass which also sustains the wild herbivores, and physically displacing both predators and prey. Every year we lose lions in retaliation for the killing of livestock, at times indiscriminately – it isn't necessarily the perpetrators who pay the penalty. Many of those who have died at the end of a spear or been poisoned earned world-wide recognition as much loved characters of *Big Cat Diary*: Scruffy, Kali, Red, White-Eye, Lispy and Clawed, to name but a few.

Little wonder, then, that estimates for lion numbers within the Reserve have dropped by around thirty per cent since Joseph Ogutu studied them here in the early 1990s, though the accuracy of his counting methods has been disputed. Gone are the large prides of thirty to forty lions: during Ogutu's study one pride near the Talek Gate numbered forty-eight. And it is not just the lions. Major declines have been recorded in other species such as giraffe, impalas, buffaloes, topi, waterbuck and warthogs.

Talk of wildlife in terms of ancient works of art to be saved at all costs, however worthy, is not going to suffice, nor are national parks run as military fortresses. Like it or not, wildlife today has to pay for its own upkeep, while conservation policies have to help communities living alongside wildlife to meet their own development needs as well as appreciating the heritage value of wild land. In this regard tourism can be hugely beneficial to conserving wildlife and fostering respect for wild creatures. How best to manage it is a question that

Kenya and the Mara are still grappling with: it is estimated that there are upwards of two hundred camps and lodges in and around the Reserve, with perhaps 7,000 beds. Where will it end?

Over-familiarity with tourists can be bad for the wildlife too. As I know only too well, cheetahs jumping on vehicles gained wide coverage in the *Big Cat Diary* years, when Amber and Kike became known to millions of people across the world due to their car-climbing antics and their relaxed and trusting dispositions. At the time we felt privileged to experience such close encounters with wild cheetahs, but were always extremely careful not to take advantage of it – we never touched the cheetahs or let them get into our vehicles.

Times have changed, though, with too many visitors now encouraging cheetahs to come close enough for them to appear in selfies, or cubs to climb into open vehicles and stand on their laps. To safeguard the interests of both cheetahs and visitors, the Reserve authorities are doing everything possible to discourage the practice of jumping on vehicles. The official advice if you see a cheetah approaching your car is to drive away slowly, keeping a careful eye out for any cubs that may be nearby.

Thinking about these issues made me realise that I had reached another crossroads. It was no longer sufficient to indulge my love of wildlife by studying the lives of Africa's big cats. I increasingly felt the need to speak out about it. It wasn't events such as the death of Half-Tail, who was killed by pastoralists for raiding their livestock, that helped prompt this transition. I understood that kind of retribution, having lived on a farm where foxes were considered vermin when they ran amok in the chicken run – regardless of how beautiful and fascinating I might find them. Nor was it the death of Honey the cheetah in a botched veterinary intervention, when she was left out in the sun rather than being pulled into the shade and cooled down with a wet wrap after being immobilised. No. It was when I heard of the plan to build a lodge along Fig Tree Ridge, home to Half-Tail and Zawadi in the 1990s, the same place where Chui had raised Dark and Light in 1983 – prime leopard country. I knew I had to raise my voice on behalf of wildlife and the future of the Mara, regardless of the consequences. I appeared as a defence witness for the leopards when the matter ended up in court. The development was stopped – for the moment at least.

Sadly there is no such thing as constructive criticism, and speaking out is frowned on – as witnessed by Craig Packer's story. When conservationists objected to a proposal for yet another lodge, this one within the Reserve in a sensitive area favoured by rhino mothers with young calves, it soon became evident that there were powerful forces arrayed against the voices of reason and a forty-four-bed luxury tented camp was sanctioned. And when I wrote an article in *Swara* about the impact of the closure of Tanzania's border with Kenya on tourism to the Serengeti and the subsequent escalation in poaching, with no other intention than to show the importance of tourism in financing conservation in both countries, the Warden of the Serengeti Justin Hando wrote to the editor to say, 'The authors of the article were either intentionally interested in creating a wrong image of the Serengeti or used your magazine to achieve hidden motives.'

Nothing could have been further from the truth – and we were able to prove it. A friend in the Wildlife Department in Tanzania who understood the politics of this kind of situation told me that someone higher up would no doubt have told the Warden to refute our comments, a knee-jerk reaction to defend the good name of the country and its policies when they were not the issue.

The reality is that most protected areas are compromised, whether by the illegal grazing of livestock, cutting down of trees for firewood or charcoal, grass being cut for thatching or cattle fodder, wild animals killed for bush meat, ivory or rhino horn. The sanctity of national parks and game reserves is a myth. Lines drawn on a map during colonial times only exist on paper. Come election time people's priorities are jobs, security, education and health care. Conservation is a sideshow and one that can cost a politician his or her job.

That is exactly what happened to former Prime Minister Raila Odinga here in Kenya when, in July 2008, he issued an eviction order for the removal of people who had settled within the Mau Forest, Kenya's largest remaining stretch of indigenous montane forest and most important water-catchment area. The Mau Escarpment is the headwaters of four major rivers, including the Mara, that feed Lake Victoria, Lake Nakuru and Lake Natron. Preserving this area should be a priority for anyone taking a long-term view of the country's future. The forest has been exploited for years, with huge areas felled illegally to feed the charcoal industry and to settle the landless – and to profit the Big Men.

The eviction was opposed by prominent Rift Valley politicians whose constituents had been the beneficiaries, and used to undercut Odinga's popularity with the masses. He failed in his bid for the presidency in 2007 and again in 2012. Reforestation and resettlement are under way once more, but the Mau is a shadow of its former glory, with serious concerns over the dramatic fall in the volume of water flowing through the Mara.

Conservation is nothing without the power to implement policies. All the emotive calls to action, the warnings that time is running out, that the wild animals are being slaughtered and the taps are running dry will continue to fall on deaf ears. We need leaders with a long-term planetary vision twinned with the ability to invest in meaningful change to ensure wise husbandry of the natural world – and not just in Africa. As Jane Goodall points out in her latest book, *Seeds of Hope*, 'In many of America's great national parks, mining and petroleum companies have been permitted to carry out their destructive operations.' And with global warming making the Arctic Ocean ever more ice free it is rapidly becoming the focus of an unseemly scramble, with political heavyweights such as Russia, China and the United States all eager to lay claim to the riches that it promises in the form of massive oil and gas reserves. But at what price to the environment?

In England, the land of my birth, pressure groups constantly have to remind the government that environmental issues are vital to people's wellbeing, that the food and water we depend on are a gift of nature, that we are wholly dependent on its largesse. In his book *Collapse*, the scientist Jared Diamond is all too persuasive about how we cling to our cultural imperatives, even when the need to embrace change and adapt to a new reality is staring us in the face – when it is abundantly clear that doing things the same old way is no longer working. Former US Vice President Al Gore was certainly right when he labelled global warming an 'inconvenient truth' – though it is telling that his voice had the greatest impact after he abandoned politics. Surely the debate over climate change is irrelevant when it is so obvious that we need to reduce pollution, rampant waste and excessive consumption. The old system of economics leaks like a sieve. It fails to identify and quantify all the infinite variables that make up the subtleties of the environment we depend on: the unforeseen and unaccounted-for costs of overly exploiting the natural world. The missing link is the one that enables workable conservation imperatives to be embraced and implemented by the political elite.

Money is not the issue. The truth of the matter is that the environment is still viewed as low priority by many world leaders and the majority of the population; as George Schaller commented, America spends $10 billion a year on the environment – and $3 billion a week in Iraq. The money is there. What is missing is the willingness – or ability – to act.

In Kenya and Tanzania we need more people like Dr Bernhard Grzimek of *Serengeti Shall Not Die* fame, people of vision who understand the need for solutions from within – for African voices to lead the way, encouraged and supported by friends and finance from the international community. Dr Grzimek had unique access to the first generation of post-independent African leaders such as Julius Nyerere of Tanzania, who cherished nature (and abhorred capitalism). For over forty years Grzimek was president of the Frankfurt Zoological Society, an organisation that continues to play an important role in supporting conservation projects in the Serengeti. Whenever foreign dignitaries visited Tanzania, Nyerere would make time to take them on safari to the country's famed national parks so that he could share the wonders of these places

with his guests. He understood their significance to Tanzania and the world, enshrining his beliefs in what became known as the Arusha Manifesto in 1961:

> The survival of our wildlife is a matter of grave concern to all of us in Africa. These wild creatures amid the wild places they inhabit are not only important as a source of wonder and inspiration, but are an integral part of our natural resources and our future livelihood and wellbeing.
>
> In accepting the trusteeship of our wildlife we solemnly declare that we will do everything in our power to make sure that our children's grand-children will be able to enjoy this rich and precious inheritance.

But is anything truly sacred? Fifty years after Nyerere spoke so powerfully and eloquently, the President of Tanzania, Jakaya Kikwete, gave his blessing to a plan to construct a paved highway across the Serengeti National Park, against the advice of conservationists around the world. With his eye on the electorate in western Tanzania, Kikwete maintained that the needs of his constituents must take precedence and that the environmental concerns were baseless – the meddling of outsiders. An alternative route running to the south was eventually agreed upon, though Richard Leakey believes that the 'Serengeti Highway' will eventually be built, and that when it is it should be an act of innovation and enterprise, an overhead skyway that will allow the animals to pass freely beneath it, and that the international community should be willing to contribute to the cost.

Nobody is sure who first said, 'It is better to light a candle than to curse the darkness' – some say it was Eleanor Roosevelt – but it is certainly a sentiment that I agree with. You cannot give up hope.

ABOVE A fish-eye view of a Maasai ceremony.

ABOVE Women singing at William ole Pere's village at Aitong. Angie gets down low to capture the shots she sees in her mind's eye.

ABOVE With William ole Pere and son David. I love this shot, a funky view taken with a Canon EF8–15mm fish-eye lens.

ABOVE At home in Nairobi. Packing Angie's Toyota for safari with the help of Slippers and our safari store manager Kioko.

ABOVE With daughter Alia…

ABOVE …and son David.

ABOVE Valley of the Dunes, Serra Cafema, Namibia.
My favourite photograph of Angie and me.

ABOVE With our grandson Michael Jonathan at home in Nairobi, 2014.

And the 2015 election of John Magufuli as the new President of Tanzania offers *real* hope. Magufuli was a surprise candidate. A trained chemist and government minister, he ran on an anti-corruption platform, having earned plaudits for his corruption-busting tactic of hiding in trucks and popping out at weigh stations to nail crooked police officers. Two months after he took office he sacked almost the entire top brass at the Tanzania Ports Authority. We await his thoughts on the Serengeti Highway.

Harold Hayes believed that human ingenuity would see us through, that we can never know what lies around the corner – for better or worse. But is that another example of the eternal optimism that enables the individual to embrace the uncertainties of life, to live with a sense of purpose and a future; that keeps us going until something changes our reality so dramatically that it stuns us into wakefulness? Or are we simply too clever for our own good?

What we do know is that there will be another two billion people on the planet by 2050. By that time Africa's population will have doubled to two billion and many of our wild places will have been submerged by this human tidal wave. The Mara-Serengeti is home to forty per cent of the world's large mammals, yet it represents barely 0.01 per cent of Africa's surface. That is how little space remains for wild creatures. Proof of this can be seen if you visualise the weight of the earth's land mammals as a single piece of A4 paper. Almost a third of the page will be taken up by humans, with virtually all the remaining two-thirds occupied by our livestock – cattle, sheep, goats, pigs and horses. Elephants – all 470,000 of them –

are symbolised by just four tiny squares. All the more shocking in the light of the Tanzanian government's announcement of the loss of 65,000 elephants between 2008 and 2013.

The hands of the clock are approaching midnight. It will soon be too late to remind ourselves that a window on to a patch of green – a single tree or fragment of garden – nourishes the human spirit, regardless of whether you have seen the wonder of a wild lion or not. Patients heal more quickly with a glimpse of Eden to nurture their soul than they do when looking on to a barren concrete jungle from a hospital bed. Reason enough to fight for every last green place, even as they slip between our fingers through wanton neglect, foolishness or greed. As George Schaller cautions, 'We don't have two planets, one to treasure and one to squander… We must make this a century of environmental enlightenment, one that expresses its loyalty to the earth with all its wonder and variety, the only home we shall ever have.'

To bring my story full circle and put things in perspective, there was a time when I longed to repeat the overland journey that first brought me to Africa in 1974, to discover for myself just how much things had changed, both for travellers and for the continent's last wild places. As I began to research such a trip it quickly became evident that I had been travelling during the golden age of overlanding. Things are far less rugged nowadays, with hard-top vehicles, seat belts and stopovers in hotels rather than camping throughout – and health and safety liable to spoil the party. Forty years ago Uganda and Chad were off-limits, while today parts of North, West and Central Africa are bedevilled by wars and terrorism, making travel there a risky venture. The Islamic terrorist group Boko Haram (whose name means 'Western education is forbidden') has come to be feared in northeastern Nigeria, not least since the abduction in 2014 of 276 schoolgirls whose fate remains uncertain. The group has followers in Chad, Niger and northern Cameroon, two of which we visited, and while we travelled safely through what is now the Democratic Republic of the Congo (DRC) today's political instability makes it a no-go zone for overlanders.

While I preferred to hang on to my memories, I was under no illusions about the battle that conservationists now have on their hands, and not only in Africa. The illegal trade in wildlife and wildlife products worldwide generates upwards of $10 billion a year and is ranked alongside the other major criminal enterprises of guns, drugs and people trafficking. It is a war that many feel cannot be won without massive support from the international community, as well as far greater commitment from governments with significant wildlife resources.

Just how difficult that will be can be witnessed by watching the Oscar-nominated documentary *Virunga*, set in Africa's oldest national park – established in what was then the Belgian Congo in 1925 as Albert National Park, now Virunga National Park and a UNESCO World Heritage Site. The film is a tale of courage, sacrifice and compassion arrayed against corruption, greed and brutality, a mix of hope and despair, of the greater good overcoming avarice and ignorance. The Virungas are the last stronghold of the mountain gorilla, a rugged mountain sanctuary shared by three countries that in the not so distant past were torn apart by civil war: Rwanda, Uganda and the DRC, where the fighting continues. From my 1970s trip I remember what was then known as Zaire (now the DRC) for its massive swathe of tropical rainforest, the barely passable roads and my first taste of malaria, which struck just as a handful of my fellow overlanders set out in search of mountain gorillas – that same population of gorillas that George Schaller first studied here in 1959 and that David Attenborough found so endearing during the filming of *Life On Earth* in the late '70s. His commentary reflected his reaction to that immensely touching meeting:

> There is more meaning and mutual understanding in exchanging a glance with a gorilla than with any other animal I know. Their sight, their hearing, their sense of smell are so similar to ours that they see the world in much the same way as we do... The male is an enormously powerful creature, but he only uses his strength when he is protecting his family and it is very rare that there is violence within the group. So it seems really very unfair that man should have chosen the gorilla to symbolise everything that is aggressive and violent, when that is the one thing that the gorilla is not – and that we are.

Virunga tells us everything we need to know about the mountain we must climb, in a story filled with characters displaying the whole range of human strengths and frailties. We meet André Bauma, the humble park ranger whose job is to care for sick or orphaned gorillas, victims of poachers and civil unrest, while his compatriots in the Parks Service daily risk their lives to try to hold back the tide of ivory poachers, the bushmeat trade and rebel militias – 130 rangers have lost their lives in the struggle. At the helm is Emmanuel de Merode, a Belgian prince married to Richard Leakey's daughter Louise. The backdrop is a stunning mix of why wild Africa continues to hold us in its thrall – the lush green landscape of the rainy season dotted with herds of elephants and buffaloes, zebras and antelopes;

rivers filled with hippos and crocodiles. Black and white photographs transport us back in time to another, less romantic reality – one that still casts its long shadow over current events. It is the world that Joseph Conrad's *Heart of Darkness* hints at, the infamous reign of King Leopold II of Belgium, founder and sole owner of what was ironically named Congo Free State.

This was an entity agreed to by the other colonial powers on condition that the administration 'improve the lives of the native inhabitants'. Instead, King Leopold imposed his will through a mercenary army called *Force Publique* that helped him plunder the Congo's riches – ivory and rubber – using forced labour to rape the land. He is said to have demanded a severed hand of a native in recompense for every bullet used to 'tame' them. One missionary was so shocked by what he witnessed during this period that he wrote to Leopold's chief agent in the Congo saying:

> I have just returned from a journey inland to the village of Insongo Mboyo. The abject misery and utter abandon is positively indescribable. I was so moved, Your Excellency, by the people's stories that I took the liberty of promising them that in future you will only kill them for crimes they commit.

King Leopold's regime lasted forty-four years (1865–1909) and was responsible for the deaths of up to ten million people.

Watching *Virunga*, we see the sleazy interface between the rival power brokers played out in seedy bars where government officials and big business try to work a system that is built on corruption and impunity. As the park becomes a battleground between the notorious M23 rebel militias and government troops, both sides are intent on securing a lucrative deal with the oil men, something worth killing for, with the prize sums of money beyond most people's comprehension. As the end credits roll we learn that Park Warden Rodrigo Mugaruka was abducted and tortured, apparently after trying to prevent employees of SOCO – the British-based international oil company seeking permission to 'explore' in the Virungas – from erecting a mobile-phone antenna in the park, and that Emmanuel de Merode was ambushed on his way back to ranger headquarters and left for dead in his vehicle, having been shot in stomach and legs – a shooting he survived a day before the film was released.

And SOCO? Hit with an online petition signed by over 700,000 people – from Sir Richard Branson (big business with a human face) to Archbishop Desmond Tutu (the voice of reason) and Sir David Attenborough (on behalf of the natural world) – SOCO have been forced on to the back foot, obliged to walk away while they still can, albeit with their reputation tarnished. The story reminds us that the power of the individual can be harnessed and magnified for the greater good, that we do all have a voice and each individual can make a difference. Or do we? There is now talk of the DRC excising part of Virunga National Park so that exploration for oil can continue.

Closer to home in Kenya, what has happened to the Maasai Mara can only be described as a travesty. It may not have a war zone as backdrop, but it is a sorry tale nonetheless. Time and again management plans have been drawn up at considerable cost to donors to try to put in place a sustainable framework that would accommodate the needs of tourism without overly compromising the environment – to create a sense of order. Little came of these initiatives. Instead the Reserve continued to be viewed as a cash cow by those who hold it in trust on behalf of the Maasai community. Vast sums of money were lost to corruption. The Maasai pastoralists whom I had come to know over the years shrugged their shoulders on finding themselves marginalised from the proceeds of tourism. 'What can we do?' they would say to me. 'We have no power, we are little people.'

With no plan and a lack of any serious intent to guard the Mara against exploitation, we have been forced to bear witness to a rash of unplanned development. Camps and lodges litter the landscape in and around the Reserve, with the tourism industry and politicians seemingly vested with greater power than the wardens and conservationists in deciding its destiny. What is all too evident is that local communities must benefit from wildlife: after all, they bear the brunt of living with wild animals, often at great cost to their livelihood, and sometimes their lives. When elephants or buffaloes rampage through crops or predators kill livestock, who is going to pay? The fact is that the ordinary Maasai landowner is still not seeing his fair share of the proceeds from tourism.

As if we needed a reminder of the challenges we face, friends of the Maasai Mara and Kenya around the world were shocked by the poisoning of eight members of the Marsh Pride in December 2015 that resulted in the death of our old friends Bibi (a seventeen-year-old lioness), Sienna (an eleven-year-old lioness, one of the trio known as the Three Graces) and the young male known as Alan. The pride had killed four cattle encroaching inside the Reserve at night. The Maasai herdsmen had then driven the lions away and laced one of the carcasses with poison.

Our distress on hearing this news must not be allowed to cloud our vision of the major issues that the killings highlight, or the reason we all feel responsible in some way for the death of Bibi and her companions. Did we do enough to try to influence change for the better in the Mara? Did we speak out when we knew that there were vital issues that needed to be raised with the authorities?

I have no doubt that many of us could indeed have done more. This situation has been brewing for years. But people close to the story have naturally been concerned about repercussions – whether a film licence would be revoked, a work permit rescinded, a research project shut down.

Now we have to honour the lives of those extraordinary big cats by putting things right. The Maasai Mara is far too wonderful a place – a rich source of both aesthetic and economic benefits – for us to allow it to descend even further into turmoil. Discussions with the Governor of Narok, Samuel ole Tunai, and his team have identified a number of key recommendations: the appointment of an independent board of trustees to oversee the wellbeing of the Mara, which would in turn appoint a highly professional management company to implement a plan that embraces the whole Reserve.

The most critical management issue is dealing with the encroachment by tens of thousands of cattle within the Reserve at night. Solving that problem will be a true test of how far we in Narok have come as a county – and how far we have come as a country. The recent

investNarok Summit drew investors from all corners of the globe and featured meat processing, contract farming, potato processing, medical supplies and educational facilities. Diversifying the county's economic landscape is to be applauded. But the Maasai Mara is already a global brand, courtesy of its famed big cats and wildebeest migration. If nurtured wisely it will yield substantial dividends in perpetuity; but *not* if a substantial part of it doubles as a night-time cattle ranch and yet more camps and lodges are sanctioned inside and outside the Reserve. Ensuring that this does not happen would be a fitting obituary to members of the Marsh Pride who died.

A day or so after the death of Bibi and her companions, the BBC film crew that has been following the Marsh Pride this past year had good news for me: nature has no time to grieve. The survivors of the poisoning incident were feasting on a buffalo they had killed during the night. The last of the Three Graces, Charm, and the two subadult males Red and Tatu, sons of Sienna and Charm, had ensured that there was food for all. The fact that Red and Tatu were still with their female relatives was a reflection of the disruption that the cattle incursions had inflicted on the Marsh Pride.

Normally young males are forced out of their natal pride by the increasing intolerance of lionesses with a new generation of cubs to nurture – and by hostility from the big pride males. This helps to prevent inbreeding. But when the pride male known as Scarface was shot in 2013 (he recovered after treatment), he and his three companions, the Musketeers, wisely started avoiding Musiara Marsh and Bila Shaka, seeking breeding opportunities with lionesses of other prides. With no resident males to protect them, the Marsh Pride females continued to tolerate the presence of Red and Tatu, perhaps even encouraged it. During the protracted dry season of 2015 Angie and I watched as two young nomadic males staked a claim to the Marsh, but having mated with Bibi they soon moved on, searching for a better territory with younger females worth fighting for: Bibi hadn't raised cubs successfully for a number of years – she was too old.

The Buddhists talk of impermanence – nothing stays the same forever. New life is already stirring in Marsh Pride territory. Sienna and Charm's five daughters had split from the Marsh Pride earlier in 2015 to carve out a territory of their own. Now they suddenly found themselves benefiting from their older relatives' demise. If recent events force the authorities to address the issue of cattle encroaching into the Reserve, then perhaps the young lionesses will be able to reclaim their birthplace along Bila Shaka and continue a lineage dating back to long before I first set eyes on the Marsh Pride in January of 1977. And they have.

While it is imperative that we do everything in our power to protect the sanctity of the Reserve for its wild inhabitants, there is hope in the form of the Wildlife Conservancies bordering the Reserve – hundreds of individually owned plots whose title holders have agreed to lease their land to tourism partners in a union that is meant both to directly benefit the land owners *and* to allow tourism to prosper; at the same time it should satisfy conservation criteria of wise and sustainable stewardship, making for a less crowded safari experience for visitors.

Within the Reserve we need look no further than the Mara Triangle – that part of the Reserve lying to the west of the Mara River – where a private management company known as the Mara Conservancy (MC), under the dedicated leadership of Brian Heath, has transformed the area. Since 2001 the MC has been implementing a professional, well-thought-out plan as to how to balance the needs of the environment with the demands of the tourism industry and those of the local

Maasai community. It has invested in road maintenance and track distribution, anti-poaching patrols in conjunction with our neighbours in the Serengeti, plus control of tour vehicles and visitors to ensure that sensitive species such as big cats and rhinos are not unduly disturbed, particularly when breeding and hunting. In the Triangle a single patrol vehicle is able to manage a large game-viewing area once all the drivers and guides become aware of its possible presence. Word soon gets round if there is a real sense of commitment on the part of wardens and rangers to enforce the rules. 'When the policeman is in town, don't go through the red light' is the message.

But to achieve this you need good infrastructure and well-maintained roads and tracks. This is apparent when you visit the Triangle. Here you can venture off road to enjoy a significant sighting – a pride of lions, a cheetah or rhino, for instance – but only five vehicles are allowed to congregate at any one time and each vehicle has to move on after ten minutes so as not to overburden the animals and to allow others to enjoy the spectacle. On leaving, each vehicle is meant to return to the main track by the same path it entered and continue on its journey. It is surprising how quickly people get used to a new way of being.

Crucially, the Mara Conservancy has helped to promote greater accountability in revenue collection and has allocated more money to enable the Triangle to be run properly. Some of the money passes to the local Maasai community, which shares the surrounding dispersal area with the wild animals.

With corruption and impunity rife in Kenya, and combating it the focus of President Uhuru Kenyatta's re-election campaign, are we both naive and foolish to hope for a better future for the Mara? As one friend with a lifetime's experience of speaking their mind in Kenya commented, 'But is anyone listening in the real world of greed, avarice and arrogance where we all operate?' Another said, 'Not much to chuckle about these days, is there? By the time we have some decent leaders and a reasonably well-off, well-fed population, who will accept, if not embrace, the idea of having some wild animals around – there won't be any left.'

Fortunately there are leaders among the younger generation of Kenyans who are determined to make a difference, some of them mixing a unique brand of entrepreneurial savvy with deep connections to the land. One such person is William ole Pere Kikanae, who realised that he could turn a visit to his traditional homestead into an event that would attract business from camps and lodges in the area. Tourists love to visit a Maasai village as part of their safari to learn more about the unique culture of the pastoralists and to buy handicrafts to take home with them. Today William is pivotal to the success of the work of an NGO from Spain called ADCAM – the Association for the Development of Alternative Trade and Microcredit – whose aim is to develop socially responsible cooperative projects and environmentally friendly infrastructure. One such project has brought in the Madrid shoe company Pikolinos to harness the skills of Maasai women in beading high-quality leather from Spain that is then sewn into sandals. Pikolinos currently provides employment for nearly 2,000 Maasai women for five months each year.

In addition, ADCAM has funded the construction of the Mara Vision School near Aitong, which offers primary education for three hundred day pupils and boarders, and constructed a small tented camp sleeping eight people and run entirely by the community. ADCAM's emphasis on empowering women is reflected in its support for women interested in self-employment, offering training and microcredits to get them started.

When we met William recently in Nairobi he was dressed in all his Maasai finery – a stunning blue *shuka* (robe) with beaded cowhide belt pulled around his waist and beaded necklaces, but minus the *simi* (short stabbing knife) and the *rungu* (wooden club) he would have carried in the bush. I loved the pride with which he wore his traditional clothing, the spring in his step and the sense of confidence in who he was and what his culture meant to him. He reminded me of the Maasai warrior I had seen in Arusha while passing through Tanzania in 1974, and the impact that had on me. I had never seen anything quite as stirring as that young man with his long braided hair and face plastered with red ochre, standing nonchalantly among his city-dwelling countrymen. Perhaps he was visiting town to buy provisions; more likely he was seeking work as a watchman alongside guards wearing helmets and dressed in overalls with pickaxe handles to deter thieves, a world away from life on the savanna where lions and hyenas were the 'thieves'.

Now, as the sun set over the world of the warrior, William was on his way to the Spanish Embassy to obtain a visitor's visa. In the course of the next three months he would be travelling to Spain, the Netherlands and the USA, meeting with friends and business associates at the ADCAM offices, comfortable in these two very different worlds, an ambassador for his people and for wildlife. Whatever the future might hold for the Mara and its wild inhabitants, I feel better knowing that men like William are there to help negotiate the way forward and to demand through their own example greater accountability from their leaders.

EPILOGUE

At the end of your life,

you will never regret not having

passed one more test… or closing

one more deal. You will regret time

not spent with a husband, a child,

a friend or a parent.

———————————————

Barbara Bush,
wife of President George H W Bush

Seeing the bigger picture is one thing, but there are times when life closes in with an immediacy that can leave you feeling isolated and despondent – where nothing else matters but the individual. In 2003, the same year that Kike jumped on my vehicle and crapped on me, I was diagnosed with cancer of the bladder. By that time I had overcome the fear of death that had haunted so much of my life before I met Angie. There was a strange sense of déjà vu, given the history of that childhood fall: it was almost a relief to have to deal with something real. Annual check-ups since surgery have so far shown no sign of a recurrence.

Five years later, we were finally able to put a name to the bewildering array of symptoms that had plagued Angie for fifteen years: the unexplained rashes, inflamed scalp, painful joints in hands and feet, the crushing episodes of fatigue that could strike without warning as if someone had drained the blood from her body. She was diagnosed with lupus, an autoimmune disease that ignites a civil war within your body. How ironical was that? For years I had struggled to separate fact from fiction when obsessing over every imaginable sign that I was unwell. Nothing escaped the lens through which I viewed my 'symptoms' and brought them to life in my imagination. By contrast, Angie's symptoms proved all too real.

The diagnosis came by chance after the filming of *Big Cat Live*, when our anchor for the show, the lovely Kate Silverton, happened to mention that she had almost died of anaphylactic shock as a result of eating seafood. Her eyes and lips had swelled and large red welts had appeared over her body – the same 'giant urticaria' that Angie sometimes suffered from but that we already knew wasn't prompted by exposure to shellfish. Kate told us to contact Professor Gideon Lack at King's College in London. When he tested Angie for lupus she was positive. There is no cure and the inflammation from a lupus flare can attack any part of the body, including the kidneys and brain. Ironically, having avoided taking malaria prophylactics all these years to protect from long-term damage to liver and eyes, it turns out that the antimalarial hydroxychloroquine is the drug of choice to help dampen down the flares – along with cortisone, which comes with its own mix of benefits and disadvantages.

Worse was to come. In 2012, twenty years after we were married, we discovered that Angie had a cranial aneurism. We were stunned. The severe headaches she had been suffering that prompted her to go for an MRI scan were caused not by the aneurism but by lupus – so they found it by chance, though we now know that lupus can predispose you to aneurisms. Angie's proved to be too complex to reach by less intrusive means and would require major surgery.

We were blessed to have Christos Tolias as our surgeon at King's College Hospital. He told us he had performed three hundred operations to repair aneurisms, thirty of them as complicated as Angie's, but that we would have to wait a month for blood thinners to clear her system before it would be safe to operate.

Those few weeks granted us the opportunity to say all the things we wanted to say to each other, to relive all the precious moments we had shared and to confront head on our fear of death and separation. Each day I wrote a card to Angie reminding her of how much I loved her, of our extraordinarily rich life and beautiful home in Kenya, of the garden, Little Cat and the dogs, of our many friends scattered around the world – and most of all our children, Alia in Nairobi and David now in San Francisco. Angie's quiet courage was beyond inspiring. It gave me hope. When they wheeled her down to theatre we found a very different Christos Tolias to the gentle, compassionate man we had spoken to in his office. Now there was no escaping the calm and focus of someone totally confident in his work.

My refuge became the quiet of the hospital chapel. There I could sit and find the peace that passeth all understanding, comforted by the words of hope, sorrow and gratitude written in the visitors' book where family and friends of patients were able to express their feelings on paper. I prayed, giving thanks for my life and for having found Angie to share it with. Whatever the 'ultimate reality' might be – certainly not the man in the sky with flowing white beard, but God nonetheless – I needed to acknowledge all that had gone before, and to muster the strength to deal with whatever might lie ahead. I felt stripped bare of artifice and pretence – just one more vulnerable human being, facing up to a new and terrifying reality. I drew on the myths of old that connect people across a myriad of diverse cultures, illuminating the pathways of the inner world we call spirituality that give meaning to life.

While Angie was in hospital I went in search of No 7 Chester Row, the house in Belgravia where my mother and father had lived after the war. I sat in their local church and reflected on their lives. I thought of how young my father had been when he died, honouring how much he had crammed into those forty-two years. He survived Dunkirk to become a decorated soldier before reigniting his career as one of the highest paid architects in London. A piece of his sculpture (a wood carving of a rearing horse) was accepted for the Royal Academy Summer Exhibition. He lived long enough to experience the joy of becoming a father again, when my sister Caroline was born twelve years after my brother Clive – and again eighteen months later when I was born. His dream of owning horses and spending time in the countryside was fulfilled with the purchase of Cuba Farm. He lived every moment to the full.

I was told that the surgery could take up to eight hours. I don't know if I had been watching too many episodes of *Gray's Anatomy*, but I envisaged a man in a white coat coming down the corridor;

I imagined trying to gauge his mood, hoping that he wouldn't speak for fear of what he might say. When my mobile phone rang it was the anaesthetist to tell me that Angie was out of the theatre and in recovery. I fell to my knees and sobbed from a place so deep inside me that I am beyond words to describe my relief and elation.

But it wasn't over. Six weeks later as we were on our way to Nairobi Airport, heading for the first check-up in London, a drunk driver in his father's four-wheel-drive ploughed into the back of our taxi, causing Angie's head to jerk backwards with a sickening thud.

Was it possible – brain surgery, then this? Shocked but still able to continue, we decided to fly that night as planned, rather than drive to Nairobi Hospital. Fortunately brain scans showed no damage to the artery that Christos Tolias had 'clipped' to shut down the aneurism.

A few months later, back at home in Nairobi, I heard a crash from upstairs and knew immediately it was Angie. Before I could reach her, Elizabeth our house help came running to fetch me, a look of pure panic on her face. Blood was pouring from Angie's head where a chunk of wood had fallen from a cupboard and hit her as she crouched on the floor. Once again we were lucky: the scans showed no serious damage. Then they discovered a second aneurism on the other side of Angie's brain – a mirror image of the first one, but much smaller. We had to wait a further six months to find out it was stable, for the moment at least, the thought of another operation almost unbearable.

Sharing life with Angie and our children put everything that had gone before into a different perspective. Being a father gave my life real meaning, transforming me from a forty-year-old neurotic into a parent. Seeing David's talents as an artist, designer and son blossom gave a new sense of energy and joy to our aspirations that is hard to describe – he created the design concept for this autobiography; while being with Alia and her partner Richard when our grandson Michael was born in Nairobi's Aga Khan Hospital was a never-to-be-forgotten experience we all treasure – the perfection of a small human being is a miracle of nature.

Michael came into the world at a time of transition for Kenya, a change in the political order and an upsurge in terrorism. Kenya had its own horrifying 9/11 moment on the morning of 21st September 2013, when the Westgate Mall was attacked by four gunmen.

We had flown to the Mara to meet guests when word began to filter through of what at first appeared to be a botched robbery. Then people realised that it was a savage attack by heavily armed terrorists that would cost the lives of at least sixty-seven people, including young children murdered in cold blood. Our immediate thought was of Alia and Michael. Alia often visited the Mall at the weekend to shop and socialise with her friends. The hours dragged by as our repeated attempts to reach her failed. Eventually we discovered that she had been helping with the organisation of the Kenya Safari Sevens rugby tournament with her phone turned off. That event attracts large crowds of spectators and an international contingent of players and officials, and was later identified as an alternative target for the Al Shabab terrorist group that claimed responsibility for Westgate. Some years earlier Alia had been hijacked at gunpoint as she sat in her vehicle along Ngong Road leading into the city. She escaped that incident physically unscathed, but we needed no reminding that life in Kenya is never straightforward.

So, as the country grapples with poor security and the demise of its tourist industry due to the threat of terrorism and travel advisories, are we thinking of packing our bags and leaving? In a word, no. We love Kenya – its people, its landscape, its wildlife. Our children went to school here; Angie and Alia are Kenya citizens; before Michael was a year old he had already made three safaris to the Mara, as well as trips to Amboseli and Tsavo National Parks, and enjoyed a memorable stay over Easter at the Serena Hotel in Mombasa on the Kenya coast. He will be swimming before we know it. We can never be certain that life will treat us kindly or that bad things will not happen. That is why it is so important not to become prisoners of our fears. I know that better than anyone.

Followers of Buddhism are taught that the answers we seek lie within us. True enough, but clarity also comes from listening to others.

To distil the wisdom of the passing years I am mindful of the knowledge of mentors and elders and their voices of reason, modern-day sages who are able to be pragmatic without abandoning moral values. David Attenborough, the doyen of natural-history broadcasters and the most respected voice in Britain, who always believed his films spoke for themselves, has become far more vocal in recent years – not least about climate change, population growth and the state of the planet. He worries about the world his grandchildren will inherit, reminding us that the environment is the most important issue facing us today, the one thing that we all share and depend on, regardless of faith or creed. It echoes the warning of Wangari Maathai that wars of the future will be fought over our precious and diminishing natural resources – trees, water, land and oil.

Jane Goodall beseeches us to treat our closest animal kin with the respect they deserve, to nurture the younger generation, encouraging them to believe that every individual can make a difference. The Dalai Lama broadens the scope of things by asking us to revere all life and to be more compassionate and mindful of the billions of people on the planet who live in abject poverty while the minority worry about whether six garages are enough to house their cars in palatial dwellings. He reminds us that the pursuit of ever more growth is doomed, that most resources are finite.

Nelson Mandela inspired us to live with courage, to have a sense of purposefulness to balance our selfish needs, maintaining that to be free of the past we have to embrace forgiveness. 'Draw your enemy close to understand him better,' he would say. Don't retreat to silence – communicate. Like Mandela, Ernest Shackleton epitomised the indomitable spirit, a leader who mixed compassion with a will of steel. Philosopher Joseph Campbell wrote powerfully about the need to identify myths to live by –

to follow our 'bliss', the welling up of the transcendent wisdom within all of us. Campbell retained his belief in humanity right to the end – that goodness would ultimately vanquish evil, that there was no giving up.

For me, among this illustrious number would be Angie, quietly encouraging me to focus my attention sufficiently to absorb the advice of these wise people. And out of the darkness my father would have spoken to me of the honour, service and gratitude embodied in the Charge that each boy accepted at the Christ's Hospital Leaving Service, a reminder never to forget the great benefits I had received and to do all that I could to enable others to enjoy the same advantages.

By some strange quirk of fate during my time at Christ's Hospital I was in the house known as Coleridge A, named after the poet Samuel Taylor Coleridge, who attended CH from the age of eight. Like me, Coleridge suffered from rheumatic fever as a child and later developed crippling bouts of anxiety and depression. He was treated with laudanum, fostering a lifelong opium addiction. I cannot help wondering what treatment would have been prescribed for my anxiety and obsessions if I'd admitted to them. No doubt medication would have been part of it. What I do know is that a search for 'feelings of unreality' on the internet made me realise how common and difficult to describe they can be. There was a forum dedicated to dissociation, with testimony from people from all walks of life, some who had experienced these disturbing feelings since childhood, others who had been attacked much later. Their accounts were so harrowing to read that it made me feel humble to know how much less unwell I had been.

Years ago I came across the work of Dr Claire Weekes, an Australian zoologist and physician who became a pioneer in the field of psychiatry, applying kindness, understanding and common sense to the treatment of nervous illness. Weekes took a highly pragmatic approach, identifying the way in which the nervous system can become 'sensitised' in certain individuals and pointing out that a great deal of nervous suffering is no more than severe sensitisation kept alive by bewilderment and fear. She distrusted psychoanalysis and medical jargon, encouraging sufferers to accept their symptoms rather than fighting them and to 'float' when fear and panic struck. I found this approach enormously helpful, particularly in coping with dissociation.

David Adam, in his fascinating and lyrical book *The Man Who Couldn't Stop*, describes his own experience of obsessive compulsive disorder: he gets to the heart of the matter when he says, 'I had to ignore the thoughts, resist the compulsion, let the anxiety build, and then let it decay to extinction all over again.' The trick, if only it were that simple, is to embrace the idea that 'feelings are not facts, thoughts are not truth'.

The greatest irony perhaps is that my father dying so young was the making of me, both literally and metaphorically speaking: the most extraordinary of gifts. If he had survived, I feel sure that, given his strong character and sense of duty, he would have wanted me to pursue a more formal career, to become a doctor or lawyer, perhaps, or an architect like himself. I would have been destined to walk in his shadow rather than follow his example, struggling to compete with his obvious and abundant talents. Instead, in the emotional and physical void left by his death, my mother created a warm and loving environment for her children, one in which my father became a never-to-be-forgotten figure of heroic proportions. She believed, like Joseph Campbell, that the real riches in life do not come in the form of a large pay packet but from each individual following their own pathway to bliss. The 'myth' of my father that I embraced as a child challenged me to make something different of myself, urging me to excel without him dictating the direction of my journey, all the while encouraged by my mother's unwavering belief in me and my dreams.

My mother died in 1999 aged eighty-nine, while Angie and I were in India filming tigers for *Wild Things*. Among her belongings I came across a letter of congratulation on the announcement of my birth from Kenneth Simon, the family doctor, in which he said, 'I hope Jonathan is told in later years that he owes his presence entirely to his mother's patience.' Despite her numerous miscarriages, she had refused to give up on her dream of having more children.

One more thing I am certain of. The personal successes and awards are nothing compared to the joy that Angie and the children brought into my life. They more than anything helped me to survive the wilderness within.

ACKNOWLEDGEMENTS

I would like to thank the governments of Kenya and Tanzania for allowing me to live and work in the Mara-Serengeti. Senior Wardens David Babu and Bernard Maregesi in Serengeti, and Simon Makallah, Michael Koikai, James Sindiyo and Brian Heath in the Maasai Mara have been generous in their support. The Honourable Lena Munge helped keep the channels of communication open with the Governor of Narok County, the Honourable Samuel ole Tunai, with her thoughtful advice and support in search of a better future for the Mara, a process nurtured by Dr Christian Turner, the British High Commissioner in Nairobi.

My brother Clive, his wife Judith and my sister Caroline have always been a source of love and encouragement, while Angie's brother David and his wife Mishi shared many happy times with us in India and France. My cousin Pauline Howe, a favourite visitor to Cuba Farm, tirelessly typed up drafts of *The Leopard's Tale*; thanks also to my nephew Mark for his help with legal matters.

The wonderful Vicky Coombe has taken nurturing to new levels of kindness, and our heartfelt thanks also go to Pippa and Ian Stewart-Hunter, Pam Savage and Michael Skinner, Sue and Michael Budden, Cissy and David Walker, Brian and Annabelle Jackman, Charles and Lindsay Dewhurst, Kelvin Lack and Simone Robertson, Paul and Donna Goldstein, Keith and Liz Scholey, Robin and Elin Hellier, and Rowena Johnson. Kiki McDonough and Margot Raggett came to our rescue when Angie was diagnosed with a cranial aneurism. We will never forget their kindness in opening their hearts and homes to us.

Brian Hall and Chris Elworthy at Canon UK, and John Brinkley, Peter Antoniou and Christine Percy at Swarovski Optik (UK) have been loyal supporters of our work.

Meeting up again with Bob Hailey, my mentor at CH, and his wife Rosemary – two remarkable people – has been a blessing. It has also been the greatest of pleasures to renew contact with the inimitable and distinguished parasitologist Emeritus Professor David Halton of Queen's University, Belfast, and to connect from time to time with my good-hearted tent mate Kim Gottlieb from our overland trip of 1974.

Keith Scholey, creator of *Big Cat Diary*, has been hugely supportive of my work, as have Robin Hellier and Alastair Fothergill. BCD's Executive Producer Sara Ford never failed to boost morale and, with Colin Jackson, secured me the role of presenter of *The Truth about Lions*.

Jock Anderson has been a dear friend and I am immensely proud to be godfather to Jock and Sue's son Robert, and godfather to Cara Evans, daughter of old friends Mike and Geraldine Evans. Boris Tismimieszky is another stalwart, and Paul Pavlidis was pivotal in helping me get established in Kenya. Hilary Mitchell, Stephen Masika, Jackie Keith, Gail Shaw, Sharon Gent and Sara Moller worked wonders on my behalf in Jock's office. The late Jack and Tubby Block were generous with fatherly advice and kindness. Geoff and Jorie Kent of Abercrombie & Kent, and Anne Taylor-Kent provided us with accommodation at Kichwa Tembo, where managers Roy Wallace, Peter and Alison Cadot, Nigel Arensen and Maurice and Monica Anami, along with David and Richard Markham, Sammy Mwaura, Alistair Ballantine and David Stogdale, were hugely supportive. Priyesh Shah at Kenya

Stationers continued his company's backing of our work with the loan of a customised Land Rover.

The Grammaticus family, who own Governors' Camp, generously provide us with a cottage in the Mara, while Patrick Beresford and his team in the workshop have kept us mobile. And George Murray at Little Governors', Patrick Reynolds at Il Moran and Dave Richards at Private Camp have been the best of friends. Kevin Gilks, Jan Thoenes, Malcolm Bater, Alan Walmsley and Shigeru helped facilitate the loan of a Toyota Landcruiser in the 1990s and 2000s. We're also grateful to Anna Nzomo at Air Kenya and John Buckley and Anu Vohra at Safarilink Aviation. The late Mehmood Quraishy and his son Shaun at Spectrum Color Lab processed our slide film for decades, and Pankaj Patel at Fuji ensured continuity of supplies. Fellow photographer and author Nigel Pavitt worked miracles with scans and prints of our work, and our great friend, Lebanese wildlife photographer and entrepreneur Michel Zoghzoghi, has supported us royally.

I owe a considerable debt to the late Dr Ed Tweddell and to Dr Carter Newton who reached out to me with patience and compassion when I was struggling with mental health issues; to physiotherapist Hilary Ahluwalia for her healing hands and compassionate ways, and to Mike Eldon, another kind mentor who applied his editing skills to my grammar. Monty Ruben and his daughters Lissa and Mandy, Danae Issaias, Jock and Sue Anderson, George and Carol Zibarras, Ed and Sue Tweddell and my brother Clive gave us permission to reproduce original drawings.

In the Serengeti and the Ngorongoro Conservation Area many people have been generous with their support, not least: Karim Hirji, Markus and Monica Borner, Charlie and Lynn Trout, Alan and Joan Root, Aadje Geertsema and Margaret Kullander,

Barbie Allen, John Fanshawe and Clare FitzGibbon, Richard Matthews and Samantha Purdy, Mark Deeble and Victoria Stone, Abnel Mwampondele, Mark Jago, Karen Lawrenson, Danny McCallum, Sandie Evans, Livia Duncan, Dick Estes, Allan Earnshaw, Nigel Dundas and Billy Winter.

Carole Wyman is godmother to our son David and made it possible for him to attend Canford School in England and university in Santa Fe and San Francisco. How can we ever express our gratitude for your love? Neil and Joyce Silverman hosted us at their beautiful home in Florida and joined us on adventures in Africa and Antarctica. Arty and the late Marion Olsen were like a second family to me at their home in East Northport in the early 1970s: two of the kindest people I have ever met.

Caroline Taggart has edited the majority of the thirty books Angie and I have worked on and is now a celebrated author in her own right. She is a sublime editor with a light touch, transforming my work into something readable without destroying the author's voice. Mike Shaw at Curtis Brown and Jonny Pegg of the Jonathan Pegg Literary Agency always went the extra mile on our behalf, while Hilary Knight of HK Management nurtured us from afar.

Myles Archibald at Collins encouraged me to believe that there was a book here somewhere, while Managing Director Adrian Philips and Commissioning Editor Rachel Fielding at Bradt Travel Guides ensured there was. The generous support of Katie Simmonds and our sponsors at Canon Europe enabled the team at Bradt to produce a truly elegant and beautiful book.

Both Angie and I would like to thank our wonderful staff in Nairobi for years of assistance: Francis Kimilu Mwania, Dem Lubo Garena, Justus Muthini Kioko, Elizabeth Kalekye and Chrispus Kioko.

And how do we thank somebody for saving Angie's life? The quiet confidence and compassion, remarkable skill and after care of Christos Tolias and his team at King's College Hospital Neurology Unit are things we will never forget.

Finally, our daughter Alia and son David have made us immensely proud. No words can express my joy in being their father. We were all stunned by the beautiful design concept that David conjured up for this book. Meanwhile, our grandson Michael Jonathan is brave and bursting with energy in anticipation of each new safari.

If you would like to know more about the medical conditions mentioned in the text, have a look at these websites:

EhlersDanlos Syndrome Support Group: www.ehlers-danlos.org/
Mind: the Mental Health Charity: www.mind.org.uk
Lupus Foundation of America: www.lupus.org

I am also a patron of the Bishop Simeon Trust, which works with those affected by poverty and HIV/AIDS: www.bstrust.org/.

PHOTOGRAPHER'S NOTE

Though my first clumsy attempts at being a wildlife photographer proved disastrous I did at least get one thing right – I chose a Canon camera. I've been using them ever since and it's because of that that Angie and I were so delighted to be chosen as Canon Ambassadors. What I failed to understand back in the 1970s was that lenses are the eyes of your camera and your most important purchase. Wildlife photography demands long telephotos: photographing from our safari vehicle, I predominantly use the EF200-400mm f/4L IS USM telephoto zoom. With the flick of a switch you can engage the built-in x1.4 Extender without taking the lens off the camera and getting dust on the sensor. Angie's workhorse is the EF600mm f/4L IS II USM telephoto. In addition to this, we love the razor-sharp EF800mm f/5.6L IS USM for extreme close-ups.

ABOVE Young elephant drinking and spraying – slow shutter speeds work wonders with water.

Today most pros travel with high-quality zoom lenses. For all-round wildlife and travel photography our favourite is the EF100-400mm f/4.5/5.6L IS II USM: an amazingly versatile lens at a very reasonable price. Add a wide-angle to your kit bag – a EF24-105mm f/4L (we might be tempted to tuck the EF16-35mm f2.8L in our pocket too!) – and you are ready to travel anywhere in the world in pursuit of great images. If you add the 1.4x extender Series III to the EF100-400mm it becomes a 140-560mm lens on a full-frame sensor camera such as the brilliant EOS-1D X Mk2; or, with the EOS 7D Mk II body with its cropped 1.6x [APS-C] sensor, the same zoom becomes an impressive 160-640mm.

Here are Jonathan and Angie's top tips for great photography:

SHOOTING FROM THE HIP. Buy a point-and-shoot camera such as the Canon Powershot and carry it with you everywhere.

SEEING THE LIGHT. Shoot with the sun coming from the side of your subject (side lit) or from behind it (back-lit) for more emotive and powerful images. Early morning and late evening are best for rich colours.

LEFT One of the Four Musketeers at dawn: side light and back light produce moody images
RIGHT William ole Pere demonstrating his jumping skills. Choose a low angle for extra impact.

ABOVE One of Honey's Boys catching a young wildebeest. Using slow shutter speeds and panning really helps to give a sense of movement.

STEPPING UP. Take control of your camera by reading the manual. Be inspired by the work of other photographers. Discover what makes their work different, then develop your own style.

UNDERSTANDING EXPOSURE AND HISTOGRAMS. Your camera doesn't always expose your photographs they way you see them. Learn about under- and over-exposure and how to interpret your camera's histogram (which analyses tone and brightness) for the best results.

DE-MYSTIFYING DEPTH OF FIELD. By adjusting the aperture of your lens you can vary how much of the image is in focus. This is called depth of field and is important for great portraits (shallow depth of field) and pin-sharp landscapes (maximum depth of field).

OUT OF THE ROOF HATCH OR DOWN LOW. Lions feasting on a kill may look best taken from the roof hatch, with the whole pride in focus. But for really imposing portraits of big game, get down low in your vehicle.

FIELD CRAFT. Knowing your subject and researching the best destinations to photograph them are the keys to great images. The Internet is a rich source of information.

GETTING CREATIVE. Slow shutter speeds of 1/15th to 1/100th second and panning (moving the camera to follow your subject as you press the shutter button) will create a partially blurred effect, ideal for conveying speed and motion. Fast shutter speeds of 1/1000th second or more will give you pin-sharp images of birds in flight or animals running. Experiment with different lenses too.

FILL-IN FLASH. Use fill-in flash to add light to subjects in shadow, but be careful not to disturb your subject.

PUTTING IN THE HARD YARDS. Processing and cataloguing your images are the final steps. We use Lightroom and, for fine tuning, Photoshop CC. Always back up your best images on separate hard drives.

ABOVE Rocky outcrop, Hartmann Valley, Namibia: the EF8-15mm fish-eye
gives a funky perspective.